THE FINANCIAL MINDSET FIX

Praise for *The Financial Mindset Fix*

"Joyce Marter's book is a generous offering to us all. *The Financial Mindset Fix* is a book about our relationship with money, but really it is a book about our relationship with ourselves. Joyce seamlessly weaves together research, clinical wisdom, personal narrative, and real-world examples, and she offers powerful tools designed to help you 'walk the talk.' This practical and wise guide is a worthwhile investment indeed!"

ALEXANDRA H. SOLOMON, PHD
faculty at Northwestern University, licensed clinical psychologist at the Family Institute at Northwestern University, and author of *Loving Bravely* and *Taking Sexy Back*

"The author's voice is calm, assuring, and empowering, and her years of experience guiding her clients through the minefield of personal finances shine through every page. This is a wonderful book on achieving financial success, without a doubt. But it's also much larger than that. It speaks to creating a full, rich life of abundance and possibility. *The Financial Mindset Fix* is a must-read."

JOHN DUFFY, PSYD
clinical psychologist and author of *Parenting the New Teen in the Age of Anxiety*

"Joyce Marter provides a useful tool for improving your money mindset. *The Financial Mindset Fix* will help put you on the path to achieving your financial goals."

CHARLENE WALTERS, MBA, PHD
author of *Launch Your Inner Entrepreneur*

"What I really like about this book is that you can work with it. It can be very valuable for anyone who seriously wants to improve their financial situation and who is willing to apply themselves. This volume gives you all the tools needed to move into greater abundance."

RICK JAROW, PHD
author of *Creating the Work You Love*

"This is the book that the money genre has needed for decades. Instead of 'to-do lists' or surface coaching, Joyce Marter blows the doors off of two typically taboo topics in our culture: money and mental health. Her gentle, honest, and knowledgeable style will guide you through a deep dive to uncover and address whatever is blocking your personal prosperity."

SHERRIE D. ALL, PHD
author of *The Neuroscience of Memory: Seven Skills to Optimize Your Brain Power, Improve Memory, and Stay Sharp at Any Age*

"Joyce Marter's book, *The Financial Mindset Fix*, should be required reading for all. Like so many things we may want to 'fix,' there is no magic pill, yet Joyce sets out to give us the tools through her proven mental fitness plan that get us on the path to a more abundant life. It is easier to visualize success with Joyce's actionable steps and doses of inspiration that leave you feeling as if you had the best meeting with your trusted therapist and financial advisor. I will be recommending this book to all my friends and colleagues."

AMY BOYLE
founder of the 52 Phenomenal Women Project, photographer,
and brand ambassador for *O, The Oprah Magazine*

"Joyce Marter's business, Urban Balance, was one of the platform acquisitions to form Refresh Mental Health, a collection of top clinical mental health practices across the country. Joyce is a national leader in the field of outpatient mental health counseling and has been a leader for Refresh from Day One. In this book, Joyce shares her clinical wisdom and entrepreneurial savvy in a way that is both straightforward and inspiring. She provides practical tools we all can use to promote both our mental and financial health and well-being."

STEVE GOLD, JD, MPH, MBE
CEO of Refresh Mental Health

"If you want to enjoy the financial journey, it starts with your mindset. In *The Financial Mindset Fix*, Joyce gives you the insights and tools you need to fix your mindset and start enjoying your financial journey."

TIM KENNY, CPA, CMA, CVA
Certified Profit First Professional

"*The Financial Mindset Fix* not only changed the way I look at money but explained *why* I was sabotaging myself and *how* to shift my thinking and behavior. Never before have I equated my mental health with wealth. Now I do. This book has changed my life."

CORRINE CASANOVA
Daily House Publishing

"The greatest barriers to compassionate people solving our greatest global challenges are issues around finances. Whether it is shame, or guilt, or anger, so many people with brilliant ideas or great intentions fail in their missions because they haven't yet resolved their own personal issues around money, myself included. I'm thrilled to see the brilliant Joyce Marter take on this issue with a holistic, action-oriented approach.

"Many people try to resolve financial issues from a strictly action-oriented approach, yet I know from my time at American Express, finances are both emotional and motivational. Many feel hopeless, or despairing and helpless, around finances because they don't have the tools necessary to get to hope, which includes both positive feelings *and* inspired action. Joyce does an exceptional job with this dual approach, sure to impact those with kind hearts so they can generate success. Wealth is a powerful tool in the right hands for solving many of our greatest global challenges. And we can't solve our global challenges until we solve our own personal challenges."

KATHRYN GOETZKE, MBA
founder of iFred, host of *The Hope Matrix* podcast, author of
The Biggest Little Book about Hope, and chief mood officer at The Mood Factory

"An abundant life is possible when we commit to establishing clear core values, which we learn from doing the work to become mentally healthy humans. *The Financial Mindset Fix* is an invitation to cultivate a solid, inside out, and holistic approach to leading the lives we most desire. Joyce Marter is our wise, unwavering, and trustworthy guide."

NADINE KELLY, MD, E RYT
founder of Yogi MD

"Joyce Marter is one of the finest mental health speakers in the country. When she incorporated her expertise into a book for those of us who sometimes struggle with balancing life and our finances, I was thrilled! *The Financial Mindset Fix* is the perfect remedy for creating more abundance and peace of mind, both inside and out."

NANCY VOGL
founder of Nancy Vogl Speakers International

"Revealing and rewarding for your mind, body, and bank account! *The Financial Mindset Fix* gets you into action from page one with power-packed mental fitness exercises to reclaim work-life balance, live in a flow of abundance, and dream big dreams again."

CARA BRADLEY
mental fitness coach and author of *On the Verge: Wake Up, Show Up, and Shine*

"Joyce Marter normalizes mental health challenges with humorous stories—that are so relatable. She shares her wisdom through practical strategies and tips to create holistic wellness and abundance. *The Financial Mindset Fix* is a tutorial for improving not only your financial health but also your emotional and relational health. As a dating and relationship coach, I will be recommending this book to all my clients who are seeking greater prosperity in their relationships and their bank accounts."

BELA GANDHI
founder of Smart Dating Academy

"Money is a story, one that too often is used against us. When you're ready to engage with intention, this book can help rewrite your story."

SETH GODIN
author of *The Practice*

"If you're trying to achieve more happiness personally and professionally, this is required reading. Joyce's wisdom connecting mental health and wealth is really a breakthrough. I learned several things about myself as a woman and our sometimes-unique feelings about money. Because of Joyce, I have been able to make a few changes with immediate results. As a public speaking and media trainer, I know how much confidence and self-worth are tied to financial success. I will be giving this book to my clients."

KATHRYN JANICEK
three-time Emmy® Award–winning media and public speaking trainer

"In this wonderful new book, successful therapist Joyce Marter gently takes you by the hand and walks you down the path toward better mental health and a more abundant financial life. Her twelve unique mindsets will revolutionize your relationship with money and significantly improve the way you view yourself. An insightful, worthwhile read!"

STEPHEN M. R. COVEY
author of *New York Times* and #1 *Wall Street Journal* bestseller *The Speed of Trust*

"WOW! I truly have not read such a powerful, compassionate, engaging book before! I love the therapeutic activities and practicality of the mental and financial wellness activities and theory applications. The next time I teach practicum and internship, this book will be required. Just simply amazingly outstanding, and what a joy!"

SANDRA L. KAKACEK, EDD, LCPC
associate professor and core faculty of the
Clinical Mental Health Counseling program at Adler University

"Well, this is quite a delicious book! A compendium, really. Joyce has taken a huge step by combining mental and spiritual well-being with twelve mindsets that are necessary to heal and empower our relationship with money. I've read scores of books on financial abundance but have never encountered one that is so thoroughly researched. Or one that so exquisitely supports us to engage authentically with guided self-assessments, called wheel exercises, that are linked to the twelve mindsets. What has all this work on ourselves got to do with our finances? Everything! Marter maintains that how we feel and think about ourselves and our ability to deserve a good life are intimately linked to these mindsets. The best part? Throughout the book, she shows us how to heal what's been holding us back from living the financial life we were meant to live."

MARIA NEMETH, PHD, MCC
founder and director, Academy for Coaching Excellence

"Joyce Marter's *The Financial Mindset Fix* provides a counselor's approach—that of well-being—to ease the ever-present stress of financial instability. Applying empirically supported tools and techniques used by professional counselors, Joyce guides you through shifting beliefs around finances with the objective of leading you to holistic success—in your wallet and your mental health! Her premise is that when you love what you do and are doing good in the world, prosperity is available to you.

"Marter's book resonated with me not only as an entrepreneur but as a career counselor for more than thirty years, helping thousands of clients reach their goals. With this accessible and impactful book, Marter's contributions to the counseling profession continue to be significant and relevant. An inspirational game changer!"

SUE PRESSMAN, PHD, LPC
president, American Counseling Association 2020–2021

"Good mental health multiplies financial worth many times. Said differently, financial wealth is a mirage without good mental health. In this book, Joyce Marter provides a brilliant mix of bite-size lessons and easy-to-use tools for everyone to achieve good mental health. The book contains examples of how good mental health has helped adults and professionals in their personal lives, careers, and finances. She even discusses her own journey from financial struggle to being a very successful entrepreneur."

MIKE ADHIKARI, MBA
mergers and acquisitions advisor

"*The Financial Mindset Fix* shows us what's truly driving our financial behavior. This is a comprehensive guide to financial wellness, and the chapter on resilience is excellent. Joyce shows us how to approach and overcome the inevitable financial setbacks."

SPENCER SHERMAN
founder and advisor, Abacus Wealth Partners, and author of *The Cure for Money Madness: Break Your Bad Money Habits, Live Without Financial Stress—and Make More Money!*

"Before reading this book, I was working very long nights, and it took a toll on my mental health. After reading *The Financial Mindset Fix*, I learned that boosting my mental health was the key to unlocking my financial dreams. By working through the mental fitness program, I began to envision and create a more abundant life for myself. Soon, I turned my passion for reading and writing into a new business in which I help authors write books. Today, I feel energetic, resilient, and confident in achieving my financial dreams."

SIMON GOLDEN, PHD
editor, book coach, and researcher

"Too many dreams are deferred because dreamers believe they lack the money to fund them or, even worse, that they can't attain financial abundance. *The Financial Mindset Fix* shows you that it's really head trash about money keeping us stuck and provides the tools to take out the trash. Read this wonderful book to clear the way for you to *finally* get to bringing your dreams to life."

CHARLIE GILKEY
author of the award-winning *Start Finishing*

Joyce Marter, LCPC

THE FINANCIAL MINDSET FIX

A Mental Fitness Program
for an Abundant Life

ST. MARTIN'S
ESSENTIALS
NEW YORK

Published in the United States by St. Martin's Essentials,
an imprint of St. Martin's Publishing Group

EU Representative: Macmillan Publishers Ireland Ltd, 1st Floor, The Liffey Trust Centre, 117–126 Sheriff Street Upper, Dublin 1, D01 YC43

THE FINANCIAL MINDSET FIX. Copyright © 2026, 2021 by Joyce Marter. All rights reserved. Printed in the United States of America. For information, address St. Martin's Publishing Group, 120 Broadway, New York, NY 10271.

While all the stories in this book are true, some names and identifying information have been changed to protect the privacy of the individuals involved. This publication is not intended as a substitute for professional medical or mental health advice, diagnosis, or treatment. If issues arise as a result of reading this book or doing the suggested activities, seek the advice of a professional therapist.

Book design by Linsey Dodaro
Illustrations by Alexis Neumann

www.stmartins.com

The Library of Congress has cataloged the hardcover edition as follows:

Names: Marter, Joyce, author.
Title: The financial mindset fix : a mental fitness program for an abundant life / Joyce Marter, LCPC.
Description: Boulder, Colorado : Sounds True, 2021.
Identifiers: LCCN 2020041383 (print) | LCCN 2020041384 (ebook) | ISBN 9781683647232 (hardback) | ISBN 9781683647249 (ebook)
Subjects: LCSH: Finance, Personal. | Wealth--Psychological aspects. | Success.
Classification: LCC HG179 .M3119 2021 (print) | LCC HG179 (ebook) | DDC 332.024—dc23
LC record available at https://lccn.loc.gov/2020041383
LC ebook record available at https://lccn.loc.gov/2020041384

ISBN 978-1-64963-278-4 (trade paperback)

The publisher of this book does not authorize the use or reproduction of any part of this book in any manner for the purpose of training artificial intelligence technologies or systems. The publisher of this book expressly reserves this book from the Text and Data Mining exception in accordance with Article 4(3) of the European Union Digital Single Market Directive 2019/790.

Our books may be purchased in bulk for specialty retail/wholesale, literacy, corporate/premium, educational, and subscription box use. Please contact MacmillanSpecialMarkets@macmillan.com.

First published in the United States by Sounds True

First St. Martin's Essentials Trade Paperback Edition: 2026

10 9 8 7 6 5 4 3 2 1

In loving memory of my mother, Madelyn Taff Brinkman, who spent her life studying psychology and spirituality, and my father, Robert James Brinkman, who was a high-powered business executive and savvy financial investor. Thank you for all your love and support. The combination of everything I learned from both of you, in essence, is the financial mindset fix.

I am a financial planner, not a psychiatrist, but I do know that your net worth will rise to meet your self-worth only if your self-worth rises to accept what can be yours.
SUZE ORMAN author of ten consecutive
New York Times bestsellers about personal finance

CONTENTS

Exercises are available for download at financialmindsetfix.com/exercises

Introduction	Wake Up! You Deserve a Greater Life	1
	The Financial Health Wheel	14
Chapter 1	Abundance: Discover Your Worth and See That We're All Beggars Sitting on a Golden Bench	19
	Therapy Session Number 1	21
	Look at Your Financial Self in the Mirror	25
	Examine Your Self-Worth	27
	Synergize for Success	30
	Record and Rewire Your Thinking	31
	The Abundance Wheel	35
Chapter 2	Awareness: Realize How Your Unconscious Is Robbing You of Riches	39
	Therapy Session Number 2	41
	Identify Your Default Role	44
	Drop Your Defenses	50
	Check Up on Your Mental Health	57
	Check Your Reality by Budgeting	59
	The Awareness Wheel	62
Chapter 3	Responsibility: Stop the Blame Game and Take the Reins of Your Life	67
	Therapy Session Number 3	69
	Author Your Best Future	72
	Take an Honest Look at Yourself	78
	Take Fiscal Responsibility	80
	The Responsibility Wheel	81
Chapter 4	Presence: Promote Fiscal Consciousness Through Being a Human Being, Not a Human Doing	85
	Therapy Session Number 4	88
	Pump the Breaks on Busyness	92
	Redirect Your Attention to the Here and Now	97
	Try a Financial Fast	99
	Spend Mindfully	100
	The Presence Wheel	101

Chapter 5	Essence: See How Your Ego Is Killing Your Cash Karma	105
	Therapy Session Number 5	107
	Align with Your Essence	110
	Cancel Your Ego Trip	118
	The Essence Wheel	122
Chapter 6	Self-Love: Tell Your Inner Saboteur to Buzz Off and Invest in Yourself with Fierce Love	127
	Therapy Session Number 6	129
	Face Your Inner Saboteur	132
	Cultivate Your Inner Dream Team	137
	The Self-Love Wheel	139
Chapter 7	Vision: Whip Out Your Magic Wand to Create a Luxurious Life and Better World	145
	Therapy Session Number 7	148
	Declare a Personal Manifesto	151
	Dream Big Dreams	152
	Develop an Action Plan	156
	Live with Intention	157
	Visualize Success	158
	The Vision Wheel	159
Chapter 8	Support: Appreciate That Giving and Receiving Are Two Sides of the Same Coin	163
	Therapy Session Number 8	165
	Replenish Yourself	167
	Remove Barriers to Receiving Support	170
	The Support Network Wheel	176
	The Support Wheel	183
Chapter 9	Compassion: Explore the Spirituality of Business and Recognize That Love Is the Currency of Life	187
	Therapy Session Number 9	188
	Increase Success Through Empathy	192
	Expand with Compassion	196
	Wield the Power of Lovingkindness	198
	Pay It Forward	201
	The Compassion Wheel	202

Chapter 10	Detachment: Disempower Fear, Negativity, and Financial Anxiety to Welcome Prosperity	207
	Therapy Session Number 10	209
	Shelve Your Worries with "The Container"	213
	Recalibrate Expectations to Zero	214
	Separate from Negativity	217
	Practice Detachment with Love	219
	The Detachment Wheel	220
Chapter 11	Positivity: Harness the Power of Extreme Optimism to Manifest Success	225
	Therapy Session Number 11	226
	Reframe Positively to Become Grateful	229
	Act "As If"	231
	Look for the Exceptions	233
	Do Some Exposure Therapy	235
	The Work Satisfaction Wheel	240
	The Positivity Wheel	244
Chapter 12	Resilience: Convert Adversity into Opulent Opportunity	249
	Therapy Session Number 12	251
	Flagging the Minefield	257
	Create a Financial Resilience Plan	261
	Focus on Growth	264
	Practice Affirmations for Resilience	266
	The Resilience Wheel	267
Conclusion	Financial Mindset Wisdom: Bringing It All Together for Complete Prosperity	271
	The Mindset Fix Wheel	272
	The Financial Health Wheel	276

Acknowledgments	281
Notes	285
Book Club Reader's Guide	303
About the Author	305

Introduction

WAKE UP! YOU DESERVE A GREATER LIFE

What you seek is seeking you.
RUMI thirteenth-century poet, Sufi mystic, and theologian

When I began graduate school at Northwestern University, I was afraid my professors would notice my struggle with anxiety and, as a result, tell me that I wasn't fit to become a therapist, which was my dream. As I read textbooks and listened to lectures about mental health, addiction, and relational problems, I recognized aspects of myself and my family. I sat in silent shame, thinking I was expected to have it all together.

Thankfully, the faculty recognized that as part of the human condition, we *all* have mental health issues and encouraged the students to participate in personal counseling. Just as we don't expect doctors or nurses to have perfect physical health, we don't expect therapists to have perfect mental health. (Phew!) We are expected, however, to take care of our mental health as best as possible, serving as healthy models and guides for others.

It was the process of my own therapy, combined with my clinical training, that opened my eyes. It gave me the language and lens to understand myself, my relationships, life, and the world around me. I learned to relax into the understanding that my anxiety was a normal response to my nature and nurture and began to practice self-compassion. I learned the tools to better manage my stress and anxiety and expanded my comfort zone so I could blossom into my best self. Of course, I'm still a work in progress, as none of us is perfect, but I'm living a more abundant life than I ever imagined. I want the same for you too!

Do you want a prosperous life filled with inner peace, support, and financial success? If so, what is keeping you from achieving a life you deserve?

We all unconsciously recreate what is familiar until we become aware of and choose something better. It took years of struggle before I chose to emancipate myself from self-limitation. To save you time and suffering, I'll share with you what I learned from more than twenty years of counseling clients, starting and selling a business, and working on myself to create transformative change resulting in greater personal and financial prosperity.

A Surprise Bonus

After several years of working in a variety of settings with a diverse array of clients, I noticed my clients were receiving unexpected bonuses due to their efforts in therapy. As they were making progress in therapy, they were receiving raises, promotions, starting successful businesses, and doing better financially.

Why was this happening?

In therapy, no matter what issues we are working on, we are always simultaneously treating underlying feelings of self-worth, or the value we place on ourselves. As my clients' sense of worth improved, so did their finances—because of increased confidence, empowerment, assertiveness, and self-care.

Renowned author Suze Orman noticed this same correlation through her work as a financial advisor and said, "Lasting net worth comes only when you have a healthy and strong sense of self-worth."[1] However, Orman cautions that it doesn't work the other way; having high net worth doesn't increase the likelihood that you will have high self-worth. Scientists have observed a similar pattern in research literature; mental health significantly predicts future wealth, yet wealth does not affect future mental health.[2] I've noticed these same trends in my practice and began sharing this knowledge through executive coaching, business consulting, corporate training, and public speaking. While financial advisors help people manage their money, as a psychotherapist, I help professionals utilize psychological skills to improve their self-worth and emotional intelligence in order to achieve work-life balance and financial success.

Curiously enough, the basics of money management is not rocket science—set a budget, make more than you spend, have a savings account, pay off your debt, and plan for the future. It's our psychology that can make our financial lives difficult. Popular radio host and author Dave Ramsey believes that financial success is 20 percent financial knowledge and 80 percent behavior.[3] He confirms that financial success is all about your ability to control the person in the mirror. As you continue to go through this program, you'll begin to see how your thoughts, feelings, attitudes, self-care, goals, motivation, and support impact your finances directly. Self-love is a big factor in your financial success.

Early on in my career, with only $500 to invest and $50,000 of student loans, I started my counseling business, Urban Balance, when my first daughter was two years old. As the practice grew, the business went through difficult financial times. I put a lien on my home, fully anticipating filing for bankruptcy. Through countless mistakes, which you'll learn more about in the chapters to come, I learned some painful but valuable lessons, including the harmful aspects of the ego, the importance of accessing support, and more. After a lot of work on myself and my relationship with money, and with the help of many talented people, we turned the ship around. Thirteen years after start-up, I successfully sold Urban Balance for several million dollars and was able to invest in the parent company, Refresh Mental Health, for continued growth in earnings.

Under the new ownership, Urban Balance continues to thrive beyond my wildest dreams. The company provides jobs for hundreds of people in several states, mental health services for tens of thousands of people per year, internships for countless therapists-in-training, and even sliding fee and pro bono counseling services for people in need.

Shift Your Financial Mindset to a Holistic View of Success

It has been an enormous blessing to learn about mental health and the psychology of money from my clients' experiences as well as my own. Through this, I've recognized universal truths and identified twelve mindsets that improve mental health, relationships, and financial prosperity when put into action.

For the past ten years, I have been sharing these insights through national speaking engagements. The response has been overwhelmingly positive, with attendees saying the content is inspiring, empowering, and even life changing. They discovered that in order to live a truly abundant life, it's essential to have both positive mental health and financial health, not one without the other. Now, you can adopt this holistic mindset and create a life of wellness and abundance by working through this engaging program from the comfort of your own home.

We are in the midst of a mental health epidemic, and we have been for quite some time. In the late 1990s, substance abuse and mental health issues were on the rise in the United States due to the opioid epidemic. In late 2007, people began experiencing immense financial stress from the Great Recession, further exacerbating the mental health epidemic. On top of these significant historical stressors, many of us were suffering from the disease of being busy. Through technology, we were plugged into a never-ending stream of news and work. We became disconnected from ourselves and one another. Our achievement-oriented and consumer-based culture taught us that money equates to happiness. This led many of us to operate from ego and become competitive, negatively impacting our ability to foster deep interpersonal connection and collaboration at home and work.

The result is an alarming and deeply concerning rise in mental illness and addiction, which is costly to each of us on a personal, community, and global level:

- Seventy-three percent of Americans experience psychological symptoms caused by stress, and 48 percent feel their stress has increased over the past five years.[4]
- In 2018, approximately 20.3 million people in the US had a substance use disorder, including 14.8 million people who had an alcohol use disorder and 8.1 million people who had an illicit drug use disorder.[5]
- According to the National Alliance on Mental Illness, one out of five Americans (nearly 44 million people) experience mental illness in a given year, and 46.4 percent will experience a mental illness during their lifetime.[6]
- Suicide completion rates have surged to a thirty-year high. Globally, over 800,000 suicides are reported each year with more unreported.[7] Suicide is the tenth leading cause of death in the US.[8]
- Less than half of US adults with mental illness received treatment in 2018, and the median delay between the onset of mental illness symptoms and treatment is eleven years.[9]

And then a worldwide pandemic started in 2020. As a society already experiencing a mental health epidemic, the pandemic was quick to ignite a global mental health and financial crisis. The plummeting economy and surging unemployment caused prolonged financial stress, panic, and fear. Mandatory lockdowns and social-distancing requirements caused people to feel isolated and lose important social support, such as in-person connection to friends and family. Normal routines like attending school or work, visiting a place of worship, working out at the gym, going shopping, and visiting friends were gone in an instant. Many people began referring to the mental health crisis as the "epidemic within the pandemic."

At the time of this writing, the following information was current. Keep in mind these figures will most likely continue to change:

- Research suggests that "deaths of despair"—deaths arising from alcohol, drugs, or suicide—could jump by up to 154,037 in the US due to the pandemic.[10] As of June 2020, one in four Americans between the ages of eighteen and twenty-four had serious thoughts about committing suicide.[11]
- Anxiety and depression have surged during the pandemic. In Turkey, for example, 23.6 percent of people experienced depression; 45.1 percent of people experienced anxiety.[12]
- The pandemic has greatly increased post-traumatic stress disorder (PTSD) in certain hotspots around the globe. In a Tunisian community, for example, 33 percent of the general population experienced PTSD. Time spent watching news about the pandemic or being exposed to details of a person's illness, death, or burial due to COVID-19 were positively associated with PTSD.[13]
- Obsessive compulsive disorder (OCD) rates have risen during the pandemic. A population in Italy, for example, showed a substantial increase in the severity of OCD symptoms during the first six weeks of their lockdown.[14]
- Intimate partner violence has surged worldwide due to increases in joblessness, economic anxiety, and physical isolation in homes during the pandemic. The United Nations Population Fund estimates that fifteen million additional cases of gender-based violence will occur worldwide for every three months of lockdown.[15]

We are learning an important lesson from the pandemic—there is an intrinsic relationship between mental health and financial health. Not caring for your mental health could cost you relationships, employment, or even your life. Financial distress accounts for 16 percent of suicides in the US and correlates with lower life satisfaction and higher stress, anxiety, and depression.[16]

We need to include positive mental and physical health, relationships, and work-life balance in our definition of success, not simply financial achievement. It's time to shed the shame and stop the blame by honoring how both world events and your unique life experiences have impacted you emotionally and financially. Good for you for deciding to work through a program that will empower you with the tools to persevere through challenges with courageous resilience and create sustainable success.

It's Not About the Money, It's About Financial Health and Well-Being

In this book, I encourage you to improve your financial health for your own good as well as for the good of others. I'm not encouraging greed, excess material possessions, waste, or the love of money. When we compassionately (by doing no harm) acquire and manage money, it can enable generosity, altruism, and positive change for the greater good. We are talking about using financial prosperity to care for ourselves, each other, and the world around us. Love is the true currency of life.

Being an active participant in life and aligning our unique gifts with a need in the world can improve our financial mindset. When we make our greatest effort to contribute with our fullest self-expression, we can both weather financial storms and reap tremendous monetary rewards.

About The Financial Mindset Fix Program

The Financial Mindset Fix is a holistic program to enhance your mindset around finances and transform the way you think, feel, and act so you can get out of your own way and achieve the success you deserve. Each chapter focuses on a different mindset that, when adopted, can improve your well-being and financial health, with empirical support to back that up. The program includes exercises and practical tools to set you up for success. The following is an overview of each chapter's mindset and how embracing this way of living will increase both your mental and financial fitness:

CHAPTER 1: ABUNDANCE

Explore your psychology of money, embrace your worth, and expand your thinking to welcome abundance into your life. Shift your perspective from scarcity to abundance. By doing so, you'll be able to recognize and unlock the doors to a more expansive, supported, and prosperous life.

CHAPTER 2: AWARENESS

Remove the blinders of defense and denial and recognize how your mental health impacts your financial health. Wake up and notice you are unconsciously repeating what is familiar and choose a more prosperous path.

CHAPTER 3: RESPONSIBILITY

Now that you are aware of the emotions and behaviors that constrain you, free yourself of resentment and anger through responsibility and forgiveness. Empower yourself to become the author of the rest of your life story. Take control of your financial future.

CHAPTER 4: PRESENCE

Further increase your awareness by giving yourself the present of presence. Experience the riches only available in the here and now. Apply mindfulness to your financial life to make decisions from a place of peace, groundedness, and clarity.

CHAPTER 5: ESSENCE

Through presence, connect with your inner light and highest self. Become aware of how your ego is hindering your contentment and prosperity. Understand how healthy self-esteem is halfway between Diva and Doormat. Align your life and work with your core values to launch yourself to tremendous heights of personal and professional success.

CHAPTER 6: SELF-LOVE

Now that you are connected with your essence, know you are innately good and deserving of prosperity. Become your own good parent, positive coach, and compassionate advocate by not sabotaging yourself. Invest in yourself through fierce love and financial self-care, so you have more to give yourself and others.

CHAPTER 7: VISION
Your outer life is a direct reflection of self-love. Develop a personal manifesto that aligns with your soul's mission. Recreate your life in new and magical ways by envisioning what you would do if you had a magic wand. For sustainable success, create work-life balance and look for the universal win-win.

CHAPTER 8: SUPPORT
To make your vision a reality, nurture and utilize your support network. Break through barriers like guilt, shame, and fear and open yourself up to receiving support. Weed out toxic relationships and welcome people into your life who raise your stock so you can do more good in the world.

CHAPTER 9: COMPASSION
Strengthen your support, loyalty, and true prosperity by having a heart of gold that expresses empathy, care, and kindness. Appreciate how opening your mind, encouraging others, and paying it forward with generosity will help you reap great rewards.

CHAPTER 10: DETACHMENT
Keep your eye on the prize and maintain a positive vibe by detaching from drama and negativity. Unplug from FUD—fear, uncertainty, and doubt—so you can weather the storms and stay on course for your personal and financial vision.

CHAPTER 11: POSITIVITY
Now that your heart is in the right place, you are unstoppable! Put yourself out in the world with cheerful enthusiasm and extreme optimism. Spin straw into gold by practicing gratitude to align with greater prosperity. Use creativity and proactive behaviors to negotiate a better life.

CHAPTER 12: RESILIENCE
Discover why progress isn't linear and adversity is the birthplace of opportunity. Develop resilience to help you move through difficulties so you can

come out stronger, more flexible, and more adaptable on the other end. Learn how to combine everything you've learned in this program to thrive, prosper, and persevere!

CONCLUSION: FINANCIAL MINDSET WISDOM
Bring all your learned skills together for complete prosperity and to improve your well-being and financial health.

Who Benefits from This Program?

The Financial Mindset Fix program is geared toward:

- People who desire an improved financial life, including those living paycheck to paycheck and those who want to increase their prosperity.
- Those who want to improve their mental health and happiness.
- Business leaders and professionals who desire new tools to improve their emotional intelligence, relationship skills, and leadership abilities.
- Entrepreneurs, business owners, and self-employed workers who want to improve their work-life balance and their bottom line.
- Business consultants and advisors who want to help their clients succeed.
- Corporate teams who want to improve communication and collaboration and increase sales.
- Companies that want to offer health and wellness programming to reduce stress at work, absenteeism, and health-care costs while increasing employee productivity and retention.
- Athletes and creative professionals who want to improve their professional performance and success.
- Caretaking professionals who want to prevent burnout and desire greater financial prosperity.
- Therapists and coaches who can use the material and exercises for themselves and their clients.
- School social workers, school counselors, and educators who can use this material to develop life skills and psychosocial programming for students.

We all need therapy or counseling at different points in our lives. If you have never had therapy or aren't currently in counseling, it might be helpful as you work the program. If you are in therapy, this program serves as a powerful supplement. However, if you aren't interested in therapy at this time, this program is like a vitamin to boost your mental health immune system. This book is not intended as a substitute for professional mental health treatment. The Financial Mindset Fix is a mental fitness program that also leads to financial gain.

What You Need to Know About Each Chapter

Each chapter focuses on one of the twelve different mindsets and explains how adopting it can improve your mental and financial health. Each chapter begins with a personal story of how the mindset helped me move through some tough situations. I'm hoping that sharing my story gets your wheels turning on how that mindset can help you too. I also share inspirational stories from my clients' experiences. To ensure confidentiality, all of the anecdotes in this book are composites of different clients with the identifying variables changed. These stories will help you discover that you are not alone in your challenges or your quest to optimize your financial mindset!

To help you best apply each principle, I dispersed short exercises throughout the chapters so you can begin to apply them to your life and work. Many of these exercises are popular tools therapists use in their practices. They come from various empirically supported therapeutic approaches, including cognitive behavioral therapy (CBT), self-psychology, narrative therapy, and others. Some of my favorite exercises are the Therapy Sessions, which allow you to imagine that you're stepping into my office for a therapy or business coaching session. I'll ask you specific questions to promote self-reflection and insight. Of course, this isn't actual psychotherapy, but you will gain significant insight into yourself and how you might need to change to improve your mental and financial health. As you go through the exercises, take your time. There's no need to rush through them.

Highly innovative (and revealing) wheel exercises review the mindsets in each chapter, assess and measure where you are at, and help you gain traction on the road to prosperity. In my speaking engagements and workshops, these wheel exercises are sometimes initially met with some resistance. However, after a few minutes, as participants get the hang of completing them and gain some unbelievable insight, they can't get enough of them. In fact, in my evaluations, people share how the wheel exercises are their favorite. That's why I've selected them to be a core component of this program. In total, this book contains fifteen wheel exercises—including the one here in the introduction, which we will get to shortly.

I've been surprised to find that even therapists who are very familiar with most of the concepts I share have found completing the wheels to be revealing—kind of like stepping on a scale and being surprised by the results! We don't often measure our mental and financial health in an honest way, which is perhaps why they can become so easily neglected. This program and the wheel exercises change that. Just as it's essential to be honest in therapy, it's vital to be honest with yourself in these exercises, even though it can be difficult or even painful to acknowledge our own areas of deficit. The more honest you are, the more you will benefit from this program. And if you become worried about particular mindsets that need a bit of work, relax. Continue to practice those mindsets just like you would exercise different parts of your body to improve your overall fitness. Working this program creates powerful life change.

In my workshops, I've noticed that when people discuss their completed wheels and exercises with a partner or a small group, they tend to make additional insights and connections. You might consider working through the program with a friend, partner, colleagues, or book club. The wheels will drive your life forward, the twelve mindsets will keep you on your path, and having support will give you greater traction.

Throughout this book, the exercises refer to journaling. You can do this in several ways. For your convenience, all of the exercises in this book are available to you at financialmindsetfix.com/exercises. I recommend saving and storing your digitally completed exercises in a file folder dedicated to this program. If you prefer paper and pen, print them out and utilize a dedicated journal or notebook. I suggest dating all your entries and exercises so you can revisit them and track your progress!

The Wheel Exercise Tutorial

The wheel exercises are self-evaluation tools that help you realize where your strengths and weaknesses lie in a given area. Don't worry about your scores—we are all works in progress. Since you'll be doing the wheel exercises throughout this program, you can turn to this tutorial for a refresher as needed. Completing the wheel exercise is easy. After you go through it once, you'll be a pro. And if you become discouraged because there is still progress to be made, always remember we are looking for progress, not perfection.

Each wheel exercise begins with a set of questions. After you read a question, simply rate yourself on the following scale: Poor (1–3), Fair (4–5), Good (6–7), Prosperous (8–10).

Each wheel diagram contains a set of spokes, similar to the spokes on a bicycle wheel. After you answer each wheel exercise question, chart your answer on the wheel. Find the spoke that matches the label of the question. Then simply place a dot on the spoke next to the number that corresponds with your answer. For example, if you rated yourself a 3, put a dot at the 3 mark on the spoke.

After scoring yourself on every spoke, connect the dots to create a circle. Note that the higher a number is, the closer it is to the outer section of the wheel, while lower scores are more toward the middle. To get an idea of how it looks, see The Financial Health Wheel Example below.

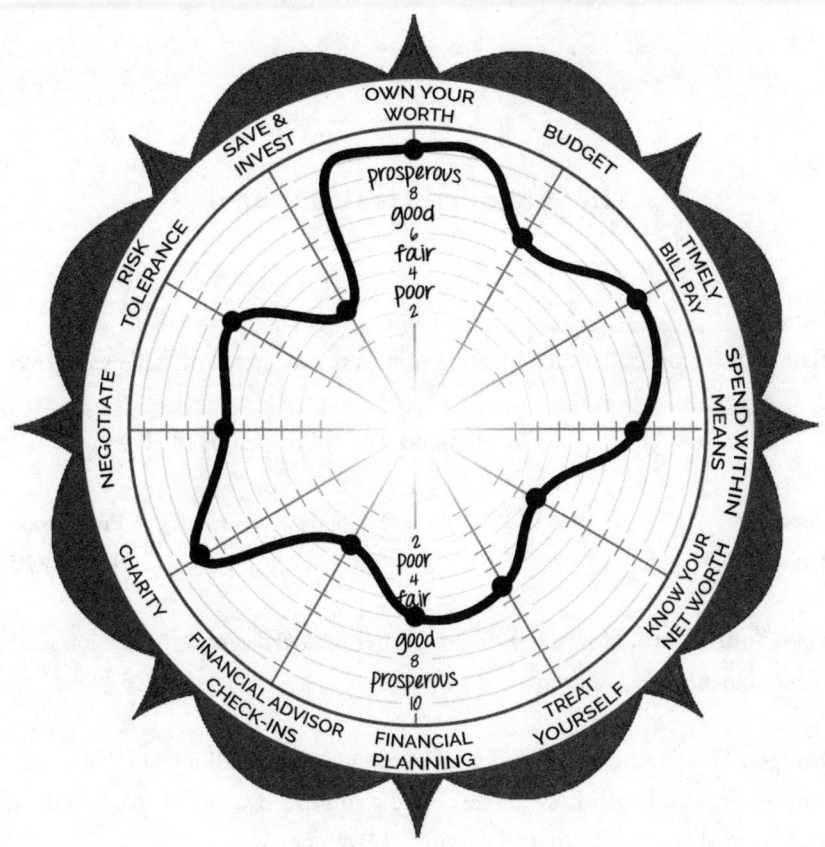

The Financial Health Wheel Example

The "dents" on the wheel represent areas where this person scored lower. This wheel was filled out by someone who doesn't have much when it comes to Save & Invest, so she scored low in that area, but she scored high when it came to Charity. This program provides the opportunity to begin working on these dents, or areas of deficit, today.

To get a base reading on how you currently handle finances, you're going to start by completing The Financial Health Wheel. Throughout this program, you'll dive into different aspects of your financial health, then revisit this same exercise at the end of the book to see all the progress you've made! I know you want to skip over this exercise, but don't! It's crucial because you are important and so is your financial health. You've got this! (Remember that all exercises are available for download at financialmindsetfix.com/exercises.)

The Financial Health Wheel
(20 minutes)

Date: _____

Rate your response after each question using a number from the following scale:

Poor (1–3), Fair (4–5), Good (6–7), Prosperous (8–10)

Poor			Fair		Good			Prosperous	
1	2	3	4	5	6	7	8	9	10

Own Your Worth: How deserving of greater financial prosperity do you feel? (Abundance) _____

Budget: How aware are you of your earnings and spending? Do you check your budget and cash flow at least once a month, live within your budget, and avoid slipping into financial denial? (Awareness) _____

Timely Bill Pay: Not paying bills on time can mean late fees and dings to your credit. How do you rate yourself on organizing and paying bills on time? (Responsibility) _____

Spend Within Means: Do you practice mindful spending? How well do you spend within your limits so you do not accrue debt? (Presence) _____

Know Your Net Worth: Net worth is the calculation of all assets (balances of all your bank accounts, value investments, and property) minus your liabilities (balances on credit cards, loans, and mortgages). How do you rate yourself at knowing your approximate net worth at any given time? (Essence) _____

Treat Yourself: How good are you at treating yourself within means when you feel you deserve it? (Self-Love) _____

Financial Planning: When it comes to your financial health, including paying off student loans or credit card debt and saving to buy a home, your kids' college, or your retirement, how would you rate yourself? (Vision) _____

Financial Advisor Check-Ins: How good are you about meeting with a financial advisor once or twice a year to keep on track? (Support) _____

Charity: How good are you at supporting causes that are meaningful to you in a doable way? (Compassion) _____

Negotiate: Negotiating includes asking for better pay or benefits, discussing the price of major purchases or contracts, and bartering services when possible in order to get a deal. How good are you when it comes to negotiating? (Positivity) _____

Risk Tolerance: When you have adequate insurance in place, it becomes easier to detach from the outcome. How would you rate yourself when it comes to having the proper amount of insurance for your health, car, house/apartment, business, and even life? (Detachment) _____

Save & Invest: Having at least three to six months of expenses in your savings and investments such as an IRA for your future is a good rule of thumb. How would you rate yourself when it comes to saving and investing for a rainy day? (Resilience) _____

Chart your responses on The Financial Health Wheel. (See The Wheel Exercise Tutorial above for instructions.) Start at the top of the wheel. For each spoke, ask yourself if you're Poor, Prosperous, or somewhere in between. Put a dot on the spoke next to the number that corresponds with your answer. Now continue going around the wheel, and after scoring yourself on every spoke, connect the dots to create a circle. Remember, just be honest with your responses.

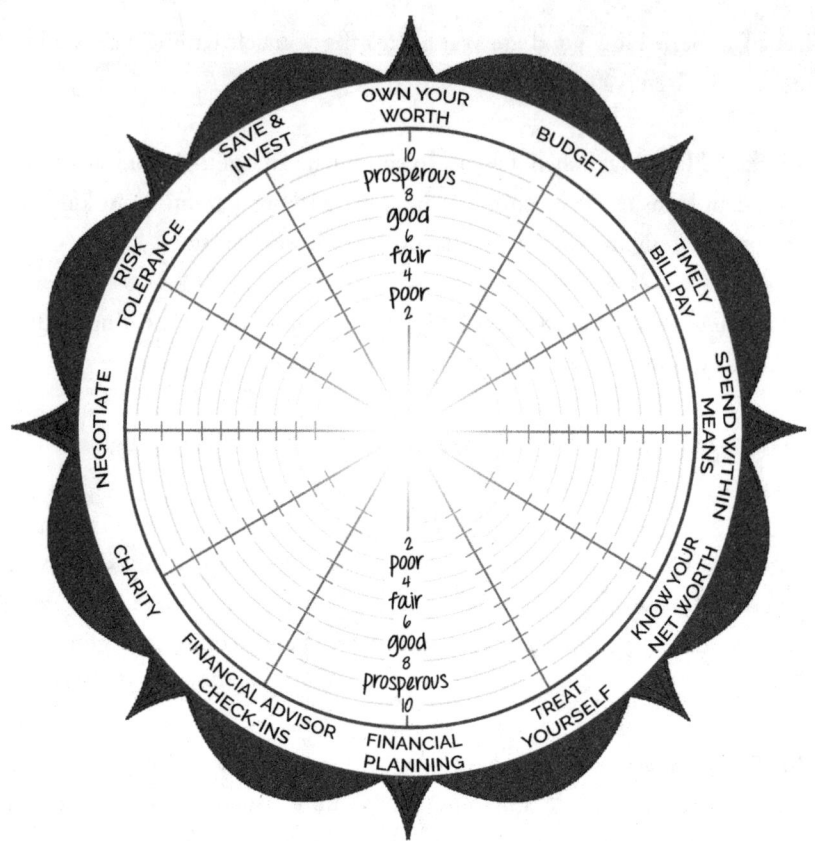

The Financial Health Wheel

Date your wheel so you can reference it when you reassess your financial health at the conclusion of the program. Congratulations! You have now completed your first exercise in this program. It gives you a good reading of your financial health now, before starting the program. Even if you rated yourself pretty well when it comes to your finances, you will learn how to continue to expand and improve your well-being and financial health. Every chapter of this book is full of practical tips, innovative tools, and inspiration.

...

How Much Time Is This Going to Take?

Each chapter's exercises should take no more than three hours to complete. For your convenience, I included approximately how long it will take to complete each exercise. Pick and choose the activities you want to do and complete them in a way that works best for you.

If your schedule permits, I recommend a twelve-week timeline, because most people can commit to twelve weeks of working on themselves. This helps with momentum and consistency. If this seems daunting, you might decide to tackle one chapter a month. Do the program in a time frame that works for you. All that matters is that you stick with it and stay dedicated to the work it takes to welcome your greater life.

Just like physical exercises can provide noticeable results in your physique, financial mindset exercises can improve your mental and financial fitness. It's okay to skip activities that do not resonate with you, but I strongly encourage you to complete each chapter's wheel exercise.

The Financial Mindset Fix as a Way of Life

Because we are all works in progress and are continuing to evolve, The Financial Mindset Fix program is meant to become a way of life. It's not a quick fix. Just like the benefits of a regular strength training regimen begin to diminish when you suddenly stop, the same applies to your financial mindset. Continue to practice and develop these mindsets to increase personal and professional success. The more you practice these mindsets, the easier it becomes.

The Financial Mindset Fix program contains tools you can use forever. You can circle back to chapters as needed when life throws you particular challenges or setbacks. Regardless of where you are at in your journey, let me be your guide to a more prosperous life. I will be with you during each step, cheering you along the way. Congratulations on investing in your self-worth and financial life. This will be the most improved year of your fiscal and emotional health!

Chapter 1

ABUNDANCE

Discover Your Worth and See That We're All Beggars Sitting on a Golden Bench

*Why are you so enchanted by this world when
a mine of gold lies within you?*
RUMI thirteenth-century poet, Sufi mystic, and theologian

"You certainly didn't choose this field for the money," scoffed my professor. It was 1994 and the first day of my master's program in counseling psychology at Northwestern University. Even though in my heart I wanted to be a therapist and help others, I felt a pit in my stomach. I had just signed a promissory note for $50,000 of student loans to pay for my graduate degree. How was I going to pay it back and support myself?

When I graduated two years later, the average starting salary for a beginning counselor was $18,000 a year. I heard a classmate had a $25,000 starting salary, so I made that my goal. I obtained a job earning exactly $25,000 a year as a counselor working with HIV positive IV drug users at a methadone maintenance clinic in downtown Chicago. It was there I learned about the traumas of growing up with poverty, violence, racism, and crime, as well as the essential goodness and resilience of the human spirit.

After two years of working at the methadone clinic, I was newly married and having a hard time making ends meet. I decided I needed at least $35,000 a year to live more comfortably. Fortunately, I obtained a job as an employee assistance program (EAP) counselor, which paid exactly $35,000 a year. I provided behavioral health services for employees working in industries ranging from labor unions to hospitals to legal and financial firms. To move forward in my career and improve my financial standing, I also worked a part-time job at a counseling group practice.

In 2002, I took a leap of faith, left my two jobs, and dove into full-time private practice. Knowing I needed support, I scheduled a coffee meeting with my friend, Dr. Steven Nakisher. He had also recently started a practice and asked me how much money I was hoping to make per year. Since I was pregnant with my first daughter and bills were piling up, I told him I would really love to increase my earnings to $60,000 a year.

Steve frowned and said, "Only $60K? I want to make over $100K a year."

I said with surprise and naivete, "Do you think that's possible?!"

Steve said with confidence, "Of course."

That year, I made $60,000, and Steve made well over $100,000.

Steve went on to start several successful businesses and was a contestant on *Shark Tank* and won. One of his products made it on Oprah's Favorite Things list. Steve's line of thinking led him to great success, while my modest aspirations seemed to set my own glass ceiling. After noting this cause and effect, I did what any good therapist would do—I made an appointment with my therapist!

In our session, Arlene Englander asked me, "What do you think of when you hear the word 'money'?" I said, "Money makes me think of stress. Money is stressful." She replied, "Well, then! Of course, you make it go away!"

Together, we explored how my beliefs about money were rooted in my childhood. My dad was born during the Great Depression and grew up in the inner city of Cleveland, Ohio, where he witnessed his parents doing grueling factory work. He chose an academic route where he worked full-time throughout college and served as a lieutenant in the Air Force to finance his master of business administration (MBA) degree from Harvard University. Although he achieved success as a division president of a large company that made gaskets, the automotive recession of the 1980s pulled the rug out from beneath him.

When I was eight, I remember playing in the living room and telling my dad I was so happy to have him home during the day, which was unusual. I looked at him and saw he was crying. He explained that he was laid off from his job. Although I didn't really understand what that meant, I could see he was not as happy as I was that he was home. He looked sad, ashamed, and afraid. Like many men, he derived much of his self-worth from his career and income.[1]

Our family relocated twice during the next three years—from Detroit to Toronto to Toledo. Multiple layoffs and unemployment triggered my father's massive financial anxiety and clinical depression. There were many arguments about money, yet we lived in a large home in a lovely suburb and belonged to a fancy country club. I wasn't sure which was our financial reality—the somewhat opulent one people saw on the outside, or the scary and shameful one I felt on the inside. In many ways, my dad was a wonderful example of financial accomplishment and resilience, as he eventually invested in the stock market and did very well. However, my upbringing felt like a financial and emotional roller coaster, leaving me with some work to do in therapy.

Through therapy, I said to hell with the message that therapists can't help people and make good money—a message I received that first day in grad school (and at least a hundred other times in my career). Even though my last name is Marter, I refused to be a financial martyr! I set the intention to start a counseling business that would not only change lives but also change my own. The beginning of my life transformation was working on my beliefs about money and trying to embrace my worth. There were many twists and turns and bumps along the path toward abundance.

As I counseled working professionals and built my practice, Urban Balance, I became increasingly interested in the psychology of money. I started to see how my clients' thoughts and beliefs about money impacted their bottom line, either positively or negatively. As their therapist, my job is to help my clients explore what's blocking the flow of money and other resources such as love and support so they can dive into the flow of abundance. And now I will share that with you so you can do the same! (Remember that all exercises are available for download at financialmindsetfix.com/exercises.)

Therapy Session Number 1
(20 minutes)

Imagine you are in my office for your first therapy session. We'll explore how your life experiences with money may have shaped and molded your relationship with money today. Write your responses to the following questions in your journal:

- What cultural, religious, and family belief systems about money were you taught?
- What are your attitudes and beliefs about people with a lot of money? With very little money?
- Growing up, did you notice expectations surrounding money were different for males than females, for the young versus the old, for different types of professions, or differing expectations resulting from ethnic or racial discrimination?
- How has this impacted your financial life today?
- What do you think of when you hear the word *money*? For me, it was stress, which is negative. Are your thoughts positive or negative when you hear the word *money*?
- Do you set income ceilings for yourself? If so, what have they been, and what is holding you back from breaking through those ceilings?
- Do you feel truly capable and deserving of having an abundance of money and other resources? If not, why?

Now, pretend you are reviewing your responses with me. Highlight the top three ways of thinking that might be preventing you from living an abundant life. For example, if you were taught that rich people are bad or men should earn more money than women, ask yourself how might you reframe those beliefs to receive abundance and take better care of yourself, your loved ones, and the world around you? Write this out. This is the type of work you need to do to start embracing The Financial Mindset Fix.

...

Bravo! Now let's dig a bit deeper into your relationship with money.

What Does Your Relationship with Your Finances Look Like?

During my thirties, if my financial life were a person, her name would have been Penny. I blamed Penny for much of my unhappiness and responded to her with irritability and anger. I treated her with horrible neglect and forgot to feed her or see how she was doing. When I did visit her, I responded with guilt, fear, and panic because of her poor appearance. I was too embarrassed and ashamed to introduce her to anyone and couldn't even look her in the eyes.

In my late thirties, when my personal and business debt was at an all-time high, I was in a place of crippling financial anxiety. Penny collapsed from exhaustion. As a caretaker and people pleaser, I racked up massive debt trying to take care of my staff, clients, and family, including my two young daughters. I attempted to give my staff whatever they asked for and made sure my girls never went without—even if it was beyond my pay grade. No wonder Penny was exhausted. Because the business was insurance friendly and there was a lag in insurance claim processing, we were in cash-flow hell. The last week of every month, I couldn't sleep, wondering if we could cover the payroll and rents due on the first of the month. My business partner and I were taking cash advances on our personal credit cards to make ends meet. Credit card companies were calling and staff therapist paychecks were bouncing. We were maxed out and living in financial terror.

At our lowest financial point, my business partner of seven years, who was one of my very best friends, sent an email to me and our entire staff stating that she was quitting and never coming back. Besides the heartbreaking deaths of my dad in my twenties and my mom in my thirties, this was the most devastating loss I ever experienced. My business partner and I always referred to one another as "soul sisters." I was sure we would still be friends when we were little old ladies. This loss felt like a spouse moving out during the middle of the night with no notice. She never said goodbye, and I shipped her personal belongings to her. There was a gaping hole in my heart, and I felt broken open.

After she departed, the staff felt like the business was a sinking ship. About a third of the thirty-five therapists quit and took their clients. While grieving the loss of my friend and business partner, I felt alone and exhausted, but I refused to throw in the towel. I still had staff and clients counting on me. In our business dissolution agreement, my former partner retained the office location and staff closest to her home. Meanwhile, I assumed responsibility for our business debts of over $100,000 and four other long-term office leases. Like a captain of a ship, I felt responsible and dedicated to the voyage, and I refused to abandon ship.

Instead of telling my staff everything would be okay, as I had in the past, I apologized for not seeking proper business and financial consultation. In truth, I was afraid that somebody would tell me the business model didn't work and that my dream company would have to close. Rather than feeling like everything was up to me to figure out, I practiced humility and asked for help. The staff that stayed loved the company and wanted to help. Instead of suffering in silence, I started speaking openly about my situation. Friends and family offered support and helpful advice.

My neighbor, an accountant with an MBA, asked if I had undergone a business valuation. He offered to have a certified public accountant (CPA) friend review my books, tell me the value of my business, and possibly offer help.

Facing my fears, I made an appointment with the CPA, Tim Kenny. With trepidation and eyes filled with tears, I handed him my QuickBooks files while he calmly asked some questions. A few days later, he called to tell me the business model worked! Tim said it truly was a cash-flow problem, and he could help me obtain the proper bank lending so I could pay my therapists and rent on time.

Tim also provided me with a reality check. He said, "Joyce, you are not running a charity to employ therapists. This is a business, and you deserve to profit." I was giving all my resources away until I had nothing left to give. I needed to start prioritizing Penny and set some healthy financial boundaries. When I did, it was better for everybody.

The bank loans and some tweaks to the business model stopped the financial hemorrhaging, but this was not a quick and painless fix. Penny was still on life support. My in-house accountant, Shelly, became my angel of daily encouragement. We took things one day at a time, and with the help of the leadership team and staff, we turned the ship around.

Tim, Shelly, and my financial planner, Bill Laipple, all got to know Penny very intimately and helped me tremendously in taking better care of her. I began to communicate openly and honestly with Penny and visit with her virtually every day. Penny's health started improving dramatically.

Today I call my financial life Prosperity. She is strong, vibrant, and powerful. She and I support one another and have each other's back. I value her, am proud of her, and take good care of her.

Penny and Prosperity are reflections of my sense of worth at two different points in my life. I had to value myself to welcome abundance. You can do this too. Really. However poor your financial health is at this time, you can have prosperity, and you deserve it.

Look at Your Financial Self in the Mirror
(20 minutes)

Answer the following questions in your journal:

- If your finances were a person, what would you name them?
- How would they look and feel?
- What is the nature of your relationship?
- What's the connection between who you see in the mirror and your financial self-worth?

...

After you've looked at your financial self in the mirror, it is time to welcome greater abundance into all aspects of your life.

Financial Health Boost: Own Your Worth

Am I good enough? Yes I am.[2]
MICHELLE OBAMA lawyer, author, and former First Lady of the United States

Because our parents are imperfect human beings, we all have unmet needs that leave us with feelings of lack of worth. By observing my clients over the years, I have recognized that high self-worth leads to increased net worth, but not the other way around. Research shows that high self-esteem is positively correlated with job performance.[3] To improve your financial health, embrace your worth.

My heart filled with pride when my client Nia vented about her toxic and low-paying job, and said, "I am worth more than this and I want better for myself." While most of us have worked low-paying jobs at various points in our lives out of necessity, they should be a stepping-stone as we grow and develop. I know this is the start of a new chapter for Nia, one that will bring greater abundance because she now knows she is deserving.

In my own journey, I also worked on embracing my worth. In 2012, I had my first invitation to provide an out-of-state keynote. As many people ascribe to the belief "You get what you pay for," I consulted my friend Ross, a successful therapist and author who frequently gives talks and presentations, about setting a fee for my presentation.

I asked Ross what he charged for an out-of-state speaking engagement. He generously shared his pricing with me. Even though the price was far beyond what I had ever asked, I borrowed Ross's self-esteem and requested that amount from the people hiring me. They replied, "Great! No problem." I was thrilled!

I called Ross and said, "I can't believe I'm getting paid that much for speaking for only forty-five minutes!" He said, "Forty-five minutes? I gave you my full-day rate."

The most you get is what you ask for. We have to value our worth, move through unnecessary guilt, and remember that when we have more, we can give more and do more good in the world.

Examine Your Self-Worth
(10 minutes; lifetime practice)

In your journal, answer the following questions:

- Imagine somebody who believes in you (like your best friend, colleague, or mother) is asked to describe your unique gifts and strengths. What would they say?
- Describe a time when you pleasantly surprised yourself on what you were able to accomplish. How did that feel? What did you learn from that experience that could translate to other aspects of your life?
- When do you feel the most valuable? In which relationships? Why?
- Write about a time when you felt you were compensated appropriately for a job well done. How did that come to be? Did that opportunity fall in your lap, or did you welcome it somehow? What can you learn from this experience?

Your self-worth reflects how much abundance you are willing to let into your life.

...

Abundance Versus Scarcity

Long-lasting and pronounced success comes to those who renew their commitment to a mindset of abundance every minute of every hour of every day.[4]
BRYANT McGILL American author

I ascribe to the theory of abundance; there is more than enough money, opportunity, goodness, love, and other resources for all of us. Therefore, when we have more, it doesn't mean somebody else has less. Abundant thinking can create new income streams and increased revenue for you while providing more for others—such as jobs, internships, sliding fee or pro bono services, and charity. Abundance isn't selfish; when you have more, you can help more.[5]

Some people live by the scarcity model. Perhaps they have experienced not having enough and understandably believe they have to hang on to what they have and protect their resources. Others were taught an "each for his own" kind of mentality, which can fuel greed, jealousy, and competition. Shifting from a scarcity mindset to an abundance mindset opens doors to possibilities, collaborations, celebrating the successes of others, and greater prosperity.

In my practice, I have seen financial trauma lead to obsessive thinking about financial losses, depression, anxiety, and PTSD.[6] My client Rachel grew up in abject poverty in the Chicago housing projects. It was common for her to go hungry and not have essential toiletries. She is a very intelligent and hardworking woman, and worked her way through college. Even with a strong salary, trauma from the past caused her to fear going without. She ate herself into morbid obesity and came to me after having gastric bypass surgery. No longer able to overeat, she replaced that compulsion with spending. Rachel began to hoard toiletries, clothing, and other household items while racking up debt. Scarcity thinking leads people to keep and hoard those objects they perceive as scarce.[7]

We worked on Rachel's underlying trauma and subsequent obsessive-compulsive behaviors and feelings of worthlessness that stemmed from neglect. Through cognitive behavioral therapy (CBT), an empirically supported therapy that is based on the belief that our thoughts precede our emotions and behaviors, she shifted to abundant thinking. She hired a financial planner so she could feel safe and secure about her future. She began to relax, knowing she was worthy and capable of providing for herself. As a result, her dating life improved because she was meeting people from a place of worth and stability instead of low self-esteem and desperation.

When people view their financial life through a lens of scarcity, spending can be terrifying. Money is financial energy, and just like other forms of life energy, such as breath or love, when we are in balance, we are in the state of flow. When we understand healthy spending is contributing to the abundant flow of life and lean in with trust and courage, we move into a greater flow of abundance with financial peace.

Life Is Not a Competition: Collaborate for Greater Reward

One of my clients didn't like to introduce her friends to each other out of fear they would like each other better and leave her out. If they did meet, she would try to control their interactions. She was selfishly hoarding her friends out of greed and fear of scarcity. Over time, her controlling behavior caused them to become annoyed and distanced from her. That's when her fears were manifested through the power of self-fulfilling prophecy.

In business, this kind of greed can lead to short-term gains, but it ends up biting you in the ass because you will lose employees and customers. Research shows that greed can lead you to doing something wrong, illegal, or getting fired.[8]

Rather than being secretive and protective over business resources, a healthy spirit of collaboration can actually improve your bottom line. I provide workshops and coaching to help other therapists build their practices. For years, people told me this was foolish because I am creating more competition for myself. Through an abundant lens, I see this differently. By helping other therapists succeed, I am staying true to my mission to promote mental health care access for all, which contributes to the greater good. My bottom line has increased from creating additional income streams through coaching and training. Also, therapists I've coached or trained often refer clients to me, recommend me for speaking engagements, and send employee candidates my way.

An abundant mindset, with accompanying action, works. Colleagues in my professional association went to insurance companies and asked for fee increases. One year, we achieved a 17 percent pay increase for all mental health providers in Illinois. By collaborating with my "competitors," my business's bottom line increased by $10,000 a month. This was one of the biggest improvements in my business, which never would have happened without collaboration with my competitors.

The last five years I owned my business, I was part of a practice management group of about ten people who owned large psychotherapy practices. We met quarterly to discuss business challenges and exchange ideas and support. I was always impressed with the spirit of generosity and the open sharing of resources. Instead of operating in silos, we shared information that helped us all grow and flourish, and we helped more clients. We received much-needed emotional support as well, as we talked openly about the challenges of managing staff or starting a new location. We maintained friendly collegiality and celebrated each other's successes. Meanwhile, we respected professional boundaries, such as areas of service, staff members, or referral sources. I recommend this type of forum to anyone interested in growing their business.

Synergize for Success
(10 minutes; lifetime practice)

In your journal, answer the following questions:

- With whom do you feel competitive? How might feeling competitive be hurting you?
- How do your competitors inspire you? What can you learn from them? Identify the blessings.
- How can you invite more collaboration into your life?
- How will shifting from competition to collaboration help you welcome greater abundance?

. . .

Stop Setting Your Ceiling! Blow the Lid Off Life with Abundant Thinking

> *A man is but the product of his thoughts. What he thinks, he becomes.*[9]
> MOHANDAS GANDHI Indian lawyer, anti-colonial nationalist, and political ethicist

When you refuse to believe something is impossible, it becomes possible. Statements or beliefs such as "I am poor" or "I am rich" can shape our financial reality, so be mindful of the power of your thoughts and words.

The stage of life you're in may impact your perspective on abundance too. For example, if you are young and starting out, you may identify as "a broke college student." How might this belief limit you? Or maybe you are retiring and are telling yourself "It is too late for me to improve my financial situation." Stop these self-limiting beliefs and know it is never too early or too late to invest in yourself.

Change your language from:

- "I don't" to "I do" (e.g., "I don't deserve prosperity" to "I do deserve prosperity")
- "I won't" to "I will" (e.g., "I won't get the job" to "I will get the job")
- "I can't" to "I can" (e.g., "I can't start my own business" to "I can start my own business")
- "I'm not" to "I am" (e.g., "I'm not very good at what I do" to "I am good at what I do")

I've noticed how negative beliefs limit people's potential and block the flow of abundance. The clients who repeatedly say "That won't work," "That won't help," and "I can't do that" tend to stay stuck. Those with open minds open the doors to infinite abundance. Instead of stopping when they hit roadblocks, they are open to new strategies, approaches, or solutions. They say *yes* to new opportunities such as online courses, community workshops, and networking. I've seen my clients embrace a shift to abundant thinking and do everything from starting a successful side hustle to becoming environmental leaders.

Let's do some activities to help you shift to abundant thinking!

Record and Rewire Your Thinking
(15 minutes; lifetime practice)

Cognitive behavioral therapy (CBT) helps people become aware of and change their negative thought patterns—or in simpler terms, to stop their stinkin' thinkin'. CBT uses thought records or thought dairies as tools to identify and change negative thinking patterns to make thoughts more neutral or positive.

In your journal, create a thought record chart like the one below. Think back to the last couple of weeks when you were emotionally distressed about something, especially your financial life, and write it down in your chart. I've included an example to get you started.

Situation	Thought	Emotion	Behavior	Alternate Thought
My coworker received the promotion instead of me.	I suck.	Anger Sadness Shame	Sulky and passive-aggressive	There will be a better opportunity for me in the future.

By changing the thought from negative to positive, the emotions you feel may be empowerment, peace, trust, or hope. These emotions lead to behaviors that are more celebratory of others' successes. Thought records are a lifelong tool that can change your thinking from negative to positive. I know this sounds simple, but it is important to train your brain to think positively. You can do this.

...

Discover Your Golden Bench

The world is your oyster. It's up to you to find the pearls.[10]
CHRIS GARDNER American businessman who went from homeless to billionaire, best known for the film based on his memoir, *The Pursuit of Happyness*

When I met with Tim, the CPA, that first time, I thought he was going to tell me to file for business bankruptcy. Imagine my surprise when he told me that the value of the business was at a healthy seven-figure amount. This was just after my former partner abandoned the business because we were only looking at the debt and what we were lacking, not the whole picture.

What gifts, resources, and assets are you not seeing because you are looking through a negative lens—what golden bench are you sitting on without realizing it? Think of the show *Antiques Roadshow*, where people discover trinkets that are sometimes treasures worth big cash. Take a deeper inventory of your strengths, resources, ideas, and talents. Identify overlooked treasures. I've had countless clients sitting on a nearly finished book they have written and shown to nobody, a business idea they have yet to pursue, a unique skill they haven't marketed to others, or an amazing talent they have yet to put out in the world. They want more in life, yet fear is blocking their flow of abundance.

My absolute favorite thing about being a therapist is mirroring people's strengths and all that is amazing, special, and beautiful about them. These are the seeds of abundance. They need to be seen, valued, and nurtured. By working through The Financial Mindset Fix program, you are watering your seeds and welcoming in the light so you can branch out and blossom into the fullest and most magnificent expression of yourself. Achieving abundance allows you to spread more seeds of prosperity that will grow into a vast orchard, providing abundance for generations to come.

Now it's time to apply abundance to your daily life. The Abundance Wheel brings together all the skills you learned in this chapter and measures where abundance shows up most for you. To get an idea of how your wheel might look, see The Abundance Wheel Example.

The Abundance Wheel Example

This wheel was filled out by someone who wasn't very Open to Possibilities for herself, so she scored low in that area; but she scored high when it came to Happiness for Others. The "dents" on the wheel represent areas where she scored lower. This program provides the opportunity to begin working on these dents, or areas of deficit, today. With significant areas of deficiency, your wheel may look more like a "constellation" than a circle, and that's okay! Revisit this exercise as you work through The Financial Mindset Fix program.

Where you are today is a starting point. Because the chapters are interrelated, as you work through the program, you will continue to make progress in the area of abundance.

To get a base reading on where abundance shows up in your life currently, complete The Abundance Wheel.

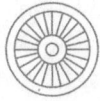

The Abundance Wheel
(20 minutes)

Date: _____

Rate your response after each question using a number from the following scale:

Poor (1–3), Fair (4–5), Good (6–7), Prosperous (8–10)

Poor			Fair		Good			Prosperous	
1	2	3	4	5	6	7	8	9	10

Self-Worth: How would you rate your ability to embrace your innate worth and feel deserving of prosperity and all that is good? _____

Positive Money Psychology: How positive are your beliefs about the meaning of money? _____

Remove Barriers: How good are you at moving past guilty feelings for wanting more and replacing self-limiting beliefs with positive statements that welcome the flow of money to you? _____

Abundant Thinking: How would you rate yourself when it comes to abundant thinking instead of scarcity thinking and trusting in an abundant flow of resources? _____

Limitless Perspective: How well are you able you see past limits (other than ethical) and think big about your life and financial future? _____

Positive Money Relationship: How would you rate yourself at having an attentive and nurturing relationship with money? _____

Collaborate: When it comes to working together rather than working in competition, how would you rate yourself? _____

Happy for Others: While celebrating the joys and successes of others, how convinced are you that this does not mean there is less for you? _____

Positive Change Belief: Do you believe that even if life is difficult now or your finances are in bad shape, things can improve? _____

Open to Possibilities: Instead of seeing roadblocks, how willing are you to look at new ways of doing things so your work, finances, and life can grow and flourish? _____

Seize Opportunities: How good are you at accepting invitations, attending events, classes, online seminars, e-courses, and other opportunities extended to you? _____

Capitalize on Assets: How would you rate yourself at utilizing the gifts, talents, and resources that are available to you? _____

Chart your responses on The Abundance Wheel. (For a refresher on how to do this, see The Wheel Exercise Tutorial on page 11.) Let's start at the top: Are you Poor, Prosperous, or somewhere in between when it comes to Self-Worth? Put a dot on the spoke next to the number that corresponds with your answer. Now continue going around the wheel, and after scoring yourself on every spoke, connect the dots to create a circle. Don't worry about your scores. Just be honest.

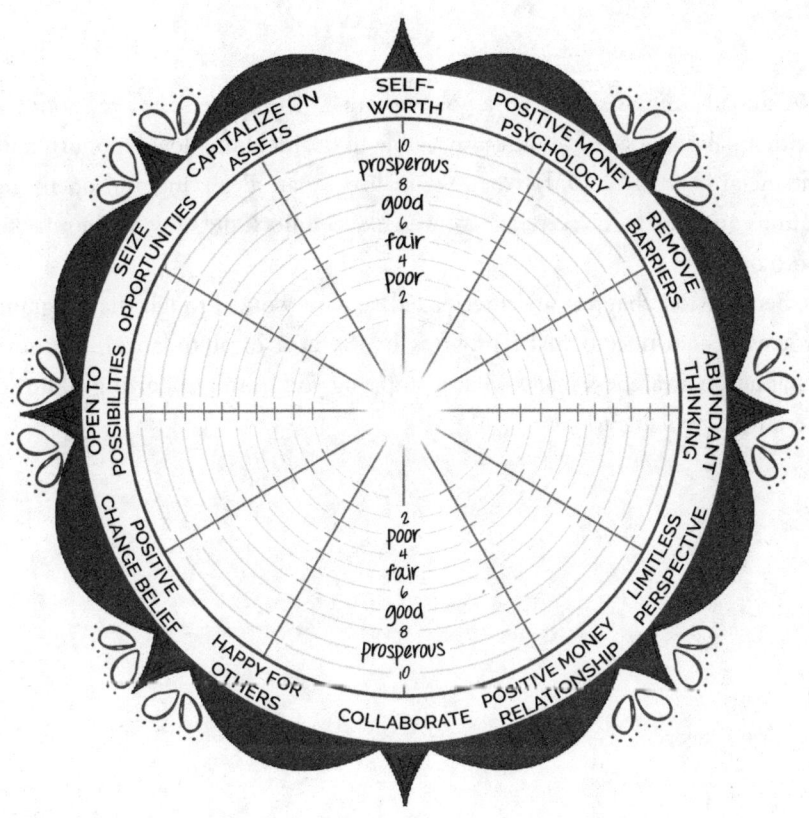

The Abundance Wheel

To see where you are at when it comes to abundance, answer the following questions in your journal:

- Where are the three biggest "dents" in your wheel?
- What do you see as the biggest obstacles to achieving a Prosperous rating in these three areas?
- Any ideas on how you can transcend those limitations?

Consider discussing your results with a friend or trusted confidant. Remember, this is deep work and it is normal to have ups and downs. Remember to date your wheel so you can track your progress over time. Keep going!

...

We are all beggars sitting on a golden bench. The universe is over-pouring with an abundance of resources available to us, including love, support, and financial prosperity. Only when we realize we are deserving and open our minds and hearts to receiving, are we able to unlock the flow of abundance into our lives.

Because the chapters are interrelated, as you work through the program, you will continue to make progress in the area of abundance. The next chapter on awareness shares what is stopping you from recognizing all those resources available to you.

Chapter 2

AWARENESS

Realize How Your Unconscious Is Robbing You of Riches

Who looks outside, dreams; who looks inside, awakes.
CARL JUNG Swiss psychiatrist and psychoanalyst, founder of analytical psychology

While sitting in a lecture on alcoholic families, I thought, "Why does this sound like my family?" While my parents didn't drink, our emotional and relational dynamics resembled an alcoholic family—arguing and volatility, feelings of shame and anger, subsequent anxiety and low self-esteem, and the existence of "family secrets."

I felt like a detective during my first year of clinical training, which was also my first year of therapy. I was searching for a deeper awareness and understanding of myself so I could become more conscious and be effective in my work. Self-awareness involves coming out of denial, being aware of our own issues (including mental health issues), and understanding our default relationship roles and patterns and how they impact our well-being and finances. Self-awareness is an essential prerequisite of conscious living and being holistically successful.

During my childhood, I learned that my mother's father, who died long before I was born, was an alcoholic. After attending the lecture on alcoholic families, I asked my mother a bit more about her father's alcoholism and her own past. Much to my surprise, she shared that she attended Alcoholics Anonymous (AA) meetings in her thirties, when my three older siblings were all under age six. Upon reflection, my mother said her drinking was probably an attempt to self-medicate her postpartum depression and painful feelings from unresolved childhood trauma.

My mom was an extremely intelligent woman with great psychological and spiritual depth and wisdom, and a witty sense of humor. Yet she was a complex person who had an enormous impact on me in some negative ways as well. When I was growing up, she was extremely critical, controlling, and strict. Whenever I experienced normal emotions of sadness or anger, instead of being empathetic, she made me feel like I was bad or wrong for having those feelings. This treatment is common for the children of alcoholics, and it trickled down to me, even though my mother didn't drink during my upbringing.

My relationship with my mom, along with my parents' constant arguing about finances and more, left me filled with anxiety and desperate for approval and peace at home. I took on the role of being a mediator in their marriage and a rescuer for anyone in our family who was suffering. (No wonder I became a therapist!)

Upon deeper reflection during my clinical training, I became aware that the result of these family dynamics was my own codependency—detrimental caretaking and people pleasing at the expense of my own well-being. In my adult life, this unconscious pattern impacted my relationships, my work, and my finances.

When Tim, the CPA, confronted me about taking care of others at the expense of myself, I realized my codependency was a big reason why my business hit financial rock bottom. In order to be more financially conscious, I needed to open my eyes to my role in creating my own misfortune. This was crunch time; I had to learn that prioritizing self-care and setting healthy limits in relationships isn't selfish, it's essential.

As I worked on myself through self-help readings about codependency, working on introspective practices such as journaling and mindfulness, and psychotherapy, I developed a greater self-awareness of why I am the way I am, and why I do what I do. This work grounded me in a more conscious reality, personally and financially. By understanding my tendency toward codependency, I've learned how to take better care of myself and set healthier limits relationally and financially, which has improved my anxiety, self-esteem, and financial standing.

I want you to have a greater awareness and consciousness so you can stop your self-defeating behaviors, take better care of yourself, and have greater success. Let's get started!

Therapy Session Number 2
(20 minutes)

Imagine you are back in my office for a second session, where we are working on promoting your awareness. As I ask you the following questions, write your responses in your journal:

- What did my story bring up for you?
- How did your family impact your mental health? Your financial health?
- Can you think about a time in your life when self-awareness helped improve both your well-being and your finances?

...

As you begin to work on your awareness, you'll need to take a closer look at yourself, just like I did. What you discover might surprise you.

We May Be Unconsciously Recreating the Familiar

> *I'm a student of patterns. At heart, I'm a physicist. I look at everything in my life as trying to find the single equation, the theory of everything.*[1]
> WILL SMITH American actor and rapper

We all unconsciously repeat roles and relational patterns we learned in earlier life experiences until we become aware and choose something better. As human beings, we are often drawn to the path of least resistance because it is comfortable and familiar.

My client Rose came to therapy to deal with her stockbroker husband's addiction to cocaine and his affinity for strippers. At the time, she was a thirty-year-old stay-at-home mom with two little kids. In therapy, she realized she was cycling through the "drama triangle" of being in the role of the victim (when she was sad), the persecutor (when she was mad), and the rescuer (when she was glad, and when trying to save her husband).[2] After multiple attempts at couples therapy, three failed interventions, and a ton of work in Al-Anon, a 12-step support group for people whose lives have been affected by someone else's drinking, she made the brave decision to divorce her husband. Like a phoenix rising from the ashes, she reclaimed her power, reentered the workforce as a paralegal, took responsibility for her financial life, and thrived like a rock star—providing for her kids and taking care of herself better than ever. This was extremely empowering for her and turned out to be essential, because her husband lost his job to addiction and stopped paying child support. Several months after we successfully terminated therapy, she called me and said, "Hey Joyce, I need a tune-up . . . I started dating—and the guy I am seeing is just like my ex-husband, except with an Australian accent."

The human tendency to repeat familiar roles and relational patterns may be affecting your relationships, career, and financial life in ways you don't realize. We are unconsciously drawn to relationships and careers that allow us to function in the same role we had in our family of origin.

According to the family systems theory, each family member has a different role in creating and maintaining balance in the familial system.[3] Because workplaces are also relational systems, we often repeat our role in the workplace. Research suggests that an individual's role in their family of origin (the family you grew up with) plays an important part in the success of their career.[4] When we become conscious of the pros and cons of the roles we tend to play in groups and organizations, we can see how our relational tendencies impact our career and finances.

The following are some examples of common roles in families, as well as how they end up impacting one's career and financial life:

Hero or Golden Child: This person is a high achiever and the pride of the family. They are often good leaders who are goal oriented and self-disciplined but may lack the ability to relax or allow others to be right or in charge. Heroes tend to become business owners and business leaders but may struggle in some of their personal relationships because of their tendency to be bossy or domineering.

Scapegoat or Black Sheep: Family members may feel this person has problems—including mental health, addiction, or social or financial issues. The scapegoat may show the signs and symptoms of underlying family problems. Their strengths may include a sense of humor, vulnerability, and authenticity. They tend to struggle to transition into adulthood and achieve less success in their career and finances.

Good Child: This is the passive, subservient child who avoids being a problem. They tend to be flexible and easygoing, but lack direction, are fearful of making decisions, and follow others without questioning. They may end up being taken for granted in relationships or working in support roles that tend to be lower paying.

Mascot or Clown: These people use humor to diffuse conflict and may not feel free to express their true selves. They tend to have emotionally immature relationships that lack a deeper intimacy, and may end up working in sales or entertainment, which can be lucrative for some, but challenging for many.

Mediator: Mediators work to keep peace in the family system and may also be rescuers. They act as communication buffers, which may or may not be healthy for them, depending on how well received or effective their efforts are. Mediators may work as attorneys, real estate brokers, or middle managers.

Nurturer: These people provide emotional support and stability in a balanced and healthy way. They can also be mediators and may work with children or in education.

Rescuer: This person takes care of other family members' problems, often to relieve their own anxiety. They tend to experience guilt and are prone to codependency and detrimental caretaking at their own expense. They may work in helping professions as a therapist, nurse, or paramedic. Overall, helping professionals do not realize their true earning potential as they tend to view their finances as being outside of their control and accept the notion that they will not make much money.[5]

Cheerleader: These rah-rah people provide encouragement and support to others while taking care of their own needs and having a positive influence on others. They may work in marketing or leadership roles to motivate customers or staff.

Thinker: These people are objective, logical, and rational, but may find it difficult to emotionally connect with others. They may be drawn to science, medicine, or mathematics and may have difficulty with the people skills needed for networking and business development.

Truth Teller: This person tells it like it is. They communicate the information that is needed, but others may not appreciate their advice. This role can be a real strength when coupled with the qualities of a nurturer or cheerleader. Journalism or law are natural career choices for these people.

You may have played more than one of these roles in your family of origin. Hang on to the good parts of your roles, but shift whatever is no longer serving you. This requires paying attention and learning new and more adaptive behaviors through counseling or coaching, and working through The Financial Mindset Fix program.

Identify Your Default Role
(20 minutes)

In your journal:

- Reflect on your role in your family of origin. Write down two to three roles from the family systems theory that you most identify with and explain why.
- How might each of these roles be affecting your personal relationships or work life?

- How might each of these roles be affecting your finances?
- Identify two strengths and two challenges of each role.
- For each role, describe one change you would like to make to enhance your relationships and one change you would like to make to enhance your professional life or finances.

...

What You Don't Know Will Hurt You

> *That which is denied cannot be healed.*[6]
> BRENNAN MANNING American author and public speaker

Defense mechanisms like denial are unconscious coping strategies that can help cushion us from the traumatic or painful aspects of life, including unpleasant thoughts, feelings, and behaviors. While they may be temporarily helpful, being defensive obstructs deeper awareness, which can prevent us from dealing with reality. We need to become aware of life's realities so we can move forward consciously in our personal, professional, and financial lives.

Unconscious contracts may also unknowingly be steering our course. These are silent agreements we have unknowingly made with family members. For example, you may feel responsible for living someone else's dream, such as a parent who made sacrifices to raise you. While the underlying intentions are good, a blind choice to follow a path that might not be what you truly want will inevitably lead to psychological distress. Another unconscious contract might be to live life as a muted version of yourself so you don't threaten somebody else within the family system. This may happen if you experience survivor guilt, are a victim of abuse, or have a narcissistic family member. Finally, you may have been raised with cultural, religious, or family beliefs that may not truly resonate with you, yet keep you from becoming your best self and living a greater life. It's important to become aware that accepting these beliefs or silent agreements is a choice.

Are you living your life for somebody else?

I work with my clients so they can live life in a way that is congruent with their true selves. As I listen to my clients' life stories, I gather pieces of the puzzle. Experience has helped me notice when there are missing puzzle pieces or if the pieces don't seem to fit due to unconscious contracts and defense mechanisms. Together, we work to break through their defenses and create positive life changes.

A few years ago, a colleague referred Colleen to me after working with her for over a year with little progress. Colleen presented with moderate, chronic depression. Despite having what many would consider a great life, she was miserable.

She described a long history of being the proverbial "good girl." She felt most loved and accepted when she did what was expected by her parents, teachers, and community. She studied law because her father told her to, married her boyfriend because she was at the time in her life when she was supposed to get married, and had kids because that's what was expected. She was ashamed to admit she didn't enjoy being a parent and hated her work. Now that her girls were almost grown, she realized she didn't even know herself or what she truly liked, felt, or wanted.

When I asked about her marriage, she said it was okay, but she felt disconnected. After I asked about infidelity, she replied that her husband had an emotional affair with his coworker. She wasn't sure how it ended but was adamant it was definitely over. I asked her, "What makes you think it was an emotional affair and not a sexual one?" She looked at me with the blank and defensive face of denial. I told her about a woman who called her husband's bluff when he said he'd had an emotional affair, saying she knew it was sexual, which led to a confession. Colleen seemed irritated with me, and when she left the consultation, I wondered if I would ever see her again.

She came back the following week. After asking her husband some pointed questions about his emotional affair, he admitted to being in a several-year romantic and sexual affair with this coworker. He was in love with her and wanted to marry her. The scaffolding of denial that held up the facade of her quintessential life came crashing down. She needed to face this truth in order to shed her false self and discover her authentic self.

Through some tough work over the next couple years, her depression alleviated and her life transformed into a reflection of her true self. It started with a newfound independence after the divorce and beginning to make decisions for herself rather than to please others. With her kids out of the house, she left the suburbs and bought a modern condo in the city. She picked up her childhood passion for art and music and began to travel the world, making diverse and interesting friends and enjoying steamy, romantic connections. Even though she had previously felt bound to her job by "golden handcuffs," she took a courageous leap of faith and left to go off on her own, focusing on an area of law that interested her more. Over time, her earnings from her own law practice—in which she was fully invested with her entire heart and soul—doubled.

Like Colleen, we all have unconscious defense mechanisms like denial, which protect us from emotional distress. They can be useful and adaptive at certain times, such as the repression or dissociation needed to survive and cope with serious trauma, but many defenses can become masks that prevent us from looking at ourselves and our lives more honestly.

Stop Lying to Yourself

My friend Lisa Lackey is a renowned trauma and sex addiction therapist. She is an intelligent, warm, compassionate woman who specializes in working with executive-level men who are dealing with porn and sex addiction. To help chip through their defenses, she presses a large red button that says "BULLSHIT!" whenever her clients are trying to fool her or themselves. Are you ready to call yourself out on your own bull?

You may be familiar with many of the following defense mechanisms.[7] But do you know when you're using them? Or how they might impair your relationships, work, and financial health? Let's review them to get your wheels turning:

DENIAL

Denial is refusing to recognize that something occurred or is happening, or failing to realize the severity of the problem. It is common for those dealing with addiction, eating disorders, depression, abuse, trauma, and other mental health issues. It can cause a person to neglect caring for certain aspects of themselves or others and can impair a sense of shared reality in relationships.

People who have a low awareness of their spending, debts, interest rates, or the fees they are being charged may be in financial denial. Denial can cause someone to live beyond their means and outside of their financial reality.

They may not be aware of their partner's financial infidelity, which may include secret savings, spending, or debt. Finally, financial denial can involve being financially illiterate (unable to understand and manage one's finances) or having a low awareness of the financial standing in one's marriage or partnership as a result of feeling disempowered in the relationship.

DISPLACEMENT

Displacement is the act of directing anger at a less threatening person than the one at whom you are actually mad. For example, you may be crabby with your partner when you are actually mad at your boss, or you may yell at your kids when you are actually angry with yourself. Because we tend to take out our anger on the people we love most, displacement can tax our most important relationships. Displacement also impairs financial consciousness. For example, blaming the economy when your finances are poor rather than taking responsibility for your own overspending.

SUBLIMATION

This is the habit of acting out unacceptable impulses by expressing them through more acceptable behaviors. For example, an angry person who wants to punch their boss might take up boxing as a way to channel frustration. With finances, this might occur when a person has an urge to gamble and they do so by investing in a business, property, or the stock market. It's important to become conscious of the underlying urge.

PROJECTION

Projection is the act of taking our own undesirable qualities or feelings and ascribing them to others. For example, you are mad at and behaving poorly toward somebody, but you blame the other person for being angry and behaving poorly. Financially, projection might occur when you call your partner cheap or accuse them of wasting money when these are actually your own issues.

INTELLECTUALIZATION

This is the act of keeping distance from the emotional reality of a situation by viewing it from a thinking perspective rather than a feeling perspective.

This might occur while making excuses about a job or financial loss from an analytical perspective rather than expressing feelings of sadness, anger, or fear.

RATIONALIZATION

This is explaining an unacceptable feeling or action in a logical manner and failing to acknowledge the true reasons for the behavior. For example, you bought a far more expensive car than you can afford, but you tell yourself it's expected to have a luxury car in your industry.

REGRESSION

Regression is reverting to old patterns of behavior from when you were younger, such as helplessness or outbursts. For example, you tell yourself you just can't understand your finances as an excuse for not trying to improve your financial situation. You may also throw a fit and refuse to deal with your financial reality.

REACTION FORMATION

This is expressing the opposite feeling, impulse, or behavior than would be authentic. For example, being overly nice to a person you dislike. With finances, this might happen when somebody is very worried about their money but spends a large amount on a fancy dinner for friends as a way of overcompensating.

Do you recognize yourself in some of these examples? If so, it's time to call yourself out on your own bullshit. Solicit and welcome feedback from people in your life who will call you out on your defense mechanisms, like your partner or closest friends. Consider seeking the help of a professional therapist, coach, consultant, supervisor, mentor, or advisor who will give it to you straight so you can chip through your defenses and live more consciously.

Drop Your Defenses
(20 minutes; lifetime practice)

Write about a time you used some of the defenses described above. If you are having a hard time coming up with an example, ask a trusted confidant like a close friend or family member, your partner, or therapist for help. Then answer the following questions:

- How did you use those defenses to justify your behaviors or decisions?
- How were those behaviors or decisions harmful to your mental health or relationships?
- Do you think it's possible that defense mechanisms like denial may have played a role in your financial issues?
- How might things have turned out differently if you dropped the defenses?

. . .

Improve Your Mental Health Awareness to Save Your Financial Life

To be self-aware, you need to be aware of your mental health issues, including any substance abuse or addictions. We all have mental health issues, just like we all have physical health issues. At times, each of us experiences stress, self-esteem issues, bouts of anxiety or depression, grief and loss, and career and relationship problems. If we develop awareness of these challenges, we may be able to prevent them from becoming more serious.

If you aren't aware of your mental health issues and/or are not taking care of them, they will likely impair many aspects of your life, including your finances. Once you are aware of your mental health issues, you can take care of them and manage them to the best of your ability, improving your overall well-being and success.

Be aware of some of the key aspects of mental health including:

Genetic predisposition may cause you to respond to stress with symptoms of anxiety, depression, or other mental health issues. Genetics account for somewhere between 40 and 60 percent of a person's risk of addiction, for example.[8]

You may not be fully aware of your family's mental health and addiction history due to shame, secrecy, and stigma. We must break through these barriers and start having open and honest conversations with loved ones about our family history of mental health and addiction so that we can become more aware of how our neurobiology might respond to stress.

Stress can trigger or exacerbate mental health issues like anxiety, depression, and eating disorders. Stress may be the result of too many demands, not enough work-life balance, sickness, dependent care, household and work responsibilities, life changes, losses, transitions, and unexpected events. Being aware of our stress levels might encourage us to make healthy life choices to reduce stress. Successfully managing stress can improve your well-being and your financial wellness.

For example, one of my clients realized her mental health was being negatively impacted by a stressful catering job that required her to work odd hours late into the night and on weekends. The schedule made it impossible for her to have routine sleep, exercise, or a social schedule, causing her great distress. It also offered inconsistent hours and no benefits, causing her to live paycheck to paycheck and cover her therapy and antidepressants out of pocket. She chose to prioritize her mental health, quit catering, and took a nine-to-five administrative position that she enjoyed and that provided structure and routine. It also gave her a regular paycheck and health insurance, which enabled her to create a budget and a small cushion of savings. Over time, she was promoted to executive assistant and made more money while maintaining a healthy work-life balance and positive well-being.

Physical health issues can impact your mental health. For example, there is a huge connection between your food and your mood, as brain and gut health are interrelated. Poor diet, sleep, or exercise can trigger or exacerbate mental health issues, while a healthy lifestyle can improve your mental health.[9] Hormonal changes and thyroid functioning also greatly impact mental health. It is important to note that many medications have mental health side effects.

Mood issues can impair your functioning at work and home, as well as affect your finances. In my practice, I've seen depression result in lost wages from low productivity and cost people their jobs. I've also seen people rack up debt during manic episodes before they were properly diagnosed and treated for bipolar disorder. One woman bought a horse, a car, and a boat in one weekend, none of which she could afford. She was mad at her husband, so it's interesting to note that the purchases were all modes of transportation! You don't think she was trying to get away from him, do you?

During my initial consultation with clients, I ask if they have ever dealt with depression, and often they say *no*. However, when I ask about symptoms such as irritability, being less interested in pleasurable activities, sleep or appetite disturbances, aches and pains, or low self-worth, they will respond *yes*, not realizing those are all symptoms of depression. Many people think that suffering from depression means you are crying all the time or feel suicidal. They don't realize depression can manifest in different ways for different people. This is why it is important to become more informed about mental health issues like mood disorders.

Trauma is something that affects each and every one of us. Traumas are disturbing events that our minds and bodies have more difficulty processing than usual life events, and they can result in symptoms that include flashbacks, nightmares, depression, or anxiety. Many people think that you have to be a war veteran or a survivor of rape or assault to qualify as a trauma survivor. Those examples are traumas with a big *T*, but all of us have been through little *t* traumas, such as a job loss, a breakup, an accident, or an injury. And unfortunately, many of us have experienced other big *T* traumas such as abuse, neglect, violence, racism, illness, natural disasters, and more.

We need to honor and process our traumas, because they are interconnected like a web. A new trauma will trigger unresolved thoughts and feelings from a previous or "root" trauma. For example, I had a client come in for therapy after she was hit by a car when crossing a crosswalk. Despite being physically okay, the event triggered a whole well of feelings from the physical abuse she experienced as a child, memories she had tucked away in the corners of her mind. The accident left her dealing with chronic insomnia, overwhelming anxiety, and the inability to work. She took an intermittent leave of absence that allowed her to take time off when she was feeling unwell without losing her job. With therapy, she was able to return to life and work within six weeks.

Personality characteristics, such as a need to be in control or to be the center of attention, may be causing us challenges at work and home. As human beings, we all have strengths and challenges with regard to our personalities, and our personalities impact our relationships with others and our financial success. Psychotherapy or other reflective practices can improve your self-awareness of any personality issues so that you can work on maximizing your strengths and building up your areas of weakness.

Attachment styles refer to how we start, maintain, and end relationships. Our attachment style is learned from our first attachments to our primary caregivers. The three main styles of attachment are: avoidant (avoiding connection and intimacy), anxious (insecure and ambivalent about being connected to others), and secure (a strong sense of self and stable and trusting connection to others). Avoidant and anxious attachment styles can impair relationships at home and at work. Learning more about your style and working on resolving the issues that cause you to operate that way can help you develop more secure attachments and relationships.

While each mental health disorder has a different group of symptoms, the following are some general warning signs of a mental health issue:[10]

- Excessive worry, fear, or overwhelm
- Problems with learning, concentration, or staying still
- Prolonged or strong feelings of irritability or anger
- Avoidance of friends and social activities
- Difficulty understanding or relating to other people
- Inability to perceive changes in one's own feelings, behavior, or personality

- Excessive use or abuse of substances like alcohol or drugs
- Multiple physical ailments without obvious causes
- Self-harm or thoughts of suicide
- Inability to carry out daily activities
- Intense fear of weight gain or concern with appearance
- Severe risk-taking behavior that causes harm to self or to others
- Drastic changes in mood, behavior, personality, sex drive, eating, or sleep

Nearly 20 percent of people dealing with a mental health issue also are substance abusers.[11]

If you have symptoms of mental health problems or addiction, schedule an appointment with a mental health professional. If you are dealing with a mental health or substance abuse emergency, dial 911, go to your nearest emergency room, or call the National Suicide Prevention Lifeline at 800-273-8255. Act swiftly and do not delay. Ask for the help you need and deserve.

If I had a magic wand, everyone would have access to counseling.

In the US, nearly half of the individuals experiencing a mental health or substance abuse disorder do not receive treatment. Barriers to care include a lack of awareness, stigma, cost, and access.

In a perfect world, every school would teach mental health awareness and every workplace would provide employee assistance programs and conduct awareness trainings through programs such as Mental Health First Aid (mentalhealthfirstaid.org). We could all become mental health advocates by stomping out stigma, having honest conversations about mental health with one another, recognize counseling as a routine and preventive form of health care, and promote access to mental health care for all.

As a therapist, I'm a big proponent of therapy. Therapy is like having a personal trainer for your emotions, relationships, and career; it can boost your mental fitness and performance in life. My client Ted has an extremely happy and successful life. He is thriving in his executive-level position, has a happy relationship with his wife and three kids, works out regularly, has a full social life, and has a strong financial profile. Whenever people ask him how he does it all, he humbly replies, "I have a really good therapist." Ted is humble, but I am not! Over the past ten years, Ted has referred more than fifty friends and colleagues to my practice. These referrals came from him talking openly about how therapy helps him continue to be his best self, both personally and professionally.

Therapy can be a preventative form of health care, like going to the dentist. Imagine how your teeth would look and feel if you never brushed or flossed or went to the dentist? (Ew!) Your mental health needs to be cared for just like your physical health. Seeing a therapist can nip mental health issues in the bud before they get worse or can even prevent them altogether, like mental floss!

How to Find an Affordable Therapist
- Your insurance likely covers mental health services. Through the Mental Health Parity Act, mental health services are covered the same as your medical care. If you have a preferred provider organization (PPO) plan, seeing an in-network provider will reduce your out-of-pocket expenses. Contact your insurance to learn about your out-of-pocket costs and to find an in-network provider. Sites like Psychology Today can also help you find a therapist who is right for you.[12] If you have a health savings or flex-spending account, you can use these pretax dollars to cover your co-pays or coinsurance.

- You may have employee assistance program (EAP) benefits from your employer (or your partner's or family member's employer). Many companies offer EAP benefits to their employees and their immediate family members or those living in the home. EAP's often cover anywhere from one to eight counseling sessions per presenting issue, per year for each covered person as well as resources and referrals for other services, such as legal or financial assistance, childcare or eldercare referrals, and more. You may be able to continue working with the EAP counselor through your insurance if you need care beyond the free sessions. To find out if you have EAP benefits, check your insurance card or contact your human resources department.

- If you do not have insurance, there are places that provide counseling on a sliding-fee scale or pro bono basis such as community mental health centers (CMHC), social services organizations, training centers for therapists, and some private practices. To find a CMHC near you, visit findahealthcenter.hrsa.gov.

- Telecounseling is another option that is often covered by your insurance (check your plan to confirm). Make sure you are working with a licensed mental health professional who is working with a HIPAA-compliant video platform.

- School counselors are available at many schools to provide free counseling services to students. Reach out if you are a student or if you have a child who may be in need of services.

- There are therapists who specialize in financial therapy and help people think, feel, and behave differently with money. For more information, visit financialtherapyassociation.org.

If therapy isn't an option or doesn't interest you, here are some other ways you can improve your awareness and take care of your mental health:

- Check out an app like Daylio, so you can track your mood and variables like exercise, sleep, nutrition, and socialization, so that you can gain insight about correlations between your mood and your menstrual cycle or nutrition so you can address these issues.[13]
- Use free assessment tools that are available through sites like Psychology Today and Psych Central.[14] You can assess everything

from your self-esteem to whether or not you might be dealing with attention deficit disorder (ADD) or depression.
- Take up journaling or create art as a cathartic expression of emotion and as a tool to increase self-reflection and insight.
- Consider joining a 12-step program for increased awareness and support around any issues with which you are struggling. There are nearly forty different 12-step groups or fellowships out there, including Co-Dependents Anonymous, Al-Anon, Debtors Anonymous, and Sex and Love Addicts Anonymous. Meetings are free and available online.
- Request feedback from friends and loved ones on how they view your mental health and invite them to speak with you openly if they ever have concerns.
- Talk with your primary care physician or a specialist about any mental health concerns you have. They may be able to improve your mental health by looking into possible medical factors, such as thyroid, hormonal, or vitamin-deficiency issues.

Check Up on Your Mental Health
(20 minutes; lifetime practice)

In your journal, answer the following questions:

- What is your family's history of mental health problems, substance abuse, or addiction? Do you have a genetic predisposition to any of these issues?
- What mental health warning signs do you recognize in yourself? Has anybody ever expressed concern to you about this?
- Have you or anybody else been concerned about your substance use or addictive behaviors?
- Have your work or finances been negatively impacted by your mental health, substance use, or addiction issues? If so, how?

Now that you've had your mental health checkup, it's time to take another look at your finances, as financial hardship can weigh heavily on all aspects of your life. Creating a budget is a great starting point. I know you probably dread it like I dread stepping on the scale at my annual physical, but it is necessary to become financially aware. I'll help you make it as painless as possible!

Financial Health Boost: Make a Budget in Six Easy Steps to Become More Financially Conscious

Financial consciousness happens when you are aware of and understand your financial reality. Financial denial is when we are not willing to face our financial reality. Not opening bills or credit card statements and being unaware of loan balances, interest rates, or your credit score are all symptoms of financial denial.

One of the best ways to overcome financial denial is to have a budget and check on how you are doing on a weekly or monthly basis. My financial planner, Bill, says that his happiest clients are the ones who live within their means, and he shared six easy steps to create a simple budget. They include gathering your financial statements, tallying your sources of income, listing your monthly expenses, recognizing fixed and variable expenses, subtracting your monthly expenses from your total income, and then reviewing your budget on a regular basis. I've created a checklist to get you started.

Check Your Reality by Budgeting
(times vary depending on how organized
your finances are; lifetime practice)

The following checklist includes the six steps you need to follow to create a simple budget.[15] Tackle the steps one at a time and check the boxes once you've completed the task. I suggest creating a spreadsheet on your computer so you can easily track and make adjustments as needed.

Note that some of the boxes under each step might not apply to you. For example, you may not have a student loan balance, so just leave that box blank under step 1.

Step 1: Gather your financial statements. This will be helpful as you calculate your monthly expenses in step 3.

- ☐ Bank statements
- ☐ Credit card statements
- ☐ Student loan statements
- ☐ Other loans
- ☐ Investment accounts
- ☐ Utility bills
- ☐ Cell phone statements
- ☐ Any other information that identifies monthly averages of income and expenses

Step 2: Tally your sources of monthly income.

- ☐ Paycheck—If taxes are automatically deducted, use the take-home pay amount. If self-employed, deduct about 20 percent from your take-home pay amount for taxes.
- ☐ A side hustle—Maybe you are an Uber driver, own an Airbnb, or sell health and wellness products on the side.

- [ ] Seasonal work
- [ ] Bonuses
- [ ] Other

Step 3: Create a list of estimated monthly expenses. The financial statements you gathered in step 1 will help you calculate this.

- [ ] Rent or mortgage
- [ ] Car payments
- [ ] Groceries
- [ ] Auto insurance
- [ ] Entertainment
- [ ] Gym membership or fitness classes
- [ ] Loan payments
- [ ] Retirement or college savings
- [ ] Professional membership fees (add them up and divide by 12)
- [ ] Charitable donations (add them up and divide by 12)
- [ ] Vacations and holiday and birthday gifts (add them up and divide by 12)
- [ ] Other

Step 4: Break expenses into two categories: fixed and variable.
Fixed expenses are those that are essential and stay relatively the same each month.

- [ ] Mortgage or rent
- [ ] Car payment
- [ ] Cable and/or internet service
- [ ] Other

Variable expenses are those that change from month to month.

- [ ] Groceries
- [ ] Dining out
- [ ] Credit card payments
- [ ] Clothes shopping

- ☐ Household shopping
- ☐ Other

Total each category in your spreadsheet.

Step 5: Subtract your total monthly expenses from your total monthly income. If your amount is positive, you are in good shape. This means you can budget to use this excess for paying off your credit cards, student loans, or mortgage, or saving to buy a home or contributing more to your retirement plan. If your amount is negative, it means you need to make some adjustments either by working more, seeking greater compensation, and/or reducing your variable expenses by cutting back on eating out or excessive spending at the salon, spa, or bars!

Step 6: Review your budget weekly or monthly. Review your budget on a regular basis to make sure you're living within your means and staying on track with your financial health. Create a routine, such as every Sunday afternoon, when you (and your partner, if you are in a relationship) compare the budgeted expenses versus what you actually spent. This reveals where you did well and where you need to improve. A good rule of thumb is to spend about 50 percent of your income on fixed expenses, 30 percent on variable expenses, and save at least 20 percent.[16]

By completing this budget checklist, you now have a starting point. Did anything come up that surprised you? Some people feel shame, fear, anxiety, or resistance about creating a budget. Others feel anger or rage because they're making less than they should be because of discrimination based on race, gender, or immigration status. This is normal. I encourage you to honor these understandable feelings, get support from others, and power through. I detest budgeting, and it makes me incredibly anxious and fuels shame. Because I care about myself and my financial well-being, I have had to push past this in order to become financially conscious. I encourage you to do the same. Although sticking to a budget is not easy, being aware of what is going on with your finances will empower you to reap financial gain over time.

...

How aware are you about what is going on in your daily life? That budgeting exercise most likely increased your awareness of your finances. The Awareness Wheel brings together all the skills you learned in this chapter and measures where awareness shows up most in your life.

The Awareness Wheel
(20 minutes)

Date: _____

Rate your response after each question using a number from the following scale:

Poor (1–3), Fair (4–5), Good (6–7), Prosperous (8–10)

Poor			Fair		Good			Prosperous	
1	2	3	4	5	6	7	8	9	10

Self-Awareness: How aware are you of your personality characteristics, your strengths and areas of needed growth, and how you impact others? _____

Relational Roles: How aware are you of the roles and patterns you often play in group dynamics—including family and work—and how this impacts your financial success? _____

Unconscious Contracts: How good are you at recognizing possible unspoken agreements? How are they impacting your mental health, work, and finances? _____

Defense Mechanisms: Are you aware when defenses like denial, rationalization, or projection pop up and impair your well-being and prosperity? _____

Substance Use: How aware are you of your substance use (caffeine, sugar, alcohol, recreational, prescription, and other drug use) and how it impacts your mental, physical, and financial health? (Please note that substance use does not necessarily mean you are a substance abuser or have a substance use disorder, which are disorders that span a wide array of problems arising from substance use.) _____

Addictions: Addiction is the use of substances or engaging in compulsive behaviors that continue despite harmful consequences. Addiction is a treatable, chronic disease that involves interactions between the brain, genetics, the environment, and a person's life experiences.[17] How aware are you of an addiction to drugs, alcohol, shopping, gaming, or sex that has negatively impacted your finances? _____

Traumas: How good are you at recognizing your history of traumas, including financial traumas, and how they might be influencing your mental and financial health? _____

Attachment Style: How aware are you of your attachment style and how it impacts your relationships and your finances? _____

Stressors: Relationship issues, financial challenges, losses, deadlines, projects, and holidays can all increase your stress level and may be negatively impacting your mental health and functioning at work. How would you rate yourself when it comes to figuring out what is stressing you out? _____

Physical Health: How aware are you of your physical health and how that may be impacting other aspects of your life, including mental and financial health? _____

Mental Health: How aware are you of the impact of your stress levels, emotional wellness, and experiences of depression, anxiety, or other mental health issues? _____

Financial Consciousness: When it comes to being aware and understanding your financial reality, how would you rate yourself? Do you combat financial denial by having and living within a budget? _____

Chart your responses on The Awareness Wheel. (For a refresher on how to do this, see The Wheel Exercise Tutorial on page 11.) Let's start at the top: Are you Poor, Prosperous, or somewhere in between when it comes to Self-Awareness? Put a dot on the spoke next to the number that corresponds with your answer. Now continue going around the wheel, and after scoring yourself on every spoke, connect the dots to create a circle.

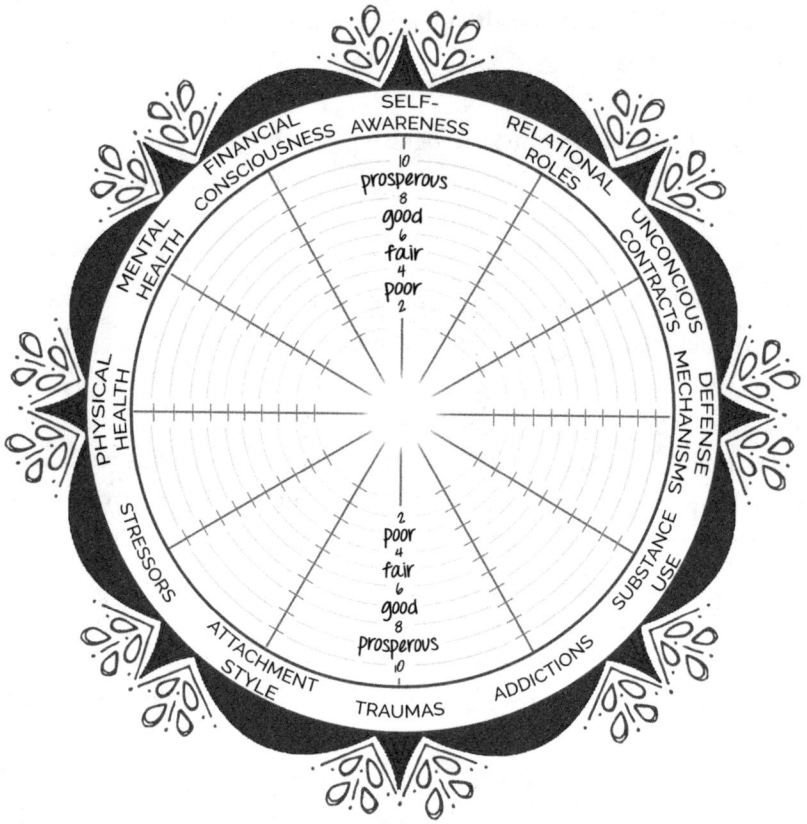

The Awareness Wheel

As always, don't worry about your scores; just be honest. Continue to practice this mindset just like you would exercise to improve your fitness. In your journal, answer the following questions:

- As you look at your completed wheel, where do you see the biggest dents? What are two things you can do better right now in those areas?
- As you look at the wheel, what three areas of your mental and financial life are you least aware of?
- Would you consider therapy, coaching, mentoring, a consultation, or training to promote more awareness?

Remember to date your wheel and file it for later reference so you can track your progress over time. Consider completing this exercise once a month or quarterly so you can live more consciously.

...

Congratulations on being brave enough to take a deeper look at yourself! It takes courage to honestly acknowledge your blind spots and know where you need to grow. Awesome job! This is the start of a greater awakening in your life.

By developing awareness, we help ourselves, each other, and the world around us. Through awareness, we shed the old skin that binds us and unfold into the greatest expression of ourselves. If each of us increases our awareness, we promote our collective consciousness and the evolution of our society as a whole.

Chapter 3

RESPONSIBILITY

Stop the Blame Game and Take the Reins of Your Life

Everything you do is based on the choices you make. It's not your parents, your past relationships, your job, the economy, the weather, an argument or your age that is to blame. You and only you are responsible for every decision and choice you make.
WAYNE DYER author of *The Power of Intention*

Because of my achievement-oriented and people-pleasing nature, I haven't been one to shy away from responsibility. Or so I thought before I took a deeper look at myself.

Early on in my career, I said *yes* to virtually any task I was asked to do and volunteered my help when I could be of service. This led to promotions with greater responsibility (like managing a team or being in charge of various programs) along with financial rewards (like salary increases and bonuses). When I transitioned to full-time self-employment, I assumed full responsibility for my career success and financial future. And when I started Urban Balance, I took on the even greater responsibility of providing a staff of therapists with office space, referrals, and administrative and billing services.

During the start-up phase of Urban Balance, I remember a career counseling session with a client who hated her corporate job but turned up her nose at some of the less sexy aspects of business ownership. As she thought about what it would take to own a business, she said, "I mean, am I supposed to seriously order office supplies, get on my hands and knees to assemble office furniture, and make cold calls to get new business?" I realized I had done all of those very tasks earlier that day.

I've purchased ten zillion boxes of tissues for therapy offices and can assemble a lamp, bookshelf, and end table blindfolded at this point. I wondered which of us was the fool. Taking on additional responsibility can lead to more financial gain, but at what cost?

In this regard, I made some serious mistakes. Healthy choices fell by the wayside. I took on more responsibility than is healthy in my roles as a therapist, business owner, wife, and mother, at the expense of my own health and wellness. The result was a serious case of burnout syndrome, which is a medical diagnosis characterized by exhaustion, depletion, negative attitudes about work, and reduced professional efficacy (which can all negatively impact financial health).[1]

In my twenties, my mother starred in most of my therapy sessions due to her hurtful criticisms. In retrospect, I was stuck in victim mode and not freeing myself through forgiveness. The second time I was in therapy was in my early thirties. I spent most of the time talking about my now former husband, complaining that I felt I was carrying more of the load. I was not looking at my own role or taking responsibility for my health and happiness.

When my world came crashing down after my business partner left, I chose to take responsibility for every aspect of my life, including my personal goals. This went beyond taking responsibility for the tasks I was supposed to do at home and work and included taking full ownership of my role in relationships and balancing work, career, and family. By taking complete responsibility for myself and not blaming others, my life and business began to transform and flourish. Taking responsibility for myself and my well-being was super empowering! It also improved my relationships, as this attitude reflects both responsibility to myself (self-respect) and responsibility to others (integrity).

Therapy Session Number 3
(20 minutes)

Welcome back to my office! This time we are working on taking responsibility for your life. Write your responses to this session's questions:

- In what ways do you already take responsibility for improving your financial success?
- In what ways do you feel irresponsible when it comes to improving your financial success?
- Do you think you err on the side of shying away from responsibility or taking on too much responsibility? What are the effects of these tendencies?
- In the past, who have you blamed when you were unhappy, underwent challenges, or experienced setbacks?
- How would you feel if you took greater responsibility for yourself, your circumstances, and your finances? What is the hard part about doing that? What are the potential positives?

Review your responses. Instead of taking responsibility for your own life, are you blaming others or making excuses? If so, it's time to call yourself out and take responsibility going forward.

...

Life Dealt You a Hand of Hardships and Blessings; How You Play It Is Up to You

A few years ago, I was telling my older sister Paula that I love the work of Wayne Dyer, whom I quoted at the start of this chapter. And she said, "You know, I think he was my driver's ed teacher."

I replied, "Umm, nooooo. He was *not* your driver's ed teacher. Wayne Dyer was a world-renowned author and speaker!"

And so to prove Paula wrong, I Googled "Wayne Dyer."

And he was, in fact, her driver's ed teacher.

It appears that early in his career, he worked as a school counselor at the high school my sister attended in Michigan. And apparently he also taught driver's ed!

His father was an alcoholic who abandoned the family when Wayne was three years old. As a result, he grew up in multiple foster homes and orphanages. When he became an author, it wasn't always easy. He pursued bookstore appearances and media interviews out of the back of his station wagon.[2]

It is remarkable to me that he would say we each need to take responsibility for ourselves, given the difficult hand in life he was dealt.

Life deals us each a hand of hardships and blessings, but each of our hands provides opportunities. While we can't control the hand we were dealt, we can control how we play it. In my practice, I have seen people squander great blessings and overcome great adversity.

My client Carl was a very successful executive in his midforties. He was well dressed, well spoken, and embodied professionalism. In our first session, Carl explained that he had been in therapy on and off at various points in his life and found it extremely beneficial. He was ready to plan his next career move.

As I conducted my initial assessment, it quickly became clear that Carl had many strengths. He was self-reflective, insightful, and therapy savvy—he knew how to take an honest look at himself and was willing to do the work. He had a full life, including a happy relationship, travel, and hobbies like cooking and painting.

When I asked him about his past, I was surprised by his response. Carl said he emancipated himself from his drug-addicted, very abusive, and financially broke parents at age sixteen. After leaving, he moved to California and became a surf bum. He gave surfing lessons during the day and partied hard at night, essentially living like a vagabond. A few years later, he had an epiphany—his partying lifestyle was going to lead him on a path to addiction, unhappiness, and financial struggle, just like his parents. He chose to take responsibility for his future and create a better life for himself. He chose to do his part—to step up and do the work it takes to foster prosperity rather than resigning himself to his current lot in life or expecting success to fall in his lap. Doing his part involved progressing his education, tending to his career goals, becoming financially literate, managing his money, and paying off debt so he could finance his education, buy a home, and so forth.

"Wow! Super impressive! How were you able to do that?" I asked.

"What choice did I have? I didn't want to be like my parents. I took responsibility and worked hard, I put myself through school, and I got in therapy. I work on myself every day," he shared.

While Carl fully honored the impact of his early childhood trauma, he never once blamed his parents in our sessions. He focused on himself and what he needed to do each day to move forward, continuing to expand and achieve greater success as he moved through life.

I've often wished I could bottle Carl's resolve—but the moral of the story is that there is no magic pill. If we want a better life with more financial rewards, we have to take responsibility and do the work.

The road to financial success is much easier for people of privilege (members of the dominant group, whether it be race, religion, socioeconomic status, etc.). Unfortunately, institutional racism, sexism, homophobia, and other forms of bias and discrimination can make the journey to financial health much more difficult. Members of marginalized populations unfairly have to work even harder than people with privilege to fiercely advocate for their own personal and financial wellness. Having the societal deck stacked against you can feel enraging, scary, horribly disempowering, frustrating, and, at times, even hopeless.

In my work with clients, we honor their experiences and traumas and how they have impacted them emotionally, relationally, spiritually, and financially. We work on facilitating deep healing and promoting positive self-esteem, empowerment, abundant thinking, and assertive communication. I'm so inspired by my brave and courageous clients who have overcome adversity to rise into the strongest and best versions of themselves and reap many rewards, including financial.

In psychology, our "locus of control" is the degree to which we believe we have control over the outcome of our life, as opposed to external forces determining our course. From a financial perspective, this is a belief that we have the power to become rich even if we weren't born that way or aren't financially healthy now. Shifting to an internal locus of control is empowering and strongly linked to high self-esteem.[3]

Narrative therapy is a form of counseling that views people as separate from their problems. This can help us develop an internal locus of control by helping us realize that we aren't just the protagonist of our own life story; we are also the author.[4] We are empowered to determine if we are a victim or a hero depending on the narrative we tell ourselves and others. So write a better narrative for yourself, a tale that leads to prosperity!

Author Your Best Future
(20 minutes)

In your journal:

- Write down the ten primary challenges life has dealt you, including financial challenges.
- On a new page, write down the ten primary blessings life has provided you, including talents, gifts, support, or resources. Highlight any blessings that may have stemmed from your challenges. For example, you are hardworking because you had to be to survive. How could you utilize your blessings to create a happier and more prosperous life?
- Become the author of your future. Write about the next five years and how your life will blossom, personally and financially, by building on all of your blessings and strengths.
- How does taking responsibility factor into your successful future?

. . .

Resentment Keeps Us Tethered to the Past; Responsibility Frees Us to Move Forward

The truth is, unless you forgive yourself, unless you forgive the situation, unless you realize that the situation is over, you cannot move forward.[5]
PRIYANKA BAGADE author

Resentment is hardened anger that keeps us tethered to our past. Blaming somebody for our unhappiness or lack of financial success gives them power and control of our happiness. Taking responsibility for what is within our control by practicing forgiveness allows us to emancipate ourselves from suffering. Over a decade of research supports the benefits of forgiveness in helping people resolve anger over betrayals, relieve depression and anxiety, and restore peace of mind.[6] If for no other reason than to free ourselves, we must take responsibility and practice forgiveness.

Some people think that therapy is about blaming your parents or your past for your struggles. Certainly we must honor how our earlier life experiences have impacted us, but then we need to take responsibility for our path going forward.

My client Sofia was angry with her ex-husband for the financial challenges that came with divorce. With deep creases between her eyebrows, she vented about him during every session for nearly a year. She spoke of living paycheck to paycheck with credit card debt and no savings. This is very normal and understandable—however, the divorce took place nearly fifteen years ago.

Even though Sofia was remarried, she spent more time complaining about her ex than focusing on her new marriage. Despite having a college degree, she worked a part-time data entry job for slightly above minimum wage. By not earning more money or celebrating her new relationship, she hung on to the victim narrative.

Sofia was so accustomed to carrying that heavy chip on her shoulder that she didn't realize she had the choice to put it down. Research shows that individuals with a victim mentality, like Sofia, have a hard time letting go of anger and changing their behavior because they do not feel in control of their life.[7] Forgiveness requires letting go, which is perhaps something she was not ready to do. But as the actress Carrie Fisher said, "Resentment is like drinking poison and hoping it will kill your enemies."[8]

Sofia isn't alone. In my practice I have seen many people expend time and energy on circumstances that are beyond their control—such as other people's thoughts, behaviors, choices, actions, or the outcome of situations. This causes them to spin their wheels and stay stuck, because we can only control our own thoughts, behaviors, emotional responses, choices, and actions. Through therapy, I help my clients recognize when they are spending energy on the uncontrollable, and I support them in practicing acceptance and surrendering responsibility for those concerns.

This mindset shift is challenging. I have struggled with acceptance and forgiveness as well, especially regarding my former business partner. A year after she ended our partnership, she sent me a text saying "It occurred to me that I might owe you an apology." A week later, we met for lunch. She apologized for leaving me in a bad place so abruptly, and I forgave her. Several months later, I learned that payments to Urban Balance from one of the insurance companies had been rerouted to her bank account just after we dissolved our partnership. A total of $160,000 had been wrongly paid to her instead of Urban Balance. When I addressed this with her, she claimed she didn't realize that had happened and had spent virtually all of the money. That's when I realized our relationship was not healthy and it was time to say goodbye forever. I was upset that my team at Urban Balance didn't notice this error, but I realized that because I was the CEO, the buck stops here—with me. I had to assume responsibility for this financial loss and move forward.

The insurance company paid me $15,000 and apologized for allowing payments meant for Urban Balance's tax ID to be routed to somebody else's bank account, while my former business partner paid me back $15,000 before filing for bankruptcy. Despite hiring an attorney, I was unable to collect the remaining $130,000 or recoup legal fees. When I think about it, it still burns me, but I choose to think of her and say to myself over and over "I forgive and release you" until the negative feelings dissipate. I focus on all the blessings that came from the challenge of her departure, which is worth more than money.

Am I 100 percent at peace about it? No.

Do I want this betrayal to make me physically ill and mentally unhappy? No.

Assigning fault to somebody else, including myself, is not productive and would cause me to stay stuck in hurt. So I practice acceptance for the events that happened, take responsibility for my part in all of it, and choose forgiveness.

My client Summer has one of the most horrific trauma histories of anybody I have ever known. When she was a child, her father chronically raped her, while her mother emotionally abused and neglected her to the extreme. Yet she does not let these traumas define her. She made this decision as a young adult, when she took responsibility for her future, feeling empowered by her capability to work, buy property, and even help build her own home and create a chosen family. She has led an extraordinary life. Now in her fifties, she describes experiencing "fierce joy" in her heart.

As author Gary Chapman says, "Forgiveness is not a feeling; it is a commitment."[9] It is a choice that takes dedication and practice. Here are some of my forgiveness tips:

- Take ownership of your role or any of your contributions to the situation.
- Practice compassion for the other party by recognizing we all are human and flawed.
- Practice gratitude for any learning or blessings that came from the experience.
- Notice when your mind focuses on the past and the negative narrative, and redirect your attention and energy to the here and now.
- Breathe out the hurt and negativity and hand it over to your Higher Power (God, the Universe, Love and Light, and so forth).
- Imagine you're surrounding yourself with a bubble of love and light that can prevent others from being able to hurt you.
- Remember, you have a responsibility to take care of yourself in the context of this relationship. You'll need to make choices about your boundaries in the relationship, including exercising your right to end the relationship.
- Remind yourself that you are choosing to forgive so you can move forward.

Now that you're practicing forgiveness, let's look at the other side of the coin—your part in relationships.

Own Your Stuff

Relationships are the key to success in life. We need strong relationships to support our success, both personally and professionally. Our personal relationships provide us with the support we need to excel in our careers. Our professional relationships are critical in helping us learn, improving our careers, establishing good productivity, and more.

To strengthen our relationships, we need to take responsibility for the challenging aspects of our personalities and own up when we don't manage our emotions well or when we make mistakes and poor choices. Doing so can facilitate trust and help resolve conflict or even prevent it.

Conflict can be costly in business. It can lead to lost customers, employee turnover, wasted time that slows productivity, and lawsuits. Because of this, a majority of my corporate training seminars are in the area of improving emotional intelligence, multicultural competence, communication skills, and conflict resolution. It takes attention and dedication to improve how we handle ourselves in our relationships.

One way to take responsibility for our role in relationships is to replace "you statements" with "I statements." This technique from Gestalt therapy encourages us to take responsibility for our feelings or deficits without blaming somebody else, which can make us defensive.[10] The following are examples of taking ownership of your stuff instead of placing blame:

Blame	Ownership
"You are working like a snail."	"I am feeling nervous that we are not going to make this deadline."
"You are not being clear."	"I am having difficulty understanding this."
"You need to handle that."	"I am not very good at digital organization and would so appreciate your help."

Another way to own your stuff is to admit your mistakes. Doing so is not a sign of weakness, it's a strength that can save time and prevent pain. Best practices for apologizing have been shown to be effective in research literature on organizational psychology.[11] These best practices include:

- The sooner, the better. If you aren't in a place where you can apologize (like during a meeting), arrange to have a private conversation as soon as possible. If it took you a bit to realize you're wrong, circle back as soon as you can.
- Face-to-face is best. It takes more courage to look somebody in the eye while acknowledging that you did something wrong. Voice-to-voice is second best. Written apologies lack nonverbal cues like facial expression and tone of voice, and may be subject to misunderstanding. Only resort to this when there are no other options or time is of the essence. A handwritten apology letter is much better than a quick email or text, if possible! If emailing or texting, suggest a follow-up meeting or call.
- Express remorse. Demonstrate heartfelt and sincere regret for your wrongdoing. Match the level of seriousness of the wrongdoing.
- Admit fault. "I am sorry you feel that way" is not a full apology. You must show that you recognize you did something wrong.
- Acknowledge hurt. Show understanding for how your actions negatively impacted the person.
- Say what you are going to do to remedy the hurt, if possible. And stay true to this commitment.
- State your intention not to repeat the wrong. Stay true to that intention as best you can.

Taking responsibility in relationships involves integrity—being ethical, honest, and true to your word even if doing so involves admitting fault or inadequacies. In business, leaders who display high integrity tend to get their teams to be more committed and perform better than leaders who display low integrity.[12] It all starts with being honest with yourself.

Take an Honest Look at Yourself
(10 minutes; lifetime practice)

Answer the following in your journal:

- What do you see as the challenging aspects of your personality? Why? How have they negatively impacted your relationships, career, and/or finances?
- How do you take ownership of these character traits? How could you do better at managing them?
- How might speaking in "I statements" help your relationships? How are you going to work on this?

...

Financial Health Boost: Take Fiscal Responsibility for Yourself

Personal fiscal responsibility involves taking care of your financial life. Financial responsibility is important because it impacts your life and your future. Making the right decisions concerning your money can help you live a more comfortable life down the road.

Taking fiscal responsibility for yourself means the following:

Taking ownership of your financial situation: Resist the urge to blame your parents, past relationships, or current partner for your financial circumstances. Accept the past, forgive who you need to, and take responsibility for yourself from here forward.

Becoming financially literate: Financial literacy is being able to understand and apply financial management skills to make informed financial decisions. Financial planning, managing debt, and calculating interest are aspects of financial literacy. In my practice, I've found that when one partner is financially literate, and one is not, there can be a big difference in power and control within the relationship. I recommend that adults become financially literate, and that the process begins as early as childhood or adolescence. It's shocking that nearly two-thirds of Americans can't pass a basic financial literacy test, so if you aren't financially literate, you aren't alone.[13] You can improve your financial literacy by reading financial literacy books, listening to money podcasts, or taking a financial literacy or basic finance class at your local community center or online. I like Suze Orman's Personal Finance Course, which is offered online at a reasonable price.

Establishing a system to manage your money: Managing your money involves having organizational systems in place, such as balancing your checkbook or using software like QuickBooks or free money-management sites like Mint to connect with your financial accounts. Utilizing systems like this allows you to see your financial situation at a glance. By doing so, you can manage your cash flow so you will have money when you need it, such as for a vacation or wedding.

Paying your bills on time: Avoid late fees. Make larger payments on your credit cards or loans when possible. Pay your debts, including money you may have borrowed from others.

Living within your budget: Check how you are doing regarding sticking to the budget you created in chapter 2.

Paying your federal and state taxes: Don't try and cheat the system. Report your earnings and pay your taxes.

Taking responsibility for your income: If you don't like what your annual income is, it is up to you to change it. Consider additional education, certifications, working more hours, asking for a raise, or starting a side hustle. Your income will not improve unless you make it happen.

> **Taking responsibility for the money you spend:** Be thoughtful about purchases. Do not blame other people for the money you spend because you have the choice to spend the money or not.

Take Fiscal Responsibility
(10 minutes; lifetime practice)

Answer the following in your journal:

- Who or what do you feel is responsible for your current financial situation? How were you impacted?
- Now, write about your part in creating your current financial life. Be both honest and gentle with yourself. The goal is for you to take ownership of your role.
- You are responsible for your financial life going forward, so it's time to take the reins. How responsible are you in managing your money? Do you have a system and does it work well? Have you incurred any late fees for bill payments within the last twelve months? Write down ways you can increase your financial responsibility—consider software like QuickBooks or free money-management sites like Mint.

...

Whew! You are doing some important work on yourself. Now, let's assess how well you take responsibility for your life on The Responsibility Wheel. The Responsibility Wheel brings together all the skills you learned in this chapter and measures how well you are doing at taking responsibility for your life.

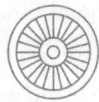

The Responsibility Wheel
(20 minutes)

Date: _____

Rate your response after each question using a number from the following scale:

Poor (1–3), Fair (4–5), Good (6–7), Prosperous (8–10)

Poor			Fair		Good			Prosperous	
1	2	3	4	5	6	7	8	9	10

Do Your Part: How willing are you to step up and do the work it takes to succeed in your relationships, work, and finances? _____

Acceptance: How good are you at embracing the hardships you have been dealt, including financial, and not blaming others? _____

Empowerment: How empowered are you to take action to determine your course in life, work, and finances? _____

Own Your Happiness: How good are you at taking responsibility for your attitude and happiness instead of assigning blame to others? _____

Forgive: How good are you at freeing yourself from resentment for any wrongdoings, financial and otherwise? _____

Apologize: When it comes to looking at your mistakes or less-than-ideal choices, how much responsibility do you take when it comes to the impact on others, work, and your finances? _____

Integrity: Integrity is being dependable and reliable, following through with commitments, doing what you said you would do, and so forth. How responsible are you when it comes to being honest, ethical, and truthful? _____

Healthy Choices: When it comes to your overall wellness, how good are you at making healthy choices? _____

Manage Money: How responsible are you when it comes to taking ownership of your financial life, paying your debts and bills on time, and taking responsibility for the income you earn and the money you spend? _____

Career Goals: How would you rate yourself when it comes to tending to your professional aspirations? _____

Personal Goals: How would you rate yourself when it comes to tending to your personal aspirations, like health goals, relationship goals, hobbies, and travel? _____

Foster Balance: How would you rate yourself when it comes to balancing your responsibilities to the best of your ability? _____

Chart your responses on The Responsibility Wheel. (For a refresher on how to do this, see The Wheel Exercise Tutorial on page 11.) Start at the top: Are you Poor, Prosperous, or somewhere in between when it comes to being able to Do Your Part? Put a dot on the spoke next to the number that corresponds with your answer. Now continue going around the wheel, and after scoring yourself on every spoke, connect the dots to create a circle.

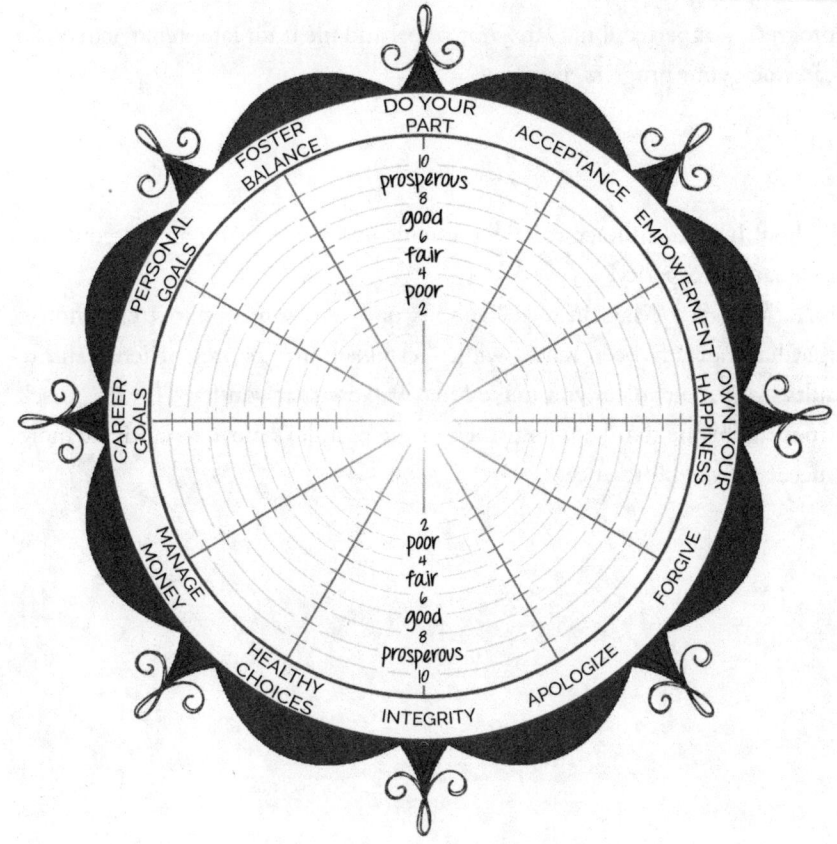

The Responsibility Wheel

In your journal, answer the following questions:

- As you look at your completed wheel, where do you see the biggest dents? What do you see as your biggest challenge to improving within these areas?
- How can you address that challenge? Is there anybody who could help you?
- What are three small changes you can make to cultivate more responsibility in both your personal and financial life?

Consider completing this exercise once a month or quarterly so you can continue to foster responsibility for your success. Remember, aim for progress, not perfection! Date your wheel and file it for later reference so you can track your progress over time.

...

Wahoo! It takes courage to take the reins in your life. You are on your way to greater prosperity!

Author Mark Manson says "fault" is past tense and results from choices that have already been made, while "responsibility" is present tense and results from the choices you make today.[14] Now that you have freed yourself from the blame that kept you stuck in the past, let's move to cultivate more success through presence.

Chapter 4

PRESENCE

Promote Fiscal Consciousness Through Being a Human Being, Not a Human Doing

Be at least as interested in what goes on inside you as what happens outside. If you get the inside right, the outside will fall into place.
ECKHART TOLLE spiritual teacher and *New York Times* bestselling author

I parked illegally, threw on my minivan's hazard lights, and dashed into the local yoga studio. I had fifteen minutes before I needed to pick up my kids from school and thought I'd use the time to do some local business networking.

Rushing into the studio in my heels and all-black business attire, the scent of lavender, soft lighting, and peaceful music was a welcoming ambiance. The owner of the studio, Lisa, was sitting elegantly behind the front desk with noticeably good posture, wearing a cozy-looking outfit and a beautiful teal pashmina that matched her eyes.

After quickly introducing myself as a therapist and owner of a group practice, I suggested we develop a relationship for business cross-referral and cross-promotion. She looked intently into my eyes as I gave my elevator pitch and took longer to respond than was comfortable, her grounded pause highlighting my manic frenzy.

"Come practice yoga," she said in a way that sounded more like a command than a friendly invitation.

I was slightly taken aback, but recovered with another smile, thanking her and going on to suggest that we could put each other's brochures in our waiting rooms.

Lisa held up her hand, stopped me midsentence, and said, "Come practice yoga." After pausing, she said, "Then we'll see about that."

"Geez, what's her deal?" I thought as I left the studio, racing to the elementary school. I felt rejected and annoyed, but I had a feeling I'd just met somebody who could be a significant teacher to me. For the next few years, I drove past the yoga studio multiple times a day as I zipped to the office, the grocery store, and my kids' after-school activities. I thought maybe I would go when I lost weight, was in better shape, and had the right leggings, because that makes so much sense, right?

After my business partner left and my stress level was through the roof, I was reminded about the many mental and physical health benefits of meditation and yoga. I recognized that the disease of being busy interfered with my judgment, so I decided to get over myself and go to the yoga studio.

My first session was a yin class, a slow-paced yoga practice in which deep stretching poses are held for several minutes each. There's a focus on the breath and releasing tension held in the body. After class, I felt like I had just had a nap, a workout, a therapy session, and went to church! I decided to attend every week and guarded that time slot on my calendar as if my life depended on it (which maybe it did!).

I signed up for a weekly mindfulness meditation class and started dropping in on other classes. As I became more involved, Lisa and I ran cross-promotional events together, which were a boost to my business.

As I began to practice yoga and meditation more regularly, I noticed powerful changes. My mode of operation shifted from manic to more mindful and from a state of constant flight to more groundedness. Through mindfulness and walking meditations, I developed a renewed appreciation for nature. By quieting my mind chatter, I noticed the beauty of the sky, trees, and flowers. I became less stressed and calmer, less reactive and more intentional as I connected with the peace and serenity that was available from deep within myself. As I became physically stronger, I was better able to handle work. If I was experiencing discomfort, I knew I could focus on my breath to help me move through the challenge. Because I was more present, virtually all of my relationships were improving and deepening.

I became more fully present and more attuned to my clients. I learned to clear my mind and body before a session through deep breathing, short body scans, and visualizations. While in session, I would connect with my breath and notice what I was feeling in my body. When I was truly present and not distracted, I could pick up on nonverbals like facial expressions and body language, or notice what wasn't being said.

Cultivating presence helped me become better at my job; I developed greater intuition so I could make better-informed business and financial decisions. This allowed me to lead and mediate my leadership team more effectively. Feeling more at peace, I became better at delegating and letting go. As a result, my business grew and flourished. When dealing with money, I checked in with the wisdom of my body rather than letting my anxious thoughts determine my choices. When my business grew strong and ripe enough to sell, presence helped me make my most important financial decision to date.

When I decided to sell Urban Balance, I worked with a business broker. We had fifty interested buyers and eight offers, and the offers varied widely not only in price but also in terms. It was important to me that I found a buyer whose heart was in the same place as mine, someone who would carry on the mission of the company.

I felt like I was on *The Bachelorette* while interviewing prospective buyers to determine who would get the final rose. Presence helped me make this critical business decision from a place of calm and conscious clarity. When sitting with prospective buyers, I noticed what I felt in my body. After dinner with one prospective buyer, I excused myself because I felt nauseous. I recognized I had a bad feeling about him even though everything on paper looked perfect. Then he asked me if the opioid epidemic was "good for business." There is a big difference between profiting by doing good work and helping people and profiting from other people's suffering. His heart was not in the right place, and I was not handing my baby over to him! *Next!*

The highest cash offer came from another prospective buyer. However, he wanted me to stay on as CEO, which I didn't really want to do. And something else wasn't feeling right to me. I told my broker that I had an inkling that this buyer didn't respect women. My broker encouraged me to have one more meeting with the buyer and asked him, "What would you do if Joyce eventually wanted to leave her position as CEO?" The buyer responded with a maniacal grin, "Leave? Oh, Joyce could never leave. If she wanted to leave, I would tie her to the bed with the bedsheets." Misogyny confirmed. No deal.

When the right buyer showed up a couple of months later, my mind, heart, and gut felt clear and aligned. While I left that transaction with less cash than some of the previous offers, I still had a sizable nest egg, a clear conscience, and the opportunity to stay in the game as an investor. Just three years after selling Urban Balance and investing in the parent company, that investment paid off tenfold, making the offer that was most aligned with my heart and mission also the most prosperous by a landslide.

After I sold Urban Balance, I participated in a six-month yoga teacher training taught by Lisa in an effort to deepen my practice and enhance my work as a therapist and corporate trainer. Yoga principles, like presence, continue to help me make important business and financial decisions benefiting my overall mental health.

Therapy Session Number 4
(20 minutes)

This session applies mindfulness to your mental and financial health. Write your responses to the following questions in your journal:

- How has the disease of "being busy" played a role in your life?
- What prevents you from being more present?
- How might being more present improve your financial wellness?

As you begin to connect with and trust that quiet wisdom within you more and more, being honest with yourself and helping yourself becomes much easier.

...

Hop Off the Busy Train

People love to brag about being on the Busy Train, flashing their busyness like a badge of honor that verifies their VIP status. Many get stuck on the Busy Train, unconsciously speeding along and failing to notice that the Busy Train is reckless, prone to breakdown and accidents, toxic, and taking them on unnecessary twists and turns. It never stops for necessary maintenance or intentional planning. Each passenger unknowingly shapeshifts from a human being to a *human doing*. The following tips will help you hop off the busy train and become more present:

Clear the clutter. The more stuff you have, the more time and energy it takes to manage it. Simplify your life by getting rid of everything you don't need in these areas of your life:

- **Digitally:** Save yourself from information overload by unsubscribing from emails. Consider programs such as SaneBox, to organize your emails according to importance. Delete apps you don't use. Shut down tabs on your browser. Stop social media alerts. Create folders for emails and files.
- **At work:** Purge and shred what you can. Consider scanning items to create space. Organize files in folders.
- **At home:** Follow Marie Kondo's advice and get rid of everything you don't need, haven't used in a year, or that doesn't bring you joy.[1] Sell items on Facebook Marketplace or by consignment, freecycle, or donate as a tax write-off, depending on what is the best use of your time.
- **Financially:** Go green on your bills and statements and set up automatic electronic payments. Freeing yourself of unnecessary stuff takes some time, so have patience and congratulate yourself as you continue to make progress!

Start your day right. Establish a morning routine that works for you and starts your day on the right foot. If you are a planner, plan your outfit, a nutritious breakfast, and set the coffee maker the night before. If not, leave yourself time in the morning for self-care. Practice a morning meditation or set intentions for the day. For example, intentions to eat healthy or make wise financial choices.

Keep separate personal and professional to-do lists. Use the Notes feature in your phone or use a project management app. Keep your personal and professional to-dos separate to avoid overwhelm.

Delegate and access support. Look at your to-do list and ask yourself, "Am I the best person to do this? Am I the only person who can do this? Do I enjoy doing this? Is this worth my time?" Outsource tasks you don't enjoy, when possible. Identify where you need help and ask for it. Consider how your partner, kids, roommate, staff, interns, or services for hire might be able to help more.

Prioritize and schedule tasks. Divide tasks into three areas: must do/critical, should do/important, and nice to do/nonessential. Then identify whether it is a daily, weekly, monthly, annual, or other time frame task. Include sleep and exercise into the "must do" section. Plug time into your calendar for your tasks and set up alerts and reminders. Don't be afraid to remove nonessential tasks.

Develop time awareness. Track your time. Are you making good use of your time? Become aware of time wasters, such as social media, too much TV, surfing the web, video games, or gossiping. Consider taking a social media or TV cleanse so you can become mindful of the habits that are sabotaging your prosperity and strive for balance.

Avoid multitasking. Multitasking reduces productivity and job performance because you waste time as your brain shifts gears from one activity to another, exacerbating stress.[2] Avoid toggling back and forth on chunk-related tasks like emails, voicemails, bill paying, and running errands.

Work on top-priority tasks first. Complete the vital few instead of the trivial many. When a big project is due, I miraculously seem to get everything else done, including cleaning my house! This kind of avoidance is counterproductive and can increase stress.

Unplug. People spend 41 percent of their total time looking at technological devices![3] Unplug from technology by setting an auto-reply on your email after work hours, on weekends, and during vacation. Take breaks from your phone, turn it off, or put it on Do Not Disturb mode. Enjoy experiencing life in the moment and resist the urge to post on social media rather than being present. If social media is a big part of your work, make sure you block out time where you unplug and are not looking at a screen or device.

Avoid overscheduling. Resist the urge to overschedule or say yes to everything. Learn to say no to what doesn't align with your values and goals or will cause you to be overly busy. Schedule time for self-care, breaks between activities, and transitions between work and home. Have realistic expectations and build in some cushion time when planning out projects.

Keep it simple. My BFF, Cherilynn Veland, therapist and author of *Stop Giving It Away*, developed a fun and useful anti-stress strategy where you assign a "Daily Ease of Functioning" score to various choices.[4] You assign a low score when something makes life more complicated and a high score when something makes life easier. For example, signing up to bring a homemade feast for an office party would have a lower score than signing up to bring napkins and paper plates. This empowering tool helps simplify responsibilities so you can avoid becoming overextended and overwhelmed. Consider asking yourself each morning, "What am I going to do to simplify my life today?"

Set time boundaries between work and life. Create balance by identifying time for work, leisure, family, and friends. It's easy to see how work can eat away your life.

End the workday on time. Use the last ten minutes of your workday to clear and organize your desk—it will help you be more efficient tomorrow. Update your to-do list, so you know what work you will focus on when you start your day tomorrow. Reflect on all you have accomplished and give yourself credit for all you have done so well.

Set a sleep alarm. Set a notification one hour before your optimal bedtime. Use the next thirty minutes to wrap up what you are doing and then put away your device for the night. Use the next thirty minutes to prepare for sleep by taking a relaxing hot shower or bath and doing some reading or a guided meditation to improve sleep. Practice gratitude for all you accomplished during the day.

Pump the Breaks on Busyness
(20 minutes; lifetime practice)

In your journal, answer the following questions:

- Which of the previous suggestions for hopping off the Busy Train do you already do well? How has it helped you be more successful?
- On a scale from 1 to 10, how overly busy do you feel? *Totally chill* is a 1 rating while *Totally crazed* is a 10 rating. If you self-scored 3 or less, you are out of danger; 4–6 you are doing well, but there is room for improvement; and 7–10 you are in the *danger zone*!
- What three ways do you plan to implement any of the suggestions for hopping off the Busy Train? Tell a friend or colleague and set a time to follow up on your progress next week.

. . .

Welcome Aboard the Peace Train

> *Health is certainly more valuable than money, because it is by health that money is procured.*[5]
> SAMUEL JOHNSON English author who was regarded as one of the greatest literary figures of the eighteenth century

Congrats on getting off the Busy Train, you might have just saved your life! Welcome to the Peace Train, where the ride is enjoyable, intentional, and safe because there is time for preventative maintenance and thoughtful planning. It runs efficiently and conserves resources like time and energy, and makes stops for healthy breaks. The conductor of the Peace Train is your inner wisdom who will guide you safely to health, happiness, and complete prosperity as long as you stay on track by being rooted in the present moment through mindfulness.

Mindfulness has been an aspect of Buddhist teachings and practices for centuries, was made popular through mindfulness-based stress reduction, and is defined as "receptive attention to and awareness of present events and experience."[6] Mindfulness helps focus your attention in the present by helping you notice when your mind is wandering so you can return your attention to the present moment.[7] For some, mindfulness can seem challenging or uncomfortable, which is why it is called a practice. It can take years to cultivate mindful awareness, so be gentle with yourself and give yourself credit for any small steps in the right direction.

Mindfulness practices include breathwork, meditation, body scans, progressive muscle relaxation, yoga, and more. Mental and physical health benefits include improving stress regulation, disease resistance, pain management, decreasing emotional reactivity, and slowing, stalling, or reversing age-related brain degeneration.[8] According to the Centers for Disease Control and Prevention, mindfulness is the fastest-growing health trend in the US, with the number of meditators tripling from 2012 to 2017.[9]

Across hundreds of cultures and thousands of years, the breath is believed to tie together the mind, body, and spirit. By slowing and deepening our breath, we can calm our minds and relax our bodies and bring our attention to the here and now. Anytime you can notice and connect with your breath, you are cultivating mindfulness.

Meditation is taking a break from your thoughts by connecting with the breath. We all have incessant mind chatter that can fuel stress and anxiety. Just like how rebooting a computer improves its operating function, meditation can reboot your mind, body, and spirit for optimal performance.

In meditation, when a thought pops into your mind, observe it and redirect your attention back to your breath. Having the thought doesn't mean you are doing something wrong, it means you are human. Saying a mantra, which is a word or statement, over and over, like a chant, gives your mind something simple to focus on while giving you a break from your thoughts. The intent of meditation is to increase the amount of time you can sit in quiet stillness focusing on your breath.

Acts of daily living, like washing dishes, doing laundry, walking the dog, gardening, making music, or creating art, can become "active meditations."

Do this by tuning in to your breath and body and focusing on your five senses with your full attention and presence.

Connecting with nature can also be a form of meditation. Nature is an antidote to technology because it is always living in the here and now. Bring your attention to your senses and notice the sky, trees, flowers, the wind on your face, and the scent of the fresh air in order to reduce stress and facilitate peace.

The more mindfulness meditation you do, the better. Ideally, practice meditation daily. Apps like Calm and Headspace can provide guided meditations, alerts, and tracking to help you develop your practice.

Mindfulness in the Workplace Optimizes Success

Mindfulness has increased in popularity in the workplace, with 22 percent of employers providing mindfulness training in 2016.[10] Organizations such as Target, Google, Aetna, Intel, Dow, and the United States Marine Corps have implemented mindfulness-based training programs with well-publicized success.[11]

Studies have shown that two-thirds of mindfulness training for organizations were helpful in reducing stress, enhancing well-being, increasing employee engagement, creating greater job satisfaction, and improving client outcomes.[12] Mindfulness at work increases motivation and job performance, positive affect and working memory capacity, problem-solving, work-life balance, focus, concentration, creativity, innovation, safety, and ethical decision-making. It also reduces absenteeism, risk of burnout, and unwanted turnover.[13]

Most corporate mindfulness programs are based on the mindfulness-based stress reduction developed in 1990 by Jon Kabat-Zinn.[14] Both staff and managers benefit from mindfulness, as it has been shown to improve communication, relationship quality, conflict management, empathy and compassion, leadership, and teamwork. Some workplaces have meditation rooms on-site or offer corporate memberships to meditation apps such as Headspace. Companies like Nike, Apple, and Goldman Sachs invest in mindfulness training because it helps attract new talent and it shows the firm is invested in people's well-being.[15]

For the past seven years, I've been facilitating mindfulness training for companies large and small. I recently conducted a mindfulness training for a global Fortune 500 company. I was training a department that worked with social media, and they needed to learn ways to unplug even more than most people because of the nature of their work. People working in customer service or roles that involve interpersonal conflict particularly appreciate the tools and techniques taught in these training sessions.

After I led the group through some breathing exercises and a short guided meditation, I asked people to share what they noticed. Most people noticed the tension they had been holding in their bodies, how shallow and short their breathing was before the exercise, or how much better and more relaxed they felt afterward. I was surprised by one participant's comment that she felt more connected to the team because it was an intimate experience to sit in silence together, eyes closed, and breathing in unison. Even those who attended via video conferencing from around the world agreed. As a department, they decided to start all their meetings with a short meditation to let go of any stressors and become synced up and present before working together. What a great idea!

Even if your workplace doesn't provide mindfulness training, this is something you can do for yourself:

- Start your day by doing a five-minute meditation at your desk.
- During meetings, calls, your commute, or anytime at all, bring your attention to your breath.
- Every hour or so, stand up and stretch. Do a short body scan, stretch, and breathe out any tension you are holding.
- If possible, step outside during your lunch break or take a break to connect with nature.
- When eating, don't do anything else, if possible. Take time to eat slowly and enjoy the smell and taste of the food.
- End your day with a short meditation or breathing exercise so you can your leave work at work and be ready for home.

Stop Ruminating about the Past and Worrying about the Future

Yesterday is gone. Tomorrow has not yet come. We have only today. Let us begin.[16]
    MOTHER TERESA Albanian-Indian Roman Catholic nun and missionary

Many of us spend significant time ruminating about the past, second-guessing our choices and wondering if the outcome would be better if we had done something differently. A study in the journal *Science* showed that people engage in mind wandering about 46.9 percent of the time, instead of thinking about what they are doing![17] They are thinking about past or future events, or events that may never happen at all. Mind wandering comes at a cost. Ruminating about negative events can lead to being counterproductive at work, which is believed to negatively impact financial success.[18] An added bonus is that people who are able to stay in the here and now and focus on the current activity tend to be happier.[19]

When my client Will was struggling with obsessive financial anxiety over his technology business and dealing with insomnia, he was second-guessing past decisions and having catastrophic thoughts about the future. I shared with him the healing power of being in the present moment and the power of breathwork and meditation. He canceled his next session, and I didn't hear from him for over a month. When we finally connected, he said, "It was that last session that got me through the last six weeks." I asked, "What do you mean?"

Following our last session, he learned he had stage four cancer. His mind immediately went to catastrophic fears about his future and mortality—of not being able to care for his wife, three children, or his business. Then he made the decision to stay in the moment.

He explained, "At that moment, I realized I was basically okay. In fact, I felt fine. I felt the same as I did before learning of the diagnosis. And I made a choice to not just take it one day at a time but one minute at a time. As I lay in the MRI machine, instead of worrying about the results, I focused on the music playing."

He said the song was Madonna's "Vogue." Can you believe that? Of all things, "Vogue." So he struck a pose and let his body go with the flow! The flow of presence—letting go of what he couldn't control, focusing on his breath, and keeping his awareness in the here and now.

Since his diagnosis, Will practices daily meditation. I'm happy to report that his cancer is in remission. He also made very significant changes to his career and ended a toxic business relationship. Presence promotes health and also provides this type of insight and clarity that some people only get from a life-threatening illness.

Will shared the most beautiful analogy for mindfulness with me. He said, "I realize now it is as if in life the needle sets on a record album the moment we are born and continues to cycle throughout our lives. If we bring our awareness to the past or to the future, we scratch our record and there is no music. The present moment is the only place we can hear our song."

Redirect Your Attention to the Here and Now
(10 minutes; lifetime practice)

In your journal:

- List three past events or choices that often occupy your mind. Implement being thankful for the lessons learned. For each event, write two valuable lessons you learned. To help you let go, consider forgiving the person(s) involved in each situation.
- List three future issues or events you worry about. For each, make a list of the things you can control and the things that you can no longer control and need to surrender. Focus only on what you can control.
- For the next day, promise yourself to raise a mental red flag when your mind takes you to the past or future events on your list. Recognize that these thoughts are perfectly normal. When you notice these thoughts, gently turn your attention to the present moment. By becoming more aware, your worries will naturally begin to subside.

...

Financial Health Boost:
Manage Your Money Mindfully and Have More

For many, thinking about finances can trigger stress, negative emotions, and obsessive thoughts about past failures or worries of future crises.[20] These negative thoughts and emotions can be financially paralyzing, causing people to abandon their financial care. Staying in the present moment can help you stop entertaining past or future worries and focus on your financial actions in the here and now. Mindfulness is especially useful for people who want to optimize their financial performance following a financial crisis because it facilitates creativity, flexibility, and adaptability, which enhances decision-making and financial outcomes.[21]

Mindfulness can also help people clarify their values and recognize what is meaningful to them, thereby reducing impulsive financial behavior, such as charging frivolous items on credit.[22] Several years ago, I had an experience that induced mindfulness in regard to my spending habits. Between two meetings in the suburbs, I spent more than an hour mindlessly shopping at a home-furnishing store the size of two football fields. I loaded my cart with candles, throw pillows, kitchen knickknacks, toys for my kids, and more. When I got to the checkout line, it was about twenty people deep, and I realized I had to leave shortly to make my meeting. I left my overflowing cart at customer service so I could come back to pay for my items later. After my meeting, I realized I truly didn't need anything in that cart.

Since that event, my mantra when I go shopping is, "I'd rather have cash than crap." It helps me mindfully stick to my list of necessities and avoid extraneous spending.

To apply mindfulness to your finances, consider the following:

Set a financial intention each morning:[23] Before you dash out the door, take a few minutes to connect with your breath and notice how you feel in your body. Set a financial intention for the day. For example, "I will spend wisely," "I will attract new business," or "I will research investment and side-hustle options."

Visualize your financial goals: Get clear on your goals—like paying off debt, saving for an emergency fund, or buying a home or car. Keep these goals top of mind.

Practice mindful spending and decision-making: Before you make any financial decisions, including spending or major decisions like

> moving or a job change, ask yourself if the choice would bring you closer to or take you further away from your goals. Check in with the wisdom of your body and notice how you feel about these choices in your gut, which is often a better guide than your thoughts. Use mindful awareness to make sure you are spending within your budget.
>
> **At the end of the day, give thanks for any wise financial choices or behaviors:** This reinforces positive choices and keeps you on the path to prosperity!

Try a Financial Fast
(7 to 21 days)

If you spend more than you should, consider a financial fast! Choose a spending ban anywhere from one to three weeks. By doing so, you'll increase your spending awareness and save some cash. During your financial fast, do not use any credit cards, if possible, and do not go to any malls or retail stores. Delete retail apps on your devices and do not purchase any restaurant food or coffee—make everything at home and pay for your groceries in cash. If you need to get a gift for a friend, consider making them something, regifting an item you haven't used, or being honest with them about your cleanse. This exercise will help you become more mindful of excess.

...

Spend Mindfully
(1 week minimum; lifetime practice recommended)

For the next week, at least, keep a log of your spending. Before you spend money, ask yourself:

- Is spending money on this item or service absolutely necessary? If not, can I afford it?
- Will this expense bring me closer or further away from my personal, professional, and financial goals?
- Does this purchase feel aligned with my values?
- Do I feel clear about this purchase in my gut?

At the end of the week, journal about anything you noticed—such as spending less money because you were more conscious of it.

. . .

The Presence Wheel brings together all the skills you learned in this chapter and measures where you are cultivating presence in your life.

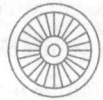

The Presence Wheel
(20 minutes)

Date: _____

Rate your response after each question using a number from the following scale:

Poor (1–3), Fair (4–5), Good (6–7), Prosperous (8–10)

Poor			Fair		Good			Prosperous	
1	2	3	4	5	6	7	8	9	10

Connect to Breath: How good are you at regularly drawing attention to your breath and connecting with the here and now: slowing and deepening your breath to reduce stress and promote relaxation? _____

Body Awareness: How good are you at bringing your attention to the present moment by noticing feelings and sensations in the body? _____

Daily Mindfulness: Recording your mindfulness practices in an app or journal can keep you on track. How good are you at setting aside at least five minutes a day for stillness, breathwork, meditation, prayer, or yoga? _____

Mindful Living: How would you rate yourself when it comes to living consciously through mindful eating, environmentally conscious choices, scheduling time for transitions, and not texting while driving? _____

Distraction Awareness: How good are you at noticing your mind chatter, diversions, and distractions that keep you from being present, and redirecting your attention to the breath and body? _____

Relationships: How present are you in your personal relationships with friends, family, your partner, and your children—for example, making eye contact and practicing active listening while not being on a device? _____

Work: When it comes to your work relationships and your attentiveness during meetings or while working on a task or project, how would you rate your ability to be present? _____

Financial Life: How would you rate yourself when it comes to applying mindfulness to your finances so you spend within your means and don't accrue unnecessary debt? _____

Single-Tasking: How would you rate yourself when it comes to focusing your attention on the task at hand: eliminating distractions by closing tabs, turning off your phone, or closing your door? _____

Unplug: How good are you at making a conscious effort to take breaks from your devices by using auto response messages, Do Not Disturb mode, or turning off your phone? _____

Connect to Nature: How often do you notice the sky, wind, trees, or flowers and spend time enjoying nature to connect with presence? _____

Intuition: How would you rate yourself when it comes to tuning in to your inner compass, connecting with the wisdom of your body and gut instincts, or noticing random thoughts or images that may be intuitive insights? _____

Chart your responses on The Presence Wheel. (For a refresher on how to do this, see The Wheel Exercise Tutorial on page 11.) Start at the top: Are you Poor, Prosperous, or somewhere in between when it comes to being able to Connect to Breath? Put a dot on the spoke next to the number that corresponds with your answer. Now continue going around the wheel, and after scoring yourself on every spoke, connect the dots to create a circle.

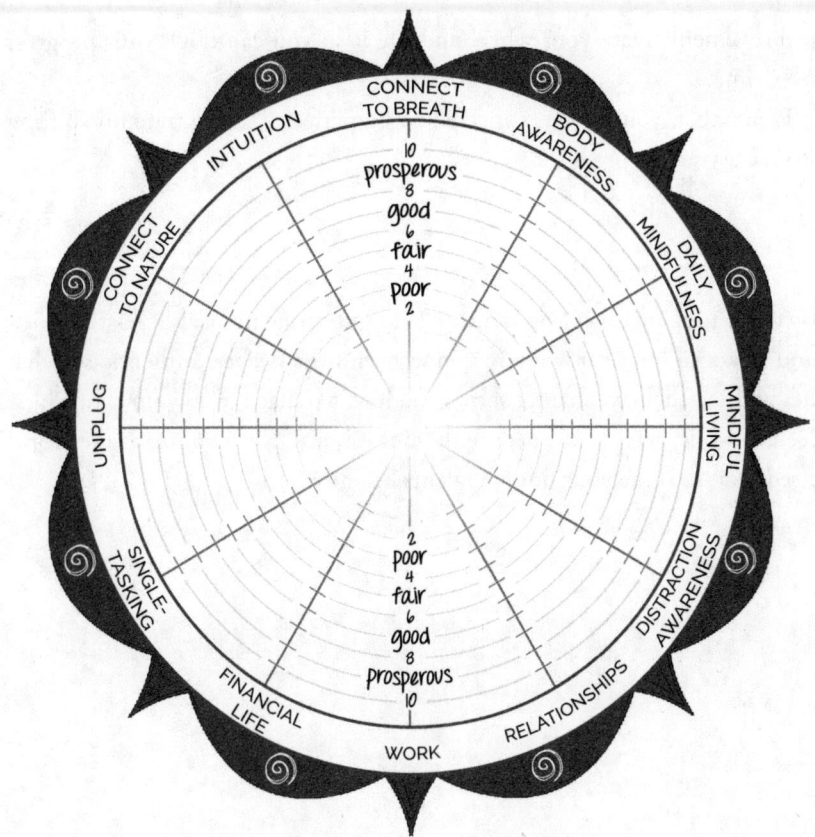

The Presence Wheel

In your journal, answer the following questions:

- As you look at the three spokes that have the lowest scores (the biggest dents in your wheel), what are two ways you can do better right now in these areas?
- How might you create some accountability for cultivating presence?
- What are two new ways to apply mindfulness to your financial life?

To become more present, consider revisiting this exercise weekly or monthly to set yourself up for greater success. Don't beat yourself up if your scores are low—we are all works in progress and have room for improvement. Date your wheel and file it so you can track your progress over time.

Remember, you are not expected to be perfect. Concentrate on shifting from busyness to presence.

...

By cultivating presence you can expect to improve your health, relationships, and financial life. You will also connect with the deeper, authentic self that lies within. The next chapter shows you how to detach from your ego, which feeds off busyness, to connect with your essence. Keep going, as the world needs you to shine your unique talents brightly!

Chapter 5

ESSENCE

See How Your Ego Is Killing Your Cash Karma

When you do things from your soul, you feel a river moving in you, a joy.
    RUMI thirteenth-century poet, Sufi mystic, and theologian

Dear Ego,

We need to talk. As a child, before you were such a big part of my life, I remember feeling like a free spirit—alive, playful, and full of joy. I was almost always present, connected to my senses, and soaking in life and the sun on my face. I danced, played, and sang, easily shining my inner light brightly without feeling judged.

As I grew, you became my constant companion. You are a mask that eclipses my inner light, making me look and behave how you think I should in order to be successful and loved. It seems all my achievements and accomplishments are never enough. You are a heavy burden to bear. Your relentless and merciless worry, anger, and angst cause me great anxiety and misery. I'm tired of wrestling with you to protect relationships with the ones I love.

With your constant negative feedback and fear of judgment from others, you first encouraged me to be a people pleaser, telling me the only way people would love me and stick around was if I squelched my own needs and desires to be of service to them. You advised me to keep my world relatively small and safe by staying in my nine-to-five job to avoid the pressures and potential failure in a full-time private practice. I worked harder and longer hours than I should have for my employer and my fees were too low.

When I began to embrace my worth through therapy, we made a wee bit of an overcorrection. Remember that huge office we rented for me and my former business partner that was on a higher floor than all our staff? You told me we deserved that even though the business couldn't support it. No wonder they didn't like us very much then! Remember when we had to swallow our pride and terminate that lease and move back in with them because it was too expensive? That piece of humble pie was a helpful correction from the universe to help us find our happy medium.

You've been with me so long that I actually started to think you were me. I forgot about my inner light until mindfulness practices illuminated it. Now I see you. Connecting to my breath helped me realize my thoughts are your incessant chatter. When I got a reprieve from them, I heard the song of my soul and connected with my heart.

You are not me. You are an aspect of me. I am my light. You are no longer in the driver's seat. The more I connect with my inner light, the more it peacefully guides me to my higher purpose and aligns my life with deeper meaning and reward. Now when I need you to help me be more confident in a business meeting or on a stage for a speaking engagement, I am glad you get me there and are by my side. When I see you are being defensive, difficult, or blocking my inner light, I kindly ask you to step aside.

My inner light is a passionate fire of love and compassion. It shines brightly to both heal myself and light the way for others. I feel connected to my light when I laugh with reckless abandon, hold those I love, move my body in dance or yoga, sing, connect with nature, create, and share with others.

The more I shine my authentic light filled with lovingkindness on my loved ones—clients, students, and attendees at my speaking engagements—the more love and prosperity I receive back. When they are stirred, awakened, or inspired in some way, that light comes back to me tenfold, bringing me into a flow of universal light, love, and financial prosperity. My soul's purpose is to promote mental and financial health. Love and faith are my guides.

So could you maybe lighten up a little? Let's keep it real. We've got stuff to do!

With gratitude,

Joyce

Therapy Session Number 5
(20 minutes)

Hello there! In this session you will become aware of how your ego is harming your financial health. You will also learn how connecting with your essence—your inner light—can catapult you into higher heights of success! Let's get started. In your journal, please write your responses to the following questions:

- What did my "Dear Ego" letter bring up for you in relation to your own ego?
- How might your ego be hurting you financially?
- In what ways do you connect with your inner light (essence) and let it shine?
- How has that connection increased your prosperity? How can you expand on this?
- What do you imagine I, as your therapist, might say about what you wrote?
- What are two or three insights you gained from this session?

Excellent self-reflection! You will benefit from having taken a deeper look at yourself.

...

Now, let's give you some tools to continue to detach from your ego and connect with your essence.

Unplug from Ego and Plug into Essence

As humans, we are comprised of mind, body, and spirit. Our ego is our sense of self through the mind's eye: our identity based on the roles we play in life and our thoughts and perceptions of ourselves. Our essence is our spirit or our inner light, where peace, love, joy, and bliss reside within us.

The relationship between essence and ego is like Aladdin's lamp: essence is the magic genie and ego is the lamp that imprisons you. When we are not living our lives in a congruent way with our essence or authentic selves, we become disconnected from ourselves and others. When we live our life in alignment with essence, not ego, we realize we are not our work titles, bank account balances, relationship status, or appearance. The more we align with essence, the better we can observe and manage ego. By realizing we have the choice to set ourselves free from the imprisonment of ego, we can expand into our highest and greatest self-expression.

Freeing yourself from ego requires separation from your pain-body, which is the energy of your emotional pain. Ego and the pain-body feed off of one another.[1] You are not your pain, depression, anxiety, or traumas. Your issues are *how* you are, not *who* you are. Your essence is your true self. Be mindful of the power of language. Do you see the difference between "I am depressed" and "I feel depressed"? You can access your inner peace and reduce your suffering by connecting with essence through presence. Therapy can also help with this.

An educated, articulate, likable guy in his forties came to me recently for counseling. He hated his lucrative job, but felt stuck in a pair of "golden handcuffs." His wife was unhappy that he didn't help more with tasks at home. They bickered often and had become emotionally and sexually disconnected. He felt bad about himself at work and at home. Some bright moments with his children kept him trudging along. Having cocktails with colleagues a few days a week was apparently how he coped with stress, disappointment, and loneliness. It seemed hard for him to even identify his feelings, let alone express them in a session. He appeared boxed in by fears, self-limiting beliefs, and thoughts of what he "should" be doing and feeling. Through therapy, he realized he had shut down and disconnected from his essence almost twenty years prior.

Through mindfulness, I helped him detach from his ego and reconnect with his inner light. As he shared his story, I felt like a miner sifting through the dirt that buried him to uncover his essence. I saw glimmers of essence when he talked about his long-lost guitar, early years in his marriage, his dream to build a house, and his desire to help nonprofits. By mirroring this all back to him, and supporting him in finding his voice, he was able to make important shifts in his marriage by being authentic. In our last session, he illustrated the idea of essence when he said, "Thank you for making me embrace my life and my light and step into who I truly am."

TIPS TO CONNECT WITH ESSENCE

Reconnect with the fire inside your heart when facing important choices and decisions through quiet reflection, meditation, mindfulness, and presence. Let your inner light be your guide.

Remember who you were before your limited thinking. Who did you want to be long ago? Live as this aspect of self.

Refuel through relationships and activities that ignite your inner fire.

Rebalance your life with hobbies and leisure by setting healthy boundaries with work.

Realign your work with your gifts and sense of life purpose.

Revitalize yourself through playfulness, cheerfulness, dance and movement, creation of art, and connection with music.

Replace fear with love, as fear is ego and love is essence. Elisabeth Kübler-Ross, psychiatrist and author of the international bestseller *On Death and Dying*, said, "There are only two emotions: love and fear. All positive emotions come from love, all negative emotions from fear. From love flows happiness, contentment, peace, and joy. From fear comes anger, hate, anxiety, and guilt."[2] Moving away the clouds of fear will allow the light of your essence to shine more brightly.

Align with Your Essence
(20 minutes; lifetime practice)

In your journal, answer the following questions to help you get back to your core self:

- What values do you hold most deeply?
- Do you live in a way that is congruent to these values? In what ways is your life incongruent with these values?
- What broad steps might you take to change your life so you can live in a way that is more consistent with your core values?

...

Now that you are seeing glimmers of your essence, I'll share why your relationship with your ego may be eclipsing your light.

Your Ego Is Your Frenemy

Spiritual teachings tell us we need to dissolve the ego so we can live as our essence, but we all have egos and it's likely they aren't going anywhere.[3] Rather than eliminating the ego, we need to manage it the best we can. Doing this is like handling a frenemy, someone with positive qualities whom you keep at arm's length because if left unwatched, they could stab you in the back.

The friendly part of your relationship with your ego is having a healthy ego or high ego strength. This part of your ego supports you in your pursuits of success in education, career, and relationships. Healthy ego strength includes the following:[4]

- A strong sense of self and the ability to differentiate the responsibility of self and others
- The ability to tolerate discomfort and regulate emotions
- Confidence and empowerment

- The capacity to problem solve
- The ability to be flexible, adaptive, and resilient

When left unmanaged, the enemy part of the ego can cause self-sabotage, including financial harm. Learning how to draw upon the strengths of your ego and keep the harmful aspects at bay requires almost constant attention and practice. You can do this by finding the happy medium between two negative manifestations of ego, the Diva and the Doormat.

Diva and Doormat: The Two Sides of Ego

> *Whenever you feel superior or inferior to anyone, that's the ego in you.*[5]
> ECKHART TOLLE spiritual teacher and *New York Times* bestselling author

Healthy self-esteem is halfway between what I call Diva* and Doormat. Dudes can be Divas too (or Divos, if you prefer). Divas are entitled and not respectful of other people's boundaries, and Doormats aren't respectful of their own. Many believe people with big egos are grandiose Divas, but ego also causes people to be Doormats. This happens when your ego tries to protect itself by avoiding criticism, failure, or even the pressures and additional exposure that come with success.[6] It might appear that Divas have a self-esteem that is through the roof, but this is just a peacock facade to hide their low self-esteem.[7] To function as your most successful self, you need to make sure your ego isn't causing you to veer toward Diva or Doormat.

Table 5.1 shows the characteristics of the two sides of ego—Diva and Doormat—and the happy medium in between, Successful Self, your optimal mode of operation.

---

* Note: The term *diva* is occasionally used in a disparaging way to refer to women who stand up for themselves. That's not the definition I'm using here.

TABLE 5.1 STRIVING FOR MIDDLE GROUND

Doormat	Successful Self	Diva/Divo
Low self-esteem, focuses on own weaknesses, often feels less than others, lacks confidence, insecure	Healthy self-esteem, balanced evaluation of strengths and weaknesses, feels good about self without feeling either inferior or superior to others, confident, secure, and humble	Low self-esteem that looks like inflated self-esteem, focuses on one's strengths and is blind to areas of weakness, often feels better than others, overly confident, arrogant
Lack of respect for self, lack of deservingness, views the needs of others as more important	Feeling deserving in a way that is respectful of self and others, balanced awareness of the needs of self and others	Lacks respect for others, entitled, views the needs of self as most important
Passive, passive-aggressive	Assertive, diplomatic	Aggressive
Doesn't build relationships that would lead to success, is often exploited by others	Has good relationships that lead to mutual and interdependent success	Exploits others, burns relationships
Sensitive to criticism, may avoid putting themselves out in the world due to self-consciousness and fear of failure and success	Responds well to constructive criticism, puts themselves out in the world with self-awareness, collaborates	Becomes enraged by criticism, is competitive and bullies, puts themselves out in the world without self-awareness
Poorly defined sense of self, easily fragments	Authentic, cohesive, and actualized self	False self, defensive mask
Blames self, everything is my fault	Takes responsibility for mistakes and apologizes, forgives others	Blames others, everything is the fault of somebody else

It's normal to recognize some aspects of both Diva and Doormat in your life. We each have certain triggers for our inner Diva or Doormat. You can keep your ego in check and find a healthy balance of self-esteem by being aware of this.

How the Diva and Doormat Are Harmful to Your Financial Situation

Working with Divas in therapy requires me to build up their self-esteem (which, remember, is actually low) as well as carefully chip through their layers of defenses. Because Divas have narcissistic tendencies, they are prone to grandiosity, materialism, and compulsive buying—issues that often come up in therapy.[8]

For example, there was a physician couple I counseled who lived in a mansion on the very expensive North Shore suburbs of Chicago, yet they were upside down on their mortgage and tearing each other apart from the stress. Selling that home and moving to a smaller one within their means required them to let go of their egos, but it was a huge relief to them in many ways. Through therapy, they became less concerned with keeping up with the Joneses and more concerned about staying authentically connected with one another. Many of us can relate to occasionally becoming possessed by our inner Diva and finding ourselves going on a spending spree we can't afford.

Working with Doormats involves helping them see how not valuing themselves has negatively impacted their finances and supporting them in becoming more assertive. For example, the guy I worked with who stayed in the modestly paying, paper-pushing job he hated for years because he thought that was the safest and most stable choice in order to support his family. When he financially chose to care about himself enough to make a career change, it ended up being far more lucrative.

Or there was the business owner who worked eighty-five hours a week and only netted $35,000 after she paid all her staff. We worked on raising her fees, becoming firmer on collecting outstanding invoices, charging for missed appointments, and setting healthy financial limits with her staff.

Table 5.2 shows how your inner Diva and/or Doormat can harm your finances, and how finding the happy medium, your Successful Self, can improve your financial health.

TABLE 5.2 STRIVING FOR FINANCIAL MIDDLE GROUND

Doormat	Successful Self	Diva/Divo
Underearner, accepts low pay, may overspend on others, neglects self	Balanced earning and spending, earns enough to thrive and prosper, balanced spending on self and others	Demands high pay, overspends on self, stingy with others
Financial struggle (*Disclaimer: Not all people who struggle financially are Doormats, but Doormat behavior leads to financial struggle.*)	Financial peace and stability, altruism, generosity, enoughness	Greed, dominance, corruption, living beyond means, living a financial lie, materialism, excess
Focuses on debts instead of assets while feeling destined to live a life of modest financial means	Knows actual net worth (assets minus liabilities) and has a realistic yet optimistic financial outlook	Focuses on assets while having delusional, grandiose visions of success

A healthy balance of self-esteem results in the middle path. Healthy self-esteem reflects respect for self and others and is a recipe for financial success.

HOW TO STOP BEING A DOORMAT

In my practice, I've helped many people recover from their Doormat tendencies by building up their self-esteem. There was the woman who actually slept under her desk at work when she worked late nights. (I made her stop that!) We worked on setting healthy time boundaries and practicing assertive communication with her boss. Or the waiter who was always taking the undesirable holiday and late-night shifts and covering for others until he worked himself into exhaustion. He eventually got sick and was fired. As we worked together, he was able to find a new job where he found a healthy balance of being supportive of others while simultaneously prioritizing his health and well-being.

Here are some tips to overcome the Doormat tendencies you find in yourself:

Hang on to your self-worth. Remember you are innately deserving of prosperity and are no less valuable or less important than others.

Acknowledge your strengths and gifts. Don't let your mind chatter focus on areas of weakness or deficit. Remember all you know and do so well. Make a list of your strengths and ask loved ones for their input; review this often until you embody it.

Be assertive. Find your voice and use your words. Avoid under-communicating and speak your truth. Advocate for yourself as you would for somebody whom you love very much. Communicate in a way that is honest, direct, clear, and demonstrates respect for yourself and others. Ask for what you need, including salary, pay, vacation time, and so forth. Being assertive is critical to performing well within a team.[9] So engage in discussions at home and at work. Avoid guilt trips and say no and set limits as needed.

I had a student intern, Ellen, who did a great job of being assertive with me. After I gave her a bunch of tasks, she replied nicely, "You have given me ten hours of work and I only have two hours left this week, so which tasks would you like me to complete?" I was so glad that she spoke up and didn't overwork herself and secretly hate me. I actually didn't realize that the work I gave her would be so time consuming, so speaking up helped her to succeed in her work and maintain work-life balance.

Reflect confidence in your language. Avoid over-apologizing. Accept compliments without dismissing or minimizing them. Use strong words that project confidence rather than passive language (e.g., "I will absolutely do that" versus "Um . . . I think I might be willing to try that").

Reflect strength in your body language. Stand tall. Keep your shoulders back. Sit up and maintain good posture. Be mindful of hand gestures that reveal insecurity or anxiety such as wringing your hands or fidgeting with your hair. Sit back in your chair rather than perched on the edge.

Shake hands firmly. Walk with purpose. Notice where you sit in meetings or groups and choose a position of strength.

Maintain eye contact. Be mindful of your facial expressions, as a huge majority of communication is nonverbal. A broad smile projects confidence. Strong eye contact reflects self-assuredness, while looking down or away may reveal self-doubt.

Avoid self-deprecating humor. While poking fun at yourself can be healthy and funny, do so in moderation and at the appropriate time. It can inadvertently lower others' opinion of you in the workplace.

Avoid personalizing. Stop blaming yourself for the mistakes of others or situations that are beyond your control.

Get support. Surround yourself with people who believe in you and build you up.

HOW TO TAME YOUR INNER DIVA

Divas with narcissistic tendencies are prone to taking more risks, have increased vulnerability to lawsuits, and can have counterproductive workplace behaviors, including theft, poor attendance, and engaging in activities that don't involve work, like being on Facebook, Snapchat, surfing the web for news, and so forth.[10]

When I was twenty-four, I worked at a group practice for a charming psychologist in his forties who talked a big game, often name-dropping important people he knew and mentioning the big business he was winning. Yet the large office suite was mostly empty, and even he was barely there. Because referrals weren't coming in, I had to find my own clients. They started alerting me that they were being double billed for their sessions. Around this same time, the phones were cut off and the owner was being sued by multiple business partners. This experience taught me never to do business with a full-out narcissistic Diva.

To avoid being a Diva, do the following:

Practice humility. Remember you are no more deserving or important than others. Recognize you are human and imperfect like us all. Ask for both help and feedback on a regular basis.

Recognize when arrogance, boastful behavior, or vanity pop up. Pull in on the reins and observe where this desire for attention or validation is coming from.

Share the spotlight. Make sure you aren't always the center of attention and create space for others to shine. Share resources and opportunities.

Focus on others. Be a good listener. Remember what is important to them. Be helpful.

Acknowledge the talents and strengths of others. Invite others to share their thoughts and expertise. Express appreciation for their contributions.

Allow yourself to be vulnerable.[11] Know that you are always worthy, even when you are imperfect. Let down the walls that you think are protecting you, as they are only limiting you and your connections with others. Admit what you don't know. Share with others your mistakes, challenges, hurts, and fears, as it eases (not increases) shame and anxiety. Open your heart to giving and receiving the love you deserve.

Be authentic. Live by your own deep values rather than what you need to portray to feel worthy. Be honest and transparent with others and be yourself. As Maya Angelou said, "If you are always trying to be normal, you will never know how amazing you can be."[12] See that authenticity will help your relationships, career, and your ability to be an effective leader.[13]

Have people in your life who will call you out, and listen to them. Solicit feedback. Set up systems of accountability to provide some checks and balances for your behaviors and keep you honest.

Let go of the need to control. Resist the urge to have the last word, micromanage, or be right.

Demonstrate respect to others. Be considerate, conscientious, polite, and cross-culturally sensitive. Affirm others. Avoid power struggles. Balance achievement and financial accomplishment with enoughness.

Resist the insatiable hunger of the ego and find balance with contentment and "enoughness." Remember this story of two men: The first man was far more successful in his career, climbing the corporate ladder, one rung after the other. The second man, who did not have all the same achievements said, "But I have something you will never have." The first man responded, "And what could that possibly be?" The second man replied, "Enough."

Cancel Your Ego Trip
(20 minutes; lifetime practice)

In your journal, answer the following questions:

- Which Diva and Doormat characteristics do you recognize in yourself?
- When do these characteristics get expressed? How has this hurt you financially?
- What will you do to re-center yourself and become your Successful Self with healthy self-esteem?

...

Don't worry if you just reflected on some negative aspects of yourself, I did too! This is tough work and I still struggle with finding that healthy balance between Diva and Doormat. We are together on this journey toward greater success and you are doing wonderfully. Now, before we finish this chapter, I want to warn you about a couple other ways your ego may be tripping you up.

Beware of Ego Traps: Imposter Syndrome and Perfectionism

Imposter syndrome and perfectionism are like sand traps that the ego has placed on your course to success, and both Divas and Doormats are vulnerable to them. While the ego has put them there to protect itself from blows and bruises, such as criticism or failure, these traps waste time and energy, which can decrease your financial gains. They may even cause you to throw in the towel. Here's how to recognize and overcome them:

IMPOSTER SYNDROME

Imposter syndrome is when we feel fraudulent about an achievement and have difficulty accepting and integrating it into our understanding of who we are.[14] It shows up in thoughts such as, "I'm only here because of luck," "I feel like a fake," and "I must not fail."[15] It's dangerous because it fuels sleep disturbance as well as depression and anxiety, psychological distress, insecurity, and poor work satisfaction and performance.[16]

While imposter syndrome is not an uncommon phenomenon, people rarely share their insecurities because they are afraid of being exposed as a fraud. It can negatively impact a person's receptivity to feedback because they fear exposure and become defensive. Embarking on new professional challenges (which may improve financial health) can be difficult because people want to reduce the anxiety, not perpetuate it.[17]

Doormats aren't the only ones who fall prey to imposter syndrome. While research shows that Divas who are overt narcissists are immune to imposter syndrome, Divas who are covert narcissists (more inhibited, sensitive, and passive-aggressive than overt narcissists) are susceptible to imposter syndrome, because at times they experience the underlying low self-esteem and insecurity of Doormats.[18]

Imposter syndrome is like a gross mold growing in the darkness. When you shed light on it and share it with others, it struggles to survive. One of the best ways to take the power away from imposter syndrome is to have a learning or workplace culture that encourages the sharing of self-doubt. When we learn that others also deal with imposter syndrome, we realize we are right with the pack and not lagging behind as our ego implies.

Here are some tips to overcome imposter syndrome and change your habits:

- Talk about your imposter syndrome with others.
- Have a mentor for support and positive feedback.[19]
- Remember your strengths and hang on to your confidence.
- Reframe any mistakes, struggles, or perceived failures as a normal part of learning to untangle performance from self-worth.[20]

PERFECTIONISM

Imposter syndrome fuels perfectionism; striving for flawlessness in order to prevent exposure as a fraud. Perfectionism reduces productivity and fuels performance anxiety, so it can be a real roadblock to success.[21] If you keep waiting for something to be perfect (like your book, business plan, website, or resume), you may never put it out in the world. At some point, it has to be good enough and you have to pull the trigger in order to receive financial gain.

In my practice, clients with perfectionism commonly have additional psychological issues including depression, obsessive-compulsive disorder, eating disorders, workaholism, extreme religiosity, and psychological rigidity (black-and-white thinking).[22]

Because low self-esteem is highly related to perfectionism, both Doormats and Divas can fall prey to it.[23] In my coaching business, I've seen some people who fall closer to the Doormat side of confidence have excessive concerns about making mistakes. They spend months, even years, putting together an intricately detailed business plan before they implement it, and some never do. It takes deep work in therapy to address low self-esteem. I remind my clients of all of their strengths, talents, and knowledge.

Those who have more narcissistic or Diva tendencies want to present themselves as perfect to validate their own grandiosity and have others respect and admire them.[24] Divas spend thousands on plastic surgeries, expensive clothes, and sports cars to support the appearance of perfection. In work, they might avoid participating in an event that might further their career if they feel they don't look their best at the time or aren't in a position that reflects well on them (like being in a support role rather than the star of the show).

In my own experience, the busier my life became, the less time and energy I had for perfectionism. Motherhood and owning a vintage home helped me realize that perfectionism is an unachievable illusion. I implemented what I call the 3.5 Rule, meaning I would like to make the honor roll, but I don't need to kill myself trying to get a 4.0. I've found this has turned down my volume of perfectionism and allowed me to have more time and energy to succeed reasonably well in more areas.

Turning down the volume on my perfectionism has also led to financial gain. For example, a news station once asked if I could provide tips for parents on how to explain the airport security process to their kids. They needed the tips and my presence within the hour. At first I was going to decline, since this was not exactly my area of expertise and I was having a very bad hair day . . . Then I dialed down the perfectionism and reminded myself that I looked basically okay, am an experienced psychotherapist, and a mother of two children to whom I've successfully explained airport security. I did the segment and it turned out just fine. The exposure led to new referrals for my practice.

Here are some tips to overcome perfectionism:

- Notice your perfectionistic thoughts and give them a reality check with a cost-benefit analysis of what perfectionism costs you in time and energy.
- Relax your standards. Remember the 3.5 Rule. In some cases, a 2.0 is just fine! Heck, don't we all have a D in our past? And failure means you are trying and is sometimes necessary on the road to greater success. It's okay not to have a 4.0. You are still awesome.
- Remember your strengths instead of focusing on the deficits.
- Allow some room for imperfection. Maybe it's as simple as leaving the unflattering photo your friend tagged you in on your social media page or giving yourself a reasonable time limit to work on a project and then submitting it.

Connecting with essence offers clarity on your deeper purpose and calling—the work you are meant to do. When you align your gifts and your essence with a need in the world, the universe will support your financial prosperity. Detach from your ego's messages of fear and judgment and let your essence explode into the world with fearless courage. The world needs you to shine your talents brightly. For this, you will be rewarded with financial prosperity.

Detaching from ego and connecting with essence will catapult you into success just like a leader, an inventor, or an artist who shines their gifts with brilliant magnificence in a way that heals, helps, and inspires others. I witnessed seeing somebody's essence in action when Florence and the Machine performed at Lollapalooza, a four-day music festival hosted in Chicago. Like a goddess, Florence moved through the crowd with presence and grace, radiating her brilliant essence and singing the song of her soul with fearless courage.

Florence Welch is one of my essence heroes. I've learned that her parents divorced when she was thirteen and her grandmother struggled with bipolar disorder and died by suicide. Florence dealt with her dyslexia and eating disorder by drinking, using drugs, and controlling her food. These issues are her pain-body, which she has not let stop her from success. In fact, these experiences may have given her powerful content and emotions to channel through her music. Florence is just one example of someone who was able to move from ego to success.

You did it! In this chapter, you've learned how to improve your success. Now, let's wrap this up by reviewing the key takeaways in this chapter's wheel exercise. The Essence Wheel brings together all the skills you learned in this chapter and measures how well you are detaching from ego and connecting with your essence.

The Essence Wheel
(20 minutes)

Date: _____

Rate your response after each question using a number from the following scale:

Poor (1–3), Fair (4–5), Good (6–7), Prosperous (8–10)

Poor			Fair		Good			Prosperous	
1	2	3	4	5	6	7	8	9	10

Essence Alignment: This is about connecting with your deepest self and unique light through presence. How are you aligning your life with essence, this core aspect of self, and choosing love over fear? _____

Ego Detachment: This is the ability to observe and separate from harmful aspects of ego such as defensiveness, competition, arrogance, feelings of superiority or inferiority, and focusing on externals, such as appearance and accomplishments. How well are you able to avoid having your financial perspective become distorted by ego? _____

Healthy Self-Esteem: This comes from feeling positive about yourself in relation to others in a balanced way, and includes healthy ego strength, confidence, and assertiveness. How good are you at celebrating your strengths and recognizing your areas of needed growth and development? _____

Humility: Humility involves a healthy awareness of all you do not know or understand, your areas of deficit, and keeping your ego in check. How good are you at remaining humble, modest, and down-to-earth even as you achieve great success? _____

Respect: How would you rate yourself when it comes to demonstrating respect for yourself and others in your communication? _____

Authenticity: How good are you at being honest, real, and genuine with others, while remaining kind and not putting up false pretenses? _____

Vulnerability: Vulnerability is about breaking down the walls created by your ego for self-protection. These walls prevent the honest communication that leads to support, connection, intimacy, and growth. How good are you at admitting what you do not know and asking for help? _____

Enoughness: I define "enoughness" as resisting the urge to feed ego with materialism and staying connected with essence as you welcome true prosperity, which includes generosity. How good are you at knowing that on the essence level, you are always enough? _____

Use Gifts: How good are you at celebrating your gifts and strengths and aligning them with a need in the world? _____

Purpose: How would you rate yourself when it comes to identifying your higher personal and professional feeling of purpose, which is fueled by your essence? _____

Values: How good are you at staying true to yourself and living your life in a way that is aligned with your core values? _____

Highest Self-Expression: How would you rate yourself when it comes to letting your inner light shine by showing up and thriving in the world as your most expansive, vibrant, and prosperous self? _____

Chart your responses on The Essence Wheel. (For a refresher on how to do this, see The Wheel Exercise Tutorial on page 11.) Start at the top: Are you Poor, Prosperous, or somewhere in between when it comes to Essence Alignment? Put a dot on the spoke next to the number that corresponds with your answer. Now continue going around the wheel, and after scoring yourself on every spoke, connect the dots to create a circle.

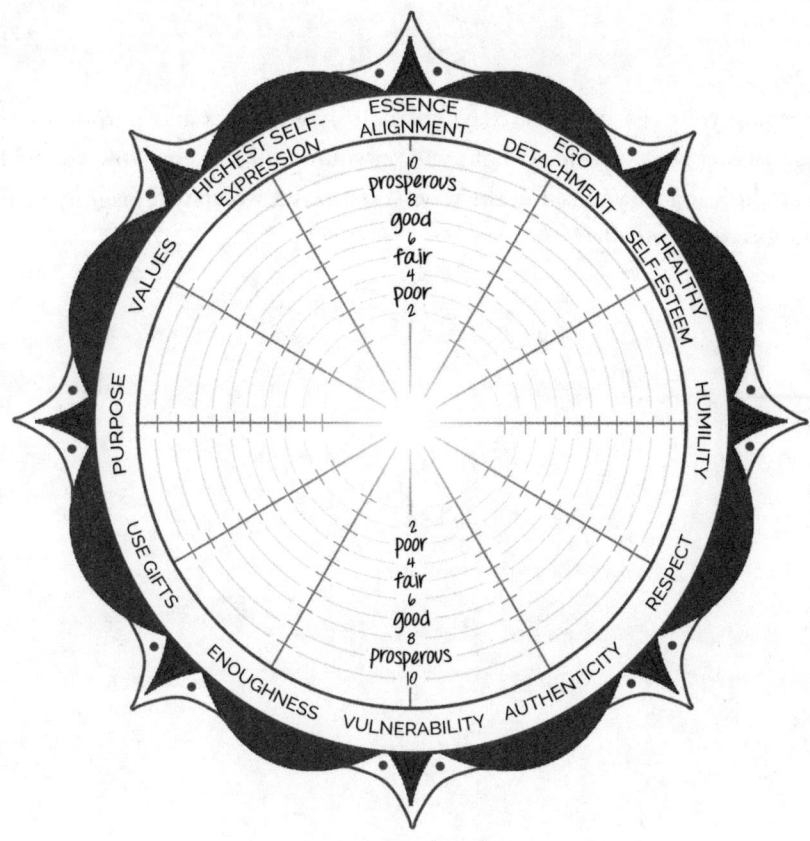

The Essence Wheel

Let's wrap this up by answering the following questions in your journal:
Look at the three spokes of The Essence Wheel with the lowest scores (the dents) and come up with two ways you can improve in each of those areas.

- What are two ways detaching from ego and aligning with essence would improve your financial life?
- How can you spend more of your time in the healthy self-esteem range?

No matter what your results are, consider revisiting this exercise monthly or quarterly to continue to keep your ego in check and ignite success by connecting with essence. Date your wheel and file it for later reference!

...

Keeping your ego in check, staying true to your values and purpose, and connecting with your inner light will set you up for success. Now you will learn how to love yourself in the ways you deserve, which will magnify your success exponentially!

Chapter 6

SELF-LOVE

Tell Your Inner Saboteur to Buzz Off and Invest in Yourself with Fierce Love

The most powerful relationship you will ever have is the relationship with yourself.
STEVE MARABOLI bestselling author of *Life, the Truth, and Being Free*

The universe was holding my feet to the fire and my mental and financial health were at stake when my business partner left and my business was in cash-flow hell. When I stopped spinning my wheels and took an honest look at myself in therapy, I saw my real enemy—my Inner Saboteur.

The voice in my head, my Inner Saboteur, was constantly telling me I wasn't enough, caused me to prioritize everyone else before myself, and almost led to financial and emotional bankruptcy. That's when I had my first turning point on my journey toward self-love. I chose to start extending myself the loving care I more easily extend to others.

Through therapy I learned to turn down the volume of my Inner Saboteur and develop self-compassion. I also started caring for myself the way I would care about somebody I love very much—emotionally, physically, and financially. I began to build up my reserves in every sense. Demonstrating love for myself in my thoughts, actions, and choices all led to higher self-worth and confidence. This led to my second major turning point.

I remember crying from the depths of my soul in the shower. Along with my sadness and grief was a deep sense of relief and an almost completely overpowering feeling of tremendous gratitude toward myself. I had just asked my husband of eighteen years and partner for twenty-five years for a divorce, yet it felt like I'd just saved my life.

My husband and I had been together since I was seventeen and he was nineteen. I'd spent the previous five years feeling like I was experiencing a psychological death in the context of my marriage. He is a good man whom I'd loved very much, and we had two incredible daughters together. I would have given myself a lobotomy if it meant I could feel happy and content in our marriage. We did a lot of work in couples therapy but remained at an impasse. There are several layers to the truth of why our marriage ended: we married young, we grew apart, we had issues around our division of labor after the transition to family, and more. Normal problems, nothing horrible.

Some friends and neighbors said I was selfish to ask for the divorce. Yet I felt like I didn't have a choice. Telling our children and families was one of the most difficult experiences I've ever been through. I won't pretend that the process was perfect, but in the world of divorces it was probably one of the best-case scenarios. During our initial conversations, we processed our hurt, anger, and loss. We finally agreed this was what needed to happen. We used one attorney to file what we had agreed upon and drove to our court date together. The judge thanked us on behalf of our children for making such fair decisions about sharing our time with them and dividing our assets. My ex-husband and I even went to brunch together afterward, honoring the end of an extremely important chapter in both of our lives.

For me, getting divorced was an opportunity to take complete responsibility for my happiness and my financial life. Because my ex-husband kept the house and virtually everything in it in our settlement, I was grateful to create a new home for myself and my girls when they were with me. That new home environment reflected my self-love and joy. I started reconnecting with nature and community too. When I started dating, I silently repeated this mantra: "Hang on to your confidence." To attract the love and life I deserved, I knew I had to hang on to my worth.

Over five years later, my ex-husband and I are both married to new partners with whom we are much better suited. Our daughters are thriving. I'm in a marriage that fuels my soul and enriches and supports my growth in ways I never dreamed possible. I now have more energy for my daughters and older stepchildren who are bonuses in our life. Some of the people who judged me for being selfish have commented on how the divorce ended up being a good thing not only for me but for all of us. I am not saying my kids haven't suffered or experienced hardship because of the divorce; of course they have, and for that my heart aches and I am forever sorry. However, I believe we all agree the blessings outweigh the challenges, and for that I give great thanks. I truly believe choosing to take care of myself, even by getting divorced, improved the trajectory of all of our lives.

The third time choosing self-love revolutionized my life was when I decided to sell my business. I felt I had completed my mission to create a company providing affordable therapy, and the responsibilities of the business were crushing my spirit. I wanted to be free for my heart's next mission—writing and speaking. During the year and a half it took to sell the business, I had to hang on to my worth as I set the price and negotiated a successful sale for more money than I once thought I would make in a lifetime. I continue to follow my heart, hang on to my confidence, and take care of myself with loving care—all of which led to this book and my speaking engagements, which are enriching both figuratively and literally. My life is blossoming into the fullest expression of myself.

Self-love is the key to how I transformed my life into one that reflects a healthy financial mindset.

Therapy Session Number 6
(20 minutes)

This session will help you feel so much better! Today you will become aware of your Inner Saboteur and start loving yourself the way you deserve. Answer the following questions in your journal:

- How has your Inner Saboteur prevented you from greater happiness and prosperity?
- What did my story bring up for you and how does this relate to your own self-love?
- How might your life look different if you embraced yourself with fierce love?

What do you think about what you just wrote? Does your relationship with yourself leave some room for improvement? Never fear! I'm here to help!

...

Self-Love Isn't Selfish

> *Contrary to what many believe, self-love is healthy. It's neither selfish, nor self-indulgent, nor egotism, nor narcissism.*[1]
> DARLENE LANCER attorney, psychotherapist, and renowned author

Self-love is caring about your own well-being and happiness, which is a basic human necessity to survive, thrive, and prosper.[2] It's both a feeling and an action and includes self-affirmation, self-compassion, and self-care.

I was concerned when one of my graduate students, Samreen, showed up for clinical supervision looking utterly exhausted. I knew she had an internship, several demanding classes, and was planning a large event for Chicago's Muslim-American community. I asked her, "If you were a cell phone, what percentage would your battery be charged?"

She replied, "One percent."

Yikes!

As human beings, a red bar doesn't warn us when our energy levels are at a dangerous low. Through self-care, we must take time to recharge our batteries so this doesn't happen.

Samreen didn't even realize she was so depleted. I asked her to identify changes she could make that day. Being the good student that she was, she excitedly said, "Okay! Number 1! Go to bed every night before one o'clock in the morning." Oh my, I thought, I guess we have to start somewhere!

What percentage would your battery be at if you were a cell phone? Of course our energy varies depending on the time of day, our health, and more. However, it's our self-love responsibility to balance life's demands without allowing our personal battery to become dangerously low. Remember, self-love isn't selfish.

Before I show you exactly how to invest in yourself with self-love, let's look at what is standing in your way.

Your Inner Saboteur Is Robbing You of Prosperity

Your relationship with yourself sets the tone
for every other relationship you have.[3]
ROBERT HOLDEN psychologist and author of *Happiness NOW!*

If you were another person in a relationship with you, would you be okay with how you treat yourself on a daily basis? Are you good to yourself? Is your mind kind to your body and soul? At times we all:

- Beat ourselves up with cruel self-talk
- Abuse our health with neglectful or harmful choices
- Deprive ourselves of prosperity through self-sabotaging behaviors like overspending and not saving for the future

Our Inner Saboteur, iSab for short, is responsible for these kinds of self-harm. An iSab tells us we aren't worthy of even our own love. As the critical and judgmental aspect of our ego, the iSab wreaks havoc in our lives with harsh comments that lead to self-sabotaging behaviors and fuel feelings of shame, inadequacy, and worthlessness. I prefer the term *Inner Saboteur* to *Inner Critic* because a critic isn't always bad and could possibly help increase one's self-awareness.

The voice of our iSab may be a combination of negative messages we received from our parents, siblings, teachers, and other formative people in our life. It might also stem from some cultural or religious teachings, or maybe it is simply our own self-loathing. We *all* have iSabs, but some of ours may be more vicious than others. For those who have survived abusive or neglective relationships, we may have especially cruel iSabs because we've internalized the negative messages.[4]

In chapter 1, we learned how self-limiting beliefs, the voice of our iSab, blocks the flow of abundance and strangles prosperity. Our iSab also criticizes and judges us by saying things like "You just said the dumbest thing ever." The more our Inner Saboteur is squawking away, the less we can concentrate and perform in our work, which negatively impacts finances.[5] To love ourselves and welcome prosperity, we need to tell our iSab to shut it.

I call my iSab Zelda. She's a real pain in the ass who I've deliberately made sure doesn't have much power over me. Recently I was interviewed on how to practice liking yourself. I explained to journalist Annakeara Stinson that by giving your iSab a name you can externalize those negative thoughts and mindfully observe them, noticing how harmful they are so you can loosen their hold over you.[6] She named her negative thoughts Terry, journaled each day for a week about her interactions with Terry, and shared how this made her feel better.

She wrote about how Terry showed up when she was at the grocery store and started giving her crap about her dating life, telling her she was a freak, and comparing her to some other woman.[7] Annakeara also used breathing exercises to separate herself from Terry after a bad argument with her mother. Annakeara's therapist agreed that naming her iSab helped her recognize how often it was showing up and causing her to feel angry, sad, shameful, jealous, and inadequate. Interestingly, Annakeara said this helped her feel sorry for Terry, essentially neutralizing her iSab through self-compassion.

You can do this too! Don't be scared; I'm here by your side.

Face Your Inner Saboteur
(10 minutes a day for 1 week minimum; lifetime practice)

Give your Inner Saboteur (iSab) a name and then visualize or even draw what your iSab looks like. (This adds to the fun!) For a week, write how your iSab impacts you. On the last day, review your entries and respond to the following questions in your journal:

- What did your iSab like to pester you about?
- Did you notice any trends around the circumstances or timing of when your iSab tends to appear?
- On a scale from 1 to 10, how badly do you think your iSab is hurting your mental health? Physical health? Financial health?

Now, close your eyes and imagine you are telling your iSab to quiet down. What happened when you attempted to do that? If you weren't able to quell your inner villain, have no fear. Your Inner Dream Team is here!

...

Cultivate an Inner Dream Team That Supports Your Success

While your iSab may always have a seat on your inner board of advisors, you can reduce its voting power by inviting an Inner Dream Team of supporters to come sit at the table. To weaken your iSab's negative influence on you, I recommend finding an Inner Dream Team to help you cultivate self-love.

The following chart shows how self-affirmation relates to the following roles:

Inner Dream Team Member	Self-Love Responsibility
Positive Coach	Self-affirmation
Best Friend	Self-compassion
Loving Parent	Self-care

POSITIVE COACH: RAH! RAH! RAH FOR YOU!

You cheer for everyone you know. Now it's time to cheer for *you*!

While your iSab insults you at every opportunity, your Positive Coach is an internal voice that supports and encourages you to be your best.

If you stumble or fumble in the game of life, it's your Positive Coach that has confidence in you and says "Shake it off! You got this!" When your self-esteem is threatened, access your Positive Coach for self-affirmation in order to maximize your performance and financial success.[8] By verbalizing your thought process as you problem solve, your Positive Coach can have a positive effect on performance, which improves finances.[9] Your Positive Coach won't let you throw in the towel when it comes to going for a promotion or starting your own business.

If you've had teachers or mentors who believed in you and encouraged you to grow, your Positive Coach may be pretty well developed. If you've had people in your life who continually put you down, you may need to foster your Positive Coach to overpower your iSab!

BEST FRIEND: YOU'VE GOT A FRIEND IN YOU!

One day, I had a realization: I am a damn good friend because I love my friends. If you are my friend, I'll have your back, normalize and validate your feelings, and want the best for you. Then it occurred to me, why am I not doing this for myself? I chose to start treating myself as if I were my own BFF—and you can do that too!

While your iSab makes you feel horrible about yourself and your actions, your inner Best Friend helps you have self-compassion, which means having a kind and caring attitude toward yourself even when experiencing difficulty or failure.[10] This is important for your financial health because people with more self-compassion have less emotional exhaustion and tend to perform better at work.[11] Self-compassion improves relationships and is positively correlated with income.[12]

Just like you love and accept your friends, your inner Best Friend accepts you exactly as you are and promotes self-acceptance: having a positive attitude toward yourself and liking yourself while acknowledging and accepting both your good and bad qualities.[13]

Your inner Best Friend can even improve your financial health as self-acceptance has a positive relationship with perceived financial performance. Studies also show that business owners with greater self-acceptance tend to have more financial success in their company.[14] People who have greater self-acceptance also tend to have higher income, and those who increase their self-acceptance over time tend to cultivate greater income over time.[15] Being your own BFF is important for your bottom line!

For members of marginalized groups, self-acceptance is especially important and may be even more difficult due to years of erosion from being devalued, discriminated against, or even hated by others. My client Cam came to me for therapy after a business coach told him he needed to speak less effeminately to land a better job. This homophobic microaggression sent Cam spiraling into a state of internalized homophobia and self-loathing. In therapy, we worked on teaching him to love and accept himself exactly as he is. Cam reprogrammed those negative messages by speaking to himself as his own best friend rather than as a harsh critic. The better he felt, the more confidence he had. After several months of hard work on embracing himself with self-love and freeing himself to be authentic, he landed a prestigious job at an organization that valued and appreciated his skills and talents and everything about him.

It's important for each of us to feel positive about who we authentically are, and our inner Best Friend can help us get there. Studies show that LGBTQIA+ people who have higher self-acceptance and positive feelings about their sexuality tend to perform better at work and have higher job satisfaction, which leads to financial success.[16]

Your inner Best Friend can also help you practice self-forgiveness. If we have done something truly wrong, we, of course, need to take full ownership, experience remorse and regret, ask for forgiveness from the ones we have hurt, and learn from our wrongs. Guilt is only useful when it helps us learn and correct wrong behaviors. However, many of us carry around guilt for mistakes we have made that goes far beyond what is appropriate, useful, or adaptive. We must free ourselves from never-ending self-flagellation so we can live in peace.

In my practice, I've worked with clients who have had to work on self-forgiveness for many different issues, including addictions. One client felt enormous guilt for turning to alcohol after the death of her father and ended up in treatment for a couple of months when her boys were small. We had to do a lot of work to help her reframe her alcoholism as a disease and not a character flaw or something she intentionally did to hurt her family. It took a while for her to respond to herself as she would somebody she loved, focusing on her awesome strength and courage to get help.

Sometimes we need to practice self-forgiveness for smaller mistakes. When I was working as the president of the Illinois Counseling Association, I sent out an email to our board of sixty members. I intended to say "It's time to get our ducks in a row for the conference."

The executive director replied back and said, "Joyce, I think you made a typo."

I had spelled ducks with an *i*.

Oops!

We all make mistakes. It's part of the human condition. We need to give ourselves the advice we would give our own best friend: to remember we are essentially good, to let it go, and to move forward with self-compassion.

We can all tap into our inner Best Friend by asking, what would I say to my best friend if they were in this situation? I have no doubt your response will be more compassionate than how you previously treated yourself.

LOVING PARENT: CARE FOR YOURSELF LIKE A PROTECTIVE MAMA BEAR!
While your beastly iSab might harm you through self-sabotaging behaviors like overworking, not taking care of your health, substance abuse, or compulsive spending, your Loving Parent will take good care of you. The Loving Parent is smart and even recognizes when your iSab is trying to fool you by disguising self-harm as self-care. For example, telling you that since you've had a hard day you deserve a cigarette or some retail therapy that you can't afford.

As adults, we must be our own Loving Parents and learn to take care of ourselves the way we would care for somebody we love very much.

Because your Loving Parent wants you to be safe and healthy in every way, they will remind you to:

Eat right. Good nutrition enhances emotional well-being and decreases anxiety and depression, which improves job performance.[17]

Get enough sleep. Sleep improves mental health and work performance.[18]

Drink enough water. Hydration is important for physical health, mental health, and performance.[19] So skip the soda and limit caffeine.

Make smart choices. Poor choices can lead to illness and injury, which are costly on every level.

Take a break from your screens. Too much screen time impairs sleep and your ability to concentrate at work. To get a good night's sleep and feel less depleted and more engaged at work the following day, do not use your smartphone late at night or send emails from bed.[20]

Stay in school. Learning drives financial performance.[21]

Get some exercise. While you might think that eating your lunch at your desk allows you to get more work done, using your lunch break to exercise can reduce stress, improve your physical health, and have a positive effect on your work performance and, subsequently, your financial health.[22]

Practice the piano. Whether you play the piano or not, create time for leisure and hobbies, including music, art, and sports. Hobbies promote mental health and wellness.

See how your Loving Parent takes good care of you? Now that you get the idea, let's see how your Inner Dream Team is doing.

Cultivate Your Inner Dream Team
(15 minutes; lifetime practice)

Rate how your Inner Dream Team members are performing on a scale from 1 to 10, with 1 being not at all supportive and 10 being fully supportive:

- Positive Coach (self-affirmation) _____
- Best Friend (self-compassion) _____
- Loving Parent (self-care) _____

Once you've determined the role with the lowest score, answer the following questions in your journal:

- Why is this aspect of inner support most challenging for you?
- How can you increase your performance in this role?

For the next day or two, imagine that this Inner Dream Team member is right alongside you. Try to hear their voice and what they might say to support you. Then answer the following questions in your journal:

- Do you notice any benefits? For example, does your Inner Dream Team member motivate you or help you feel better?
- With the help of your Inner Dream Team, did you notice a decrease in the influence of your iSab and the negative emotions it triggers?

Remember to call upon your Inner Dream Team members whenever you need them!

...

Financial Health Boost: Practice Financial Self-Care

It's time to practice financial self-care with the help of your Inner Dream Team. Financial self-care involves taking care of your finances in a way that reflects true self-love.

Accruing debt to buy items for yourself that you can't afford, such as expensive salon treatments or a fancy car, may be self-harm disguised as self-care. This is Diva behavior. It's like a client of mine who bought a new sports car every six months just to prove his worth, even when he had no savings in the bank.

On the other hand, pinching pennies and depriving yourself of what you need or what would be good for you is also self-harm disguised as self-care. This is Doormat behavior. It's like a client of mine who hadn't bought clothes for herself or had a haircut in five years! Even though she was living paycheck to paycheck, I pointed out that perhaps she didn't need to buy her toddlers expensive clothes and leather cowboy boots from the department store and she could use some of that money on herself. After a haircut and purchasing five new outfits and some new makeup, her self-esteem and self-love increased dramatically.

I've routinely confronted clients on both ends of the spectrum to help them find that happy medium—spending money in a way that reflects healthy self-esteem. True self-care is financially taking care of yourself and treating yourself well within your means. It is finding

> that healthy balance of taking excellent care of yourself both in the present and in the future. This includes earning a solid income and making sure you have everything you need and some or most of what you want, as well as taking care of your future self by having insurance and savings for safety and security. Choosing to spend discretionary income on items that promote your mental and physical health and wellness is money well spent. Examples would be purchasing a good mattress to promote better sleep, buying exercise equipment or a gym membership, making your home a sanctuary, or purchasing books and mindfulness apps.

The Self-Love Wheel brings together all the skills you have learned in this chapter and measures how well you are doing with self-love practices.

The Self-Love Wheel
(20 minutes)

Date: _____

Rate your response after each question using a number from the following scale:

Poor (1–3), Fair (4–5), Good (6–7), Prosperous (8–10)

Poor			Fair		Good			Prosperous	
1	2	3	4	5	6	7	8	9	10

Self-Compassion: Self-compassion is the ability to silence your Inner Saboteur, practice self-forgiveness and self-acceptance, and be your most compassionate advocate. It is the opposite of self-flagellation or excessive guilt and regret—it is a mental state where you recognize mistakes, learn from them, and get back on track. How would you rate yourself when it comes to self-compassion? _____

Self-Affirmation: How would you rate yourself when it comes to honoring your strengths, gifts, and unique abilities and seeing all that is beautiful and good about you? _____

Grow & Learn: When it comes to investing in activities, classes, and independent learning to help you grow and develop, how would you rate yourself? _____

Nutrition: Healthy eating includes limiting sugar and processed foods, cooking at home, eating balanced meals, taking multivitamins, and portion control. How would you rate yourself when it comes to nutrition? _____

Hydrate: Skipping the soda and energy drinks and drinking enough water is important for good health. How good are you when it comes to hydration? _____

Physical Activity: When it comes to physical activity, how would you rate yourself? _____

Appearance: How would you rate yourself when it comes to grooming yourself with love and care and putting yourself together so that you feel like the beautiful person that you are? _____

Health Care: This includes annual physicals, dental care, mental health counseling, and specialty care or holistic care as needed. What's your priority when it comes to your own health care? _____

Moderate Substance Use: How would you rate yourself when it comes to moderating caffeine, alcohol, sleep aids, or other substances in your life? _____

Solitude/Reflection: This is stillness and quiet time when you can connect with yourself. How good are you at prioritizing time for solitude and reflection? _____

Connect to Nature: This includes connecting with the outdoors, animals, or plants. How would you rate your ability to connect with nature? _____

Sleep: Making sure you get enough sleep and have the ability to fall asleep easily and stay asleep is also important for good health. How would you rate yourself when it comes to prioritizing your sleep? _____

Leisure/Hobbies: It's important to relax and enjoy activities such as art, music, or sports. How would you rate yourself when it comes to making time for leisure and hobbies? _____

Manage Time: Time management is all about setting healthy time boundaries between your work and your personal life. Make sure to unplug from technology—turn off your phone before bedtime and during mealtimes, do not respond to work emails after work hours or while on vacation, and limit screen time. How would you rate yourself when it comes to striking a nice balance in terms of connecting with others and allowing time for solitude? _____

Home Environment: Keeping your home clean, organized, and functional is important when establishing a pleasant sanctuary for yourself. How would you rate your home environment? _____

Tend to Finances: Making sure there is a healthy balance between the flow of saving and spending, and treating yourself within your means is very important. How would you rate yourself when it comes to taking care of your financial life? _____

Chart your responses on The Self-Love Wheel. (For a refresher on how to do this, see The Wheel Exercise Tutorial on page 11.) Start at the top: Are you Poor, Prosperous, or somewhere in between when it comes to Self-Compassion? Put a dot on the spoke next to the number that corresponds with your answer. Now continue going around the wheel, and after scoring yourself on every spoke, connect the dots to create a circle.

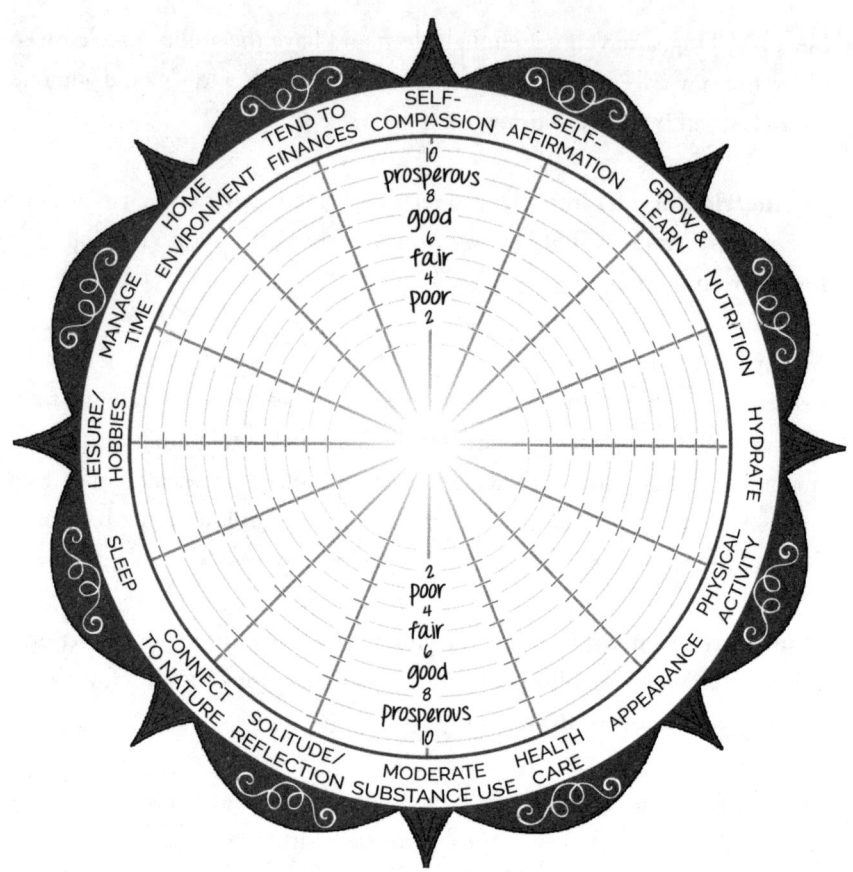

The Self-Love Wheel

Don't worry if you didn't score as well as you hoped. That just means you can look for opportunities to do better when it comes to loving yourself. In your journal, answer the following questions:

- As you review your wheel, identify the three spokes with the lowest scores (the biggest dents) and list two ways you can do better right now for each spoke.
- How might you create some accountability for increasing your self-love?
- What are two ways to improve your financial self-care?

Consider revisiting this exercise weekly or monthly to continue to cultivate self-love and to welcome greater prosperity. Don't forget to date your wheel and file it for later reference so you can track your progress over time.

...

Your self-love practices refuel and recharge your energy and self-worth, which has a direct impact on your mental health and net worth.[23] When we love ourselves, we know that we can give without becoming resentful, exhausted, and depleted, and we can receive because we know we deserve it. Self-love is the prerequisite for complete immersion in the abundant flow of love and prosperity in the world around us. Now that you are embracing yourself with love, let's envision the kind of life you deserve.

Chapter 7

VISION

Whip Out Your Magic Wand to Create a Luxurious Life and Better World

To realize one's destiny is a person's only obligation.
PAULO COELHO author of *The Alchemist*,
the world's most translated book by a living author

My career counselor, Arlene Hirsch, told me, "You must plan your career in the context of your life, not the other way around." I consulted with her while feeling conflicted about wanting to start a group practice and a family simultaneously. Her words of wisdom not only confirmed that I needed to prioritize my personal life (my life life) over my career (my work life), but they became my business's mission statement and plan. Having a vision or plan is a critical component of creating an abundant life.

In college, I dreamed about a marriage and a family, but also of an enriching and lucrative career. On my bucket list was building a therapy practice that could provide some flexibility in my schedule to create an abundant life that wasn't all about work and included time to enjoy my relationships, hobbies, and new experiences, like travel.

When I was approaching thirty, my husband and I started talking about having a baby. Due to a family history of pregnancy complications, miscarriages, and genetic disorders, my doctor suggested having children before the age of thirty-five, if possible. As a result, I felt we should prioritize starting a family. We were extremely fortunate and thrilled to welcome Celeste a year later.

While I wanted to be with Celeste as much as I could, I also wanted to be a good breadwinner. During Celeste's first two years, I saw twenty-five clients a week over the course of three days, which many consider to be a full-time practice. On Mondays and Wednesdays we paid for childcare, and on Saturdays, my husband, who worked full time as a software developer during the week, stayed home with her, which was good for all of us and reduced childcare costs. I stayed home with Celeste on Tuesdays, Thursdays, and Fridays and did my billing and marketing work during her naps. Meanwhile, I subleased my office to others on the days I was at home. Surprisingly, I earned nearly 50 percent more than my previous full-time, salaried position.

My practice was thriving in part because I chose to be in-network with most insurance plans. Despite a lower contracted rate, I was making up the difference in volume. Therapy should be accessible and affordable to people and they should be able to use their insurance to help pay for it. I received a higher volume of referrals and my treatment outcomes were better as people were able to afford to stay in treatment rather than coming for a few sessions during a crisis and then dropping out. I had more referrals than I could place, so I was sending them to friends and colleagues. I realized I could have both the family and the business I wanted as long as I continued to plan the business in the context of my life.

One colleague suggested starting a group practice sooner rather than later and said she would help. As a single person who loved to travel, she also desired work-life balance, so we came up with the name Urban Balance. Our intention was to provide work-life balance to ourselves as owners, our staff, and our clients.

We started our practice by replacing our sublessees with subcontracted therapists, one hire at a time. We provided the referrals, the office space, and billing services. Within three months we were earning more from our subcontractors than we had from our sublessees. The business continued to grow. We took ownership of our four-office suite and jokingly called it our global headquarters with playful excitement of what we hoped would come.

One year after starting Urban Balance, my husband and I welcomed our second daughter, Claudia. We moved to Evanston, a northern suburb of Chicago where Northwestern University is located. When I was in graduate school there, I had babysat for a young family in Evanston that had two little girls and a cute little house and yard. I had dreamed of someday raising a family there too. I loved that Evanston is close to the city, is on the lake, has a diverse community, and feels more like an "urburb" than a suburb because you can walk to restaurants and coffee shops and take two different trains into the city.

Soon after having Claudia, I realized that I hated my commute into the city. It was a time suck, and I wanted to be closer in case there was an urgent situation with the kids. I decided to open a small satellite office in Evanston, less than a mile from my home. When Celeste started kindergarten and Claudia was two, I switched my schedule from three long days to working only during school hours.

I recall meeting the older psychologists in the office next door and telling them I was only going to see clients weekdays from nine o'clock in the morning to three o'clock in the afternoon. They kindly explained that it wasn't possible, as most clients want to be seen evenings or weekends. I stayed the course and hired therapists to work in my office during the evenings and weekends. Over time, my schedule filled with people who have flexible schedules, and I was able to take my kids to and from school and had the flexibility to participate in school activities as desired. When Celeste was in second grade, she said I was at the school the perfect amount—not too much and not too little. Phew! It took some effort to achieve that balance.

As Urban Balance grew, we expanded our original vision with more locations and services. Sometimes the universe supported those efforts and sometimes it did not. One suburban office that tanked taught us that offices do well when they are located where many people work, not in residential areas. As a result, we regrouped and reshaped our vision. Before my business partner left, only the two of us were involved in visioning and business planning. After she left, I involved the Urban Balance leadership team as well as outside consultants, which added to its richness and integrity.

In a meeting with my CPA, he asked me what my exit plan was. Exit plan? I was so focused on building the business that I never thought about the endgame. After my business partner left, I scaled back clients to focus on marketing the practice through speaking and writing. I far preferred that work over overseeing the legal, financial, and staff management aspects of the practice. I checked in with my gut and realized I had about five years worth of energy to devote to strengthening the business in order to prepare it for sale. I wanted to sell when the business was at a high point, when I could free myself to do the work that I love and felt called to do.

While preparing to sell the business, I got divorced, a reminder that life does not always go according to plan. During this time, I reflected on what was and wasn't working in my life and created a life vision, set goals and intentions, and tried my best to align my choices with my highest path.

During one of my darker days before the divorce, I wrote a letter in present tense about my life as if it was happening exactly as I wished. I wrote about a loving and supportive partner, thriving kids, financial peace and prosperity, supportive friends, time for self-care and travel, and public speaking and writing. Today, my life closely reflects what I wrote more than six years ago. My persistent attention to envisioning my best possible life is a large part of what helped me achieve many of my dreams.

Therapy Session Number 7
(20 minutes)

Welcome back to my office. Today we are going to look at your life's vision or plan. Use this session to write a letter to yourself where you envision your best life, just as I did while going through my divorce. Act as if you are already living your best life and share what that looks like. To get started, ask yourself:

- In that best life, how would you spend your time at work?
- In that best life, how would you spend your time away from work? Include details about your family, social life, and hobbies that you enjoy.

Now read through your letter and journal about any themes you notice. It's time to make your vision a reality.

...

Instead of Going with Life's Current, Pick Up Your Oars and Create a Beautiful Journey

Creation and destruction are the two ends of the same moment and everything between creation and the next destruction is the journey of life.[1]
AMISH TRIPATHI diplomat and author

Some people go with the current in life, letting outside forces determine their destiny. Others envision their greatest path and empower themselves to make their way on a higher trajectory with faith and courage.

Our highest vision serves as a compass pointing us to our true north as we move through our life's journey. We can create and choose that vision, but because life is ever changing, traveling toward our vision is a journey of ups and downs, ebbs and flows, twists and turns. It's our job to safely guide ourselves through these challenges, striving for balance, wholeness, and self-actualization.

Life doesn't always listen to our plans. It challenges us with storms, floods, and droughts, causing our vision to shift and evolve over time. Because of this, it's more important than ever to have a vision or we can get permanently thrown off course. No matter our age or where we are on our journey, our learning and growth are not finished; we need to continue to expand our vision. By doing so, we can create the life we want, whatever that may be.

Our vision is not a destination; it is a path. As we move forward, we see new horizons, perhaps more beautiful and expansive than we ever knew existed. And as we charter new frontiers, we can lead others along the way.

Having a life vision is always important, but it is invaluable when you:

- Are starting out on your journey (perhaps as a young adult or business owner).
- Realize that something in your life isn't working and needs to change.
- Are experiencing a milestone or life transition that requires reinventing yourself.
- Identify a need in the world and want to be part of creating positive change.
- Are seeking the greater consciousness that comes with growth.

The sooner you create a vision, the better, but it is never too late to improve your course. An older attendee at one of my speaking engagements didn't agree with this, and said to me, "I wish I heard you speak forty years ago. My whole life would have been different." However, a seventy-year-old woman at the next talk came up to me excitedly and said, "I can't wait to apply all your suggestions for planning this next chapter of my life!" Do you hear the difference in responses? How do you think that might impact their vision of the future? Empower yourself to create the best of what is left of your precious life.

A life vision includes your personal and professional plans for the future. I've been awed and inspired by countless clients who've empowered themselves to radically recreate their life into something they never thought possible. You can do this too! Recall what you learned in chapter 5 about how being present connects you with your inner light and highest self. As you continue to align your life and work with your core values, your vision begins to shine.

My client Jake, who worked for his father's lawn-care business and still lived at home at age twenty-nine, was depressed and not feeling confident about his dating life. When we explored what his earlier life passions were, before his father applied pressure to work for the family business, he talked about his dreams of starting a house-painting business.

After working on healthy assertiveness, Jake told his father he was going to start painting houses on his days off and hired a couple friends to help. Soon his father's landscaping clients were hiring him and he had more work than he could handle, so he hired more people. After several months, he had new painting clients who he then referred to his father's business. His dad then needed to increase his staff, including hiring someone to replace Jake. Jake's dad was impressed with Jake's marketing and management skills, and began to relate to him man-to-man rather than father-to-son. Jake's self-esteem improved and so did his bottom line. As a result, he was able to move out and rent a nice home of his own, which made dating much easier. Through vision, Jake was able to accomplish all of this.

I've prepared some exercises to help you clarify your life vision. Before you get started on these exercises (and the others in this chapter), do some deep breathing exercises or a short meditation to help you become grounded in the present moment. Creating a vision is most effective when you are mindfully present. When you connect to your deeper self, it helps you choose goals that are inherently rewarding rather than pursuing goals that someone else wants you to choose.²

While working on these exercises, imagine you are the artist of your life's masterpiece. You'll want to make your vision as big, beautiful, and vibrant as your heart's desire. Remember what you learned about abundance: having more does not mean less for others, so don't set your own limits! Okay, let's begin.

Declare a Personal Manifesto
(10 minutes)

A Personal Manifesto is a declaration of your core values, what you stand for, and how you intend to live your life. It provides a foundation to build or rebuild your life, motivates you to live more fully, and reminds you to stay on course even during challenging times.³

My Personal Manifesto is: "I live with loving compassion, fearless courage, and vibrant joy. I share myself in everything I do with the highest intention to provide inspiration and support to ease suffering and promote connection and growth. I live a supported, balanced, joyful, and prosperous life."

Experts provide best practices for writing a manifesto.⁴ As you prepare to write your manifesto, ask yourself:

- What are my unique gifts and strengths?
- What are my strongest beliefs and values?
- How do I want to live my life?
- What do I most enjoy? What do I find most meaningful and rewarding?
- What changes do I need to make to live my best life?

Now give it a go! In three to five sentences, declare the highest intention for your life. Keep it positive and write in the present tense with confident language. Include aspects of your personal, professional, and financial life.

Consider printing out your manifesto and hanging it on your fridge or corkboard, or use it as your screensaver.

...

Dream Big Dreams
(30 minutes; lifetime practice)

In your journal, answer the following questions:

- If you had a magic wand, what would your life look like? What are your dreams and ambitions? Include personal, professional, and financial aspirations.
- What's on your bucket list? Write five to ten things you would like to experience, including travel goals.
- Finally, what do you want your legacy to be? What positive mark do you want to leave on the world? What are your philanthropy goals?

Now, here's the kicker: I want you to tell somebody about what you wrote. This makes it real and puts it out into the universe as a formal request. While this can be uncomfortable, especially when you think you are asking for too much, remember that you aren't! Telling a loved one or a trusted confidant is a critical step toward committing to your vision.

...

Create a Work-Life Balance Plan for Sustainable Success

Your health and personal relationships are the foundation of prosperity, so you must be very protective of them or all of your career and financial accomplishments could come tumbling down. As part of your vision, it's critical to develop a plan for work-life balance and well-being in order to find sustainable success.[5] Your career and financial success should be harmonious with your personal life, including your health, relationships, hobbies, and more.

Work-life balance may look different at various life stages depending on:

- Work requirements
- Household duties
- Self-care, which includes sleep, nutrition, exercise, and leisure
- Dependent care for children, aging parents, or pets
- Social/family obligations
- Unexpected events such as illness or accidents, or a global crisis

For single people without dependents, the primary challenge in creating work-life balance may be learning to set healthy time boundaries with work. Many of my clients who are single or without children have reported being repeatedly asked or expected to stay late to cover for colleagues who are parents.[6] This makes it harder for them to take care of themselves and develop their personal lives. I work with them on assertive communication and setting healthy limits.

For single parents, work-life balance is especially challenging. Relational and financial support may be low and responsibilities are high, so well-being often suffers. For couples without children, sharing the responsibilities of home and finances, and balancing those with one another's work requires communication, collaboration, and compromise. For couples with children, the challenges of creating a mutually agreed upon division of labor is compounded. For this reason, one of the partners may work part-time or be a stay-at-home parent. The value of that role can't be understated. According to salary.com, the annual salary of a stay-at-home parent in 2018 should be $162,581. In 2018, about 11 million parents chose to stay at home with kids (7 percent of these were fathers, which is up from 4 percent since 1989).[7] Millennial parents are particularly likely to stay at home—21 percent of millennial parents opted to stay at home, compared to 17 percent of Gen X parents.[8]

Whether one partner is at home or both partners work, work-family conflict often arises. Interestingly, work interfering with family, like missing your daughter's play because of business travel, causes more work performance problems than family problems.[9] These findings should motivate you and your employer to find the work-life balance that will keep you happy and productive. Conversely, family interfering with work causes more family problems than work problems.[10] One couple came to me for marital therapy because the lawyer husband tried to work from home and was chronically upset with his wife for allowing interruptions from their children. For this reason, it is important to create a harmonious work-family plan.

Work-family conflict is most common for people with school-age and preschool-age children as compared to those in later family life stages. The harmful effects of work demands were greatest for people transitioning to parenthood or those with preschool-age children. Job flexibility, like having control over where and when you work, was most beneficial in reducing work-family conflict for people in this stage of life. Because of this, work-life balance planning is especially important during these earlier stages of parenthood.[11]

Remember, maintaining balance in your life is your responsibility. You are the potter shaping and molding your life into your unique masterpiece as time spins. Life will throw you ebbs and flows of responsibilities, and you and your loved ones need to consciously collaborate and make choices about work and life to maintain wellness and balance.

Financial Health Boost: Create a Financial Plan

Having a financial plan involves establishing both short- and long-term goals and a plan to achieve them. Short-term goals might include paying off a smaller credit card balance, saving money for your vacation next month, or starting a business in the upcoming months. Long-term goals might include paying off your student loans, buying a home, or saving for retirement.

Create separate lists for short- and long-term goals, with target dates and the money you will need to make them come to fruition. A financial planner can help you crunch the numbers and come up with a realistic plan. They will also help you track your progress over time.

> Don't worry, when I was a young newlywed living in a one-bedroom apartment with my husband, I remember short-term goals like buying a bike or television felt difficult, let alone buying a house, paying off my hefty student loans, or starting a family. Rome wasn't built in a day and financial planning and achievements take time. The sooner you start planning, the more likely you are to attain your financial goals. What helped me was to look around at everybody who had something I desired, and to realize that if they figured it out, so could I. You will too!
>
> I realize this is macabre, but another aspect of financial planning is preparing how your finances will be handled after your death. It is important to create a will if you own property or have dependents, so that your loved ones will know your wishes. Estate planning occurs with an attorney who can help you arrange for the management of your estate (property and assets) during your life and after your death, in order to minimize gift, estate, generation skipping transfer, and income taxes. While this may be something difficult to think about, it is important for your loved ones and your legacy.

Make Your Vision a Reality

First say to yourself what you would be and then do what you have to do.[12]
EPICTETUS Greek philosopher

Now that you are becoming clearer on your vision and legacy, you can increase the likelihood of your dreams coming to fruition by taking these three steps:

1. Create an action plan with goals.

2. Live with intentions that support your vision.

3. Visualize success.

Each of the following exercises will help you accomplish these three steps.

Develop an Action Plan
(45 minutes; lifetime practice)

Developing an action plan for your personal, professional, and financial vision can seem overwhelming, but it doesn't have to be complicated or time consuming. In fact, it's best to keep it simple. Just follow these instructions:

- In your journal, write four to six personal, professional, and financial goals for the next year and then rank them in order of importance. Make sure to include at least two financial goals.
- Make sure they are Specific, Measurable, Achievable, Realistic, and Timely (SMART) goals.[13] For example, "Invest $15,000 in my retirement fund this year" versus "Save a gazillion dollars before I am ninety-nine."
- Break down goals into smaller objectives or tasks, such as calling your financial advisor within the next week to share your goals so they can help put together a plan to help you get there or setting up automatic monthly payments of $1,250.
- Create some accountability by sharing your goals, especially with your financial planner and/or therapist, and scheduling regular follow-ups to keep you on track.

By completing this exercise, you are gaining traction on your vision, congratulations!

...

Live with Intention
(10 minutes; lifetime practice)

An intention is a way of being or living, stated in the present, that supports the likelihood of your goals coming to fruition. Wayne Dyer, author of *The Power of Intention*, said, "Our intentions create our reality."[14]

Okay, let's do this.

- In your journal, create separate pages for your personal, professional, and financial intentions. Your financial intention may be "I am not wasteful and spend wisely."
- On each page, write three to five short and positive intentions that support you in achieving your goals. Consider reviewing or reciting your intentions before your daily morning or nighttime meditations. The more you repeat them, the more likely they are to come true.
- Create daily practices to support your intentions. In the yogic tradition, the term *sadhana* refers to the daily practices that are a means for accomplishing something. Yogi Jaggi Vasudev, also known as Sadhguru, says "Everything can be sadhana. The way you eat, the way you sit, the way you stand, the way you breathe, the way you conduct your body, mind and your energies and emotions—this is sadhana. Sadhana does not mean any specific kind of activity, sadhana means you are using everything as a tool for your well-being."[15] Make your intentions your way of life.

. . .

Visualize Success
(15 minutes; lifetime practice)

Visualizing a positive outcome has long been utilized in sports psychology—if you can envision yourself making the goal, the chances are more likely that you will. Many neuroscientists have found that visualization helps the body respond better in its pursuit of desired outcomes, including financial goals like saving and accumulating wealth.[16] That's why bank managers and financial consultants should set clear goals that are easy for clients to visualize. It can motivate them to maximize their effort and performance so they can maximize their savings.[17]

To reduce nervousness, give me more confidence, and improve my performance, I envision my speaking engagements and media appearances going well. Now, it's time for you to give positive visualization a try. With your eyes closed, pretend you already achieved your life's vision. Envision your greatest life filled with prosperity, love, health, support, success, and anything you desire. This includes your personal and professional life. How does it feel to achieve your life vision?

. . .

Now that you've had a glimpse into your future success, it's time to complete this chapter's wheel exercise. The Vision Wheel brings together all the skills you have learned in this chapter and measures how well you are doing with vision in different areas of your life.

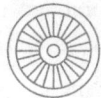

The Vision Wheel
(20 minutes)

Date: _____

Rate your response after each question using a number from the following scale:

Poor (1–3), Fair (4–5), Good (6–7), Prosperous (8–10)

Poor			Fair		Good			Prosperous	
1	2	3	4	5	6	7	8	9	10

Life Plan: A life plan is an overarching life vision that includes a Personal Manifesto by which you live. How well are you doing at creating a life plan? _____

Professional Plan: This is a career or business plan that will help you align your gifts with a need in the world. How would you rate yourself at coming up with a professional plan? _____

Work-Life Balance: A work-life balance plan protects your personal life, including your relationships and overall well-being. When it comes to work-life balance, how would you rate your ability to come up with a plan? _____

Financial Plan: This is your plan for your financial future. How would you rate yourself when it comes to creating a financial plan with goals, action items, and accountability? _____

Intentional Living: Living with intention is living according to positive statements that reflect ways of being that will help you achieve your goals and vision. How would you rate yourself when it comes to living with intention? _____

Visualize Success: This is the practice of regularly envisioning yourself achieving success in various aspects of your life. How good are you at visualizing success in all aspects of your life? _____

Daily Practices: Having daily personal, professional, and/or financial behaviors or routines will help you achieve your vision. How well do your daily practices help support your vision? _____

Health Goals: Your mental, physical, and spiritual wellness and aspirations are your health goals. How well do your health goals apply to your overall well-being? _____

Relationship Goals: These are your needs and ideals for love, connection, and support aspirations. How much thought have you put into what you want your relationships to look like? _____

Fulfill Hobbies: Do you take time for fun and leisure activities that you enjoy? How much priority do your hobbies have in your life? _____

Philanthropy Plan: Do you have a plan for how you are going to be of service to the world in a greater way; are you clear on the legacy you want to leave behind? How would you rate yourself when it comes to creating a philanthropy plan? _____

Bucket List: This is a list of experiences that you want to be sure to get out of life. How good have you been at identifying what you want on your bucket list? _____

Chart your responses on The Vision Wheel. (For a refresher on how to do this, see The Wheel Exercise Tutorial on page 11.) Start at the top: Are you Poor, Prosperous, or somewhere in between when it comes to having an overarching Life Plan? Put a dot on the spoke next to the number that corresponds with your answer. Now continue going around the wheel, and after scoring yourself on every spoke, connect the dots to create a circle. Remember, you are measuring if you have created a plan for that vision, not if you've achieved that vision. That will come in time!

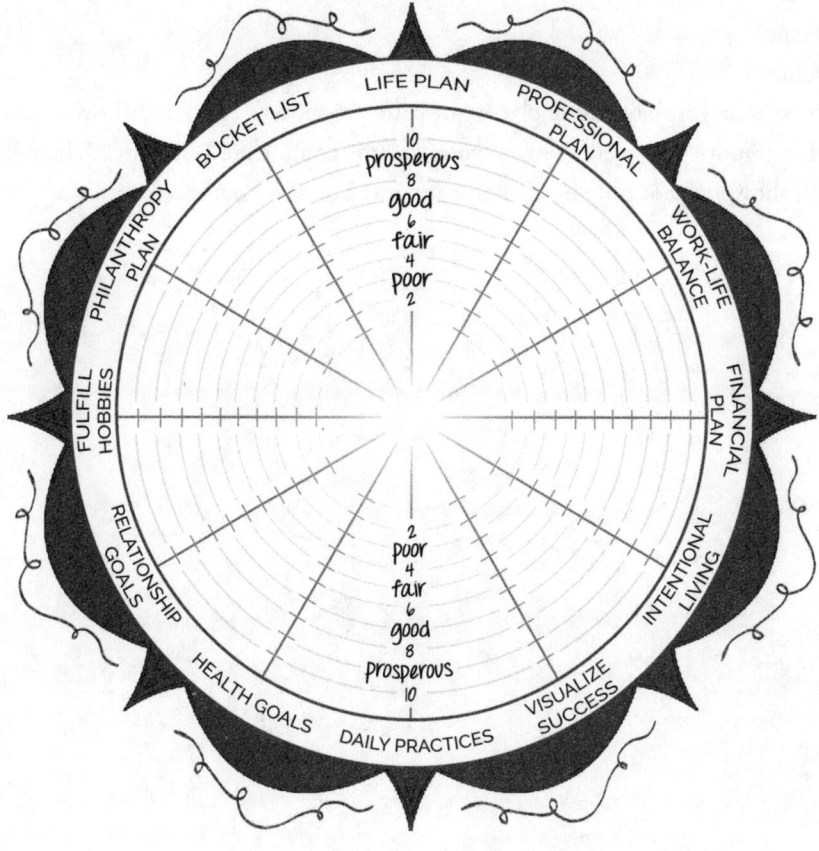

The Vision Wheel

In your journal, answer the following questions:

- As you look at the biggest dents in The Vision Wheel, what areas are in most need of attention when it comes to creating a vision?
- What roadblocks or challenges are you experiencing when it comes to improving your vision in certain areas?
- What kind of support do you need?

Consider revisiting this exercise quarterly to continue to clarify your vision of a full and abundant life. Date your wheel and file it for later reference so you can track your progress over time.

⋯

Now that you have more clarity on your vision, let's talk about how to get the support you need to make your dreams come true! In the next chapter, I'll show you not only how to give support but also how to ask for it.

Chapter 8

SUPPORT

Appreciate That Giving and Receiving Are Two Sides of the Same Coin

Alone we can do so little; together we can do so much.
HELEN KELLER author and political activist

Like many women, I defined my worth by how much I could give others. I was taught to be a good girl and not an imposition, so I didn't really ask for much in relationships. This was no longer sustainable when I became a mother.

"I need more support," I said to my then-husband a month after our first child was born. One month later, after nothing changed, I herniated a disk in my spine while putting Celeste in the crib. My back giving out was a physical manifestation of my unsupported life. Sciatic nerve pain screamed down my leg for six months until I made some important shifts in my life.

Accessing good health-care providers, like a chiropractor and acupuncturist, were instrumental in getting me back on my feet. I joined some new mom groups and reached out to my girlfriends, learning to better balance giving support with receiving support. I continued to ask my husband for what I needed and if those needs weren't met (like help with laundry or errands), I hired someone to help.

In my professional and financial life, it has taken a village of support to get me where I am today. My supportive sister Teresa encouraged me to apply to Northwestern University. I told her I would never be accepted to such a prestigious school, but I applied anyway. In a strange twist of fate, Northwestern was the *only* graduate program to accept me. Thank you, Teresa! And take that, University of Akron!

After a depressing job interview at a nursing home for the chronically mentally ill, where a resident smashed a handful of Cheetos on my black suit, I called Teresa crying. I felt destined to stay a waitress buried in student loans. She showed up at my apartment with a bouquet of tulips and a bag of Cheetos. She pulled out the yellow pages, found a counseling center just two blocks away, and encouraged me to contact them. I was immediately hired part-time, giving me my start in private practice. Teresa's support radically improved the trajectory of my life.

It was at that group practice that I met my mentor, Mark, who has been my professional consultant throughout my career and has become like a family member. When I first started my own private practice, I told Mark I wasn't going to bill insurance because it was too complicated. He replied with some tough love and said flatly, "Yes, you are." He taught me everything I needed to know about working with insurance, which became central to my work with Urban Balance.

Years later, after my business partner left, I moved past the barriers of shame, pride, and guilt to receive more support for my business and finances. By asking for support, our revenue increased by 20 to 30 percent per year and we opened new offices and increased our staff to an army of over one hundred therapists. It took a village, and I realized I had that village available to me all along. Because I provided jobs, internships, mentoring, and more, the support came back to me threefold once I was open to receiving. I no longer felt alone in the responsibility of the company's success.

In my new marriage to my husband, Jason, whose kind and gentle way of being has soothed my soul, I've had to learn how to be more open to receiving. In the first few years of our relationship, I found it almost painful to receive support. Eventually I realized I had never had that kind of support, even earlier in my life. Learning how to receive support has allowed me to come into a space of feeling loved, safe, and connected. This has gifted me with so many blessings, including more bandwidth for patience and kindness as a parent, friend, and colleague.

My life is now a supported life of ongoing growth and evolution. I balance my love of giving and building others up with allowing the love, support, and prosperity to flow back into me.

Therapy Session Number 8
(20 minutes)

Hello again! Today we are going to help you welcome more support in your life. In your journal, answer the following questions:

- Name two major challenges you have had in your life. Who helped you get through these challenges and how did they help?
- What four people have been most instrumental in supporting you in achieving your personal and professional vision? How did their input change your life's trajectory?
- Do you have a mentor who helps guide your career? How have they helped you achieve success?
- Where in your life could you use some additional support?
- Think back to your life vision from the previous chapter. If you could add anyone to your support team, who would it be and how would they help you achieve your vision?

...

Now let's learn how to optimize support for your mental and financial health.

Find a Balance of Giving and Receiving Support to Increase Prosperity

> *All of us, at some time or other, need help. Whether we're giving or receiving help, each one of us has something valuable to bring to this world. That's one of the things that connects us as neighbors—in our own way, each one of us is a giver and a receiver.*[1]
> FRED ROGERS American television personality and Presbyterian minister

Think of your support network like a bank account. You need to invest in it in order to have something to withdraw. Similarly, since support is reciprocal in nature, you need to give support in order to receive it.

Have you ever known someone who is a bit of a user? My client Joe seemed to tap out his network rapidly. He was always asking friends for rides or to cover the check, and asking colleagues to cover his shifts or work late for him. Soon he found himself depressed and alone. To better balance what he was giving and receiving, he had to learn how to take responsibility for himself as best he could, express appreciation for support he received, and reciprocate support to others. These changes improved his support network, alleviated his depression, and led to better performance at work. The more Joe offered help to others, the more he experienced the mental and physical health benefits of altruism. As a result, over time he started developing a strong and loyal support network.

A note of caution: There's a downside to giving too much support. It can lead to poor well-being, exhaustion, greater anxiety, irritation, depressed mood, emotional strain, job dissatisfaction, higher job turnover, and burnout.[2] That's why giving support needs to be balanced with self-care and receiving support from others.

Naturally, the balance of giving and receiving support changes over time. During times of adversity, great challenge, or tragedy, you might need a bit more support. When one of my best friends went through a serious battle with breast cancer, she had an army of friends running her to the doctor, sitting with her during chemo, and more. She had this support because she has always been a great friend to others. Thank God she is well today and continues to live her life in a way that ensures she's there for others and being supported by others as well.

Sometimes the support we offer somebody is returned by somebody else. I'll never forget the mom I met while volunteering for my daughter's Brownie troop who offered to drive my daughters to and from school and made us family meals after my mother passed away. Wow. Completely unexpected and powerfully moving to receive such meaningful support from somebody I barely knew.

The stages of life also affect our needs for support. From birth through adolescence, we move from being entirely dependent to becoming more and more independent. As we start to develop friendships, partnerships, and collegial relationships, we learn to develop mutually supportive and interdependent relationships. When we add pets, kids of our own, and aging parents, we start to become the primary support for others in every way, including financially. Early on in our careers we may have a greater need for mentoring, while later on, we may have more to offer as a mentor. For all of these reasons, it's important to continue to assess your balance of giving and receiving support on an ongoing basis.

Now, let's do some work to get you in that optimal balance of giving and receiving!

Replenish Yourself
(15 minutes; lifetime practice)

In your journal, answer the following questions:

- If your support network was a bank account, would you have a positive balance or be overdrawn? Why is this?
- Do you routinely give more than you receive? If so, how can you better replenish yourself by receiving support?
- What would your life look like if you had a healthy balance of giving and receiving support? How can you make this happen?

...

To help you achieve that healthy balance between giving and receiving support, let's start by removing any barriers that may get in your way!

Break Through Barriers and Open Yourself Up to Receiving Support

Until we can receive with an open heart, we are never really giving with an open heart. When we attach judgment to receiving help, we knowingly or unknowingly attach judgment to giving help.[3]
BRENÉ BROWN bestselling author, researcher, and professor

Virtually all of us would benefit from more support, yet many of us unknowingly or knowingly push support away. Here are the ways I've seen my clients (and myself) block support and how we can overcome these barriers:

Barriers to Support	How to Overcome the Barriers
Low self-esteem, not feeling deserving	Self-worth, self-love
Guilt, feeling flawed for needing help	Self-compassion, self-acceptance
Fear of being an imposition on others, fear of making somebody mad, fear somebody will hold the help over you	Self-confidence (to choose support wisely), trust
Shame, embarrassment, feelings of inadequacy	Self-compassion, self-acceptance
Learned helplessness (there's nothing I can do, including asking for help)	Empowerment, trust
Hopelessness (nothing will help)	Optimism, trust
Difficulty trusting (normal response to trauma)	Self-confidence (to choose and navigate support wisely), trust, faith

Hyper-independence, excessive value placed on autonomy (this may be cultural)	Interdependence, fostering mutual and reciprocal relationships
Rigid, firm boundaries that prohibit connection	Openness, authenticity
Loss of power or control (ego)	Collaboration, trust
Loss of credit (if I do it myself, I get all the praise)	Collaboration
Arrogance (my way is best)	Humility
Pride	Humility, vulnerability
Early life messages such as: • Needing help is a sign of weakness. • Be a good girl, not an imposition. • Your worth as a woman lies in being a nurturer and a giver. • Man up, power through, do it yourself.	Self-compassion (understanding you are human and therefore need and deserve support), self-affirmation (changing these beliefs to positive self-talk that encourages you to receive the support you need and deserve)
Expense (of hiring support)	Investment in yourself, resourcefulness, creativity
Introversion	Accessing support in ways that are comfortable to you (perhaps one-on-one or online)
Lack of resources available (especially in rural areas where there are less people and community services)	Accessing online support and using video conferencing to obtain consultation, therapy, mentoring, and more

The good news is that throughout this program you have been building most of the skills in the right column. The more you love and care about yourself, the more support you can give and receive.

Now it's time to access the support you deserve.

Remove Barriers to Receiving Support
(25 minutes; lifetime practice)

In your journal, answer the following questions:

- Which three to five barriers do you feel are your biggest obstacles to receiving support?
- In what ways do these barriers negatively impact your life?
- What are three ways to transcend these barriers this week?

Wonderful! In the next week, ask for support three times when you normally would not. Journal about how it felt. It's okay if some of the feelings were uncomfortable, as seeking support is a skill that takes practice and needs to be developed.

...

Improve Your Mental Health by Nurturing Your Network

Your support network is like a garden of resources that needs to be tended to by mindfully weeding out toxic relationships and planting seeds for making new connections.[4]

WEED OUT TOXIC RELATIONSHIPS

We have all had toxic relationships. They may have been with friends, family members, partners, neighbors, colleagues, or bosses. These relationships deplete your energy, infuse you with negativity, bring unnecessary drama or conflict to your life, and trigger feelings of low self-esteem, insecurity, resentment, frustration, or irritability. I like the expression "Relationships are like elevator buttons; they either bring you up or bring you down." Freeing yourself from toxic relationships creates space to establish and nurture positive relationships.

To deal with toxic relationships online, first limit the amount of time you spend on social media. Unfollow people who regularly post content that feels toxic to you. If those people post toxic comments on your page, unfriend, unfollow, or block them. Avoid engaging in debates online. If you feel you must respond to a toxic comment, respond with something neutral, such as "I see it differently. Let's agree to disagree." Avoid trying to loop other people into the conflict. This only worsens the toxicity. Remember, you have the right to delete comments on your social media pages. Avoid posting political, religious, or deeply personal content because you may be opening yourself up to toxic responses. Misunderstandings can happen easily without tone of voice, inflection, and other nonverbal cues that clarify messaging. You may be misinterpreting the comment by assuming somebody is being sarcastic when perhaps they were not.

Dr. Phil says "We teach people how to treat us."[5] Like attracts like. The healthier we are, the more we attract healthy people and positive relationships into our lives. People come into our lives for a reason. Even difficult relationships are blessings, as they are opportunities to learn and grow in a positive direction.

When it comes to toxic relationships either in-person or online, I advise clients to ask themselves the following key questions:[6]

Is the person/relationship temporarily or chronically toxic? If you are in a relationship with somebody who is going through a difficult life challenge, such as a divorce, an illness, or the death of a loved one, they may be in a bad space and temporarily toxic. However, if the person's toxicity is more of a chronic personality style or relationship pattern, it's likely not going to pass and needs to be addressed more seriously. Abuse is never okay.

How close and important is the relationship? The closer a toxic relationship is to you, the more important and difficult it may be to address. For example, a toxic relationship with your partner or parent is more challenging than a toxic relationship with a neighbor or coworker. Ask yourself, "Does what I gain from the relationship outweigh the costs?"

What can you control and not control? You can control your own boundaries (the amount of time, information, or frequency of contact), communication, behaviors, and responses. You cannot control the other person.

You can do your part by speaking honestly, assertively, diplomatically, and using "I" statements to express your feelings and set healthy boundaries. It is then up to them to change or not. You get to decide if you want them in your life or not. If you find yourself repeatedly expressing the same needs and setting the same limits over and over again to no avail, seriously consider relationship counseling or ending the relationship altogether.

A relationship that's ending can be hard for both parties. Have faith that by letting go of toxic people, you are freeing up your energy for new and positive people.

In my own life, every time a certain colleague and I got together outside of work, I found myself reaching for Advil. Eventually I realized this was not a reciprocal or mutually supportive relationship. I thought, "Why am I spending my time in this relationship when I could open myself up to relationships that are more positive, mutually supportive, and nurturing?" I stopped scheduling our quarterly brunches and instead invited her to the occasional continuing education training or a networking event. By changing my interactions, I could keep the positive professional pieces of the relationship intact but limit the personal burden. I created space in my personal life for friends who fill my cup rather than empty it.

PLANT SEEDS FOR MAKING NEW CONNECTIONS

Some people leave our support network through death, a breakup, by growing apart, or moving away. When this happens, it is our job to enlist new support in our lives. One client lost two sisters within the same year. In addition to the grief, she lost the people she checked in with daily, even about the silly minutiae of life. To get that support back, she asked some of her friends if they would be willing to become her new "sisters." She was amazed by how much support she received by simply being courageous enough to ask for it. After a year or so, one of those friends became an even better support than her sisters had been.

Since you can't predict the future, always be looking to enrich your support network. It can be awkward trying to make new friends as an adult. It can be especially challenging for those who are shy, more introverted, or struggle with social anxiety. Here are my suggestions:

- Commit to being social at least one night a week in order to meet new people or strengthen existing relationships. Consider using sites like Meetup to find events in your area.
- Attend a weekly club, class, or meeting of some kind (such as trivia or game nights, book clubs, or intramural sports). Challenge yourself to chat with at least one or two new people each week.
- Partner up with an extraverted friend to attend events so they can help you make connections.
- If you are uncomfortable talking, ask other people questions. People love to talk about themselves!
- Give yourself permission to leave early. Attending an event for even an hour can help to increase your support.
- If you are limited to virtual connections, consider online support groups, watch parties, social gaming, or connecting with friends and making new ones on social media apps for fitness such as Peloton, or business apps like LinkedIn. Join different groups, contribute posts, and find like-minded people.
- Plant the seed for a follow-up interaction. Suggest exchanging information and connecting in the future. I know this can feel vulnerable and be anxiety provoking, but it's worth the temporary discomfort or even some rejection to find relationships that provide lasting support.
- Reward yourself with some healthy self-care, like curling up with a good book for a couple of hours.

To seal the deal, be authentic, positive, empathetic, kind, and a good listener. Look for what you can give the person, such as a resource, introduction, or referral rather than what you can get. Research shows that social support from contacts in your network is significantly and positively associated with salary and promotions.[7]

Now that you've learned how to strengthen your social support network, it's time to see how you can do the same for your finances.

Financial Health Boost: Create a Supported Financial Life

When it comes to creating a supported financial life, you need trusted people and organizations that can help you take care of your financial health. Here are some factors to consider:

You become like the company you keep:[8] The people we associate with effect what we consider to be normal. So are you in the company of people with good financial health? Or do you surround yourself with people who live beyond their means? I am not suggesting you change your friends, but at least become conscious of how they might be impacting you and develop some relationships with people who have good financial health.

If you have a partner, you must communicate with them about your shared financial life: Different couples have different ways of organizing their finances—some keep everything separate and live like roommates, some combine everything, and others agree on some combination of the two. Financial challenges are one of the top issues couples address in couples therapy and one of the primary reasons cited for divorce.[9] Therefore, you need to learn how to communicate, present, and resolve conflict around money. You can work on this on your own, by establishing a weekly or monthly financial check-in time, or you can enlist the help of a therapist or a financial consultant to moderate and mediate your discussions and decisions.

If you are single, consider getting an accountability partner: Identify a friend who might also be working on their financial health and set up regular check-ins to hold one another accountable for your financial goals.

Seek out a financial advisor, financial planner, debt consolidation counselor, or other type of financial consultant: Even if you are financially literate, it can be invaluable to have the advice of an expert. Having a financial advisor is like having a personal trainer or coach for your finances; somebody who will motivate you, educate you, and hold you accountable. The challenge with the financial industry, however, is that some financial advisors work for organizations that want to sell you their financial products, like life insurance. You want to find someone who is more invested in coaching you to financial freedom. You may have to interview a couple people before you find the right advisor.

Consider classes or support groups: If you are serious about improving your financial health, consider taking financial classes to improve your knowledge. If you are struggling with low earnings, compulsive spending, or debt accumulation, consider a 12-step support group.

What's it going to take to give you a much-needed financial boost? Having a strong support network gives you an advantage.

Not sure how your support network measures up? Use this wheel to find out. This exercise helps you identify who is in your support network, the types of support they provide you, as well as any areas of deficit or need.

The Support Network Wheel
(20 minutes)

Date: _____

Rate your response after each question using a number from the following scale:

Poor (1–3), Fair (4–5), Good (6–7), Prosperous (8–10)

Poor			Fair		Good			Prosperous	
1	2	3	4	5	6	7	8	9	10

Physical Health: Those who help you take care of your physical health include your primary doctor, specialty doctors, holistic health providers, dentist, eye doctor, healer, massage therapist, nutritionist, personal trainer, physical therapist, and workout buddy. When it comes to having the right support system to take care of your physical health, how would you rate yourself? _____

Mental Health: Those who help promote your mental health include your therapist and psychiatrist, your significant other, family, life coach, support groups, and 12-step sponsor. When it comes to your mental health, how is your support system looking? _____

Emotional: Those who provide you with emotional support might include your partner, family, and friends. How would you rate yourself when it comes to having the right emotional support? _____

Career: People who provide professional support include your career counselor or coach, consultant, mentor, peers in professional associations, and your supervisor. If you are a student, this support team would include academic advisors, teachers, and supportive classmates. If you are a stay-at-home parent, this would include people who support you in your parenting community. How would you rate yourself when it comes to having a support system for your career? _____

Financial: People who help keep you on track financially can include your accountant, asset manager, a debt consolidation service, support group, estate planning attorney, accountability partner, or financial planner. You might also list organizations or people who help you out financially through loans, grants, loan forgiveness, or other financial assistance. How supported do you feel when it comes to your financial life? _____

Family Connection: This includes your parents, siblings, children, chosen family, extended family, your partner's family, and your pets. How would you rate your family support system? _____

Friendship: For this section, think of meaningful friends who serve as trusted confidants and provide comradery, companionship, loyalty, care, and fun. When it comes to supportive friends, how would you rate your network? _____

Partnership: If you have a significant other, list them here. If you are dating or romantically involved with more than one person, you can list them all here. If you don't have a significant other and don't want one, rate yourself a 10 instead of answering the question. If you are in a partnership, how would you rate the support you receive? _____

Social/Community: These are groups or events that provide social support and could include your place of worship, community events, concerts, gatherings with friends, gym, meditation groups, membership in organizations, your neighborhood, prayer group, 12-step group, yoga studio, parenting group, or online support system. How well are you utilizing the support that you could receive from your community? _____

Hobbies: This section is for the people who support you in doing your hobbies, including your band members, a tennis partner, an intramural sports team, a running group, an art studio, or a gaming group. How well are you doing when it comes to receiving support from people who participate in your favorite hobbies? _____

Logistics Helpers: By logistics helpers, I mean people or services that help you with the tasks related to daily living. For example, your roommate, partner, kids, neighbors, or babysitting co-op. Include people or services you hire, such as a childcare provider, dog walker, housekeeper, lawn service, grocery delivery, meal prep service, and so forth. How would you rate yourself when it comes to asking for support with specific daily tasks? _____

Spiritual: List those who provide you with spiritual support including God or your Higher Power, your priest/rabbi/pastor/spiritual advisor, meditation coach, psychic/medium, yogi, energy healer, shaman, soul coach, or other. When it comes to your spirituality, how would you rate yourself when it comes to asking for support? _____

Chart your numbered responses and then connect the dots. (For a refresher, see The Wheel Exercise Tutorial on page 11.) Start at the top: Are you Poor, Prosperous, or somewhere in between when it comes to having a support network to boost your Physical Health? Put a dot on the spoke next to the number that corresponds with your answer. Now continue going around the wheel, and after scoring yourself on every spoke, connect the dots to create a circle.

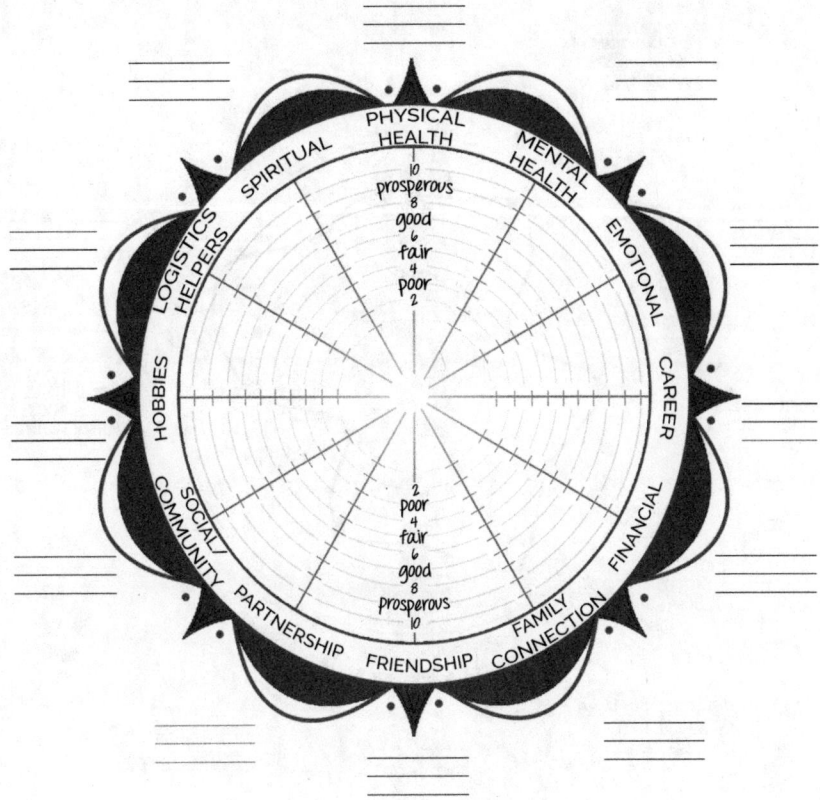

The Support Network Wheel

Now, at the end of each spoke, list the names or titles of people or organizations that provide you with this type of support. It's okay to list the same person, title, or organization in more than one spoke. See the example on the following page.

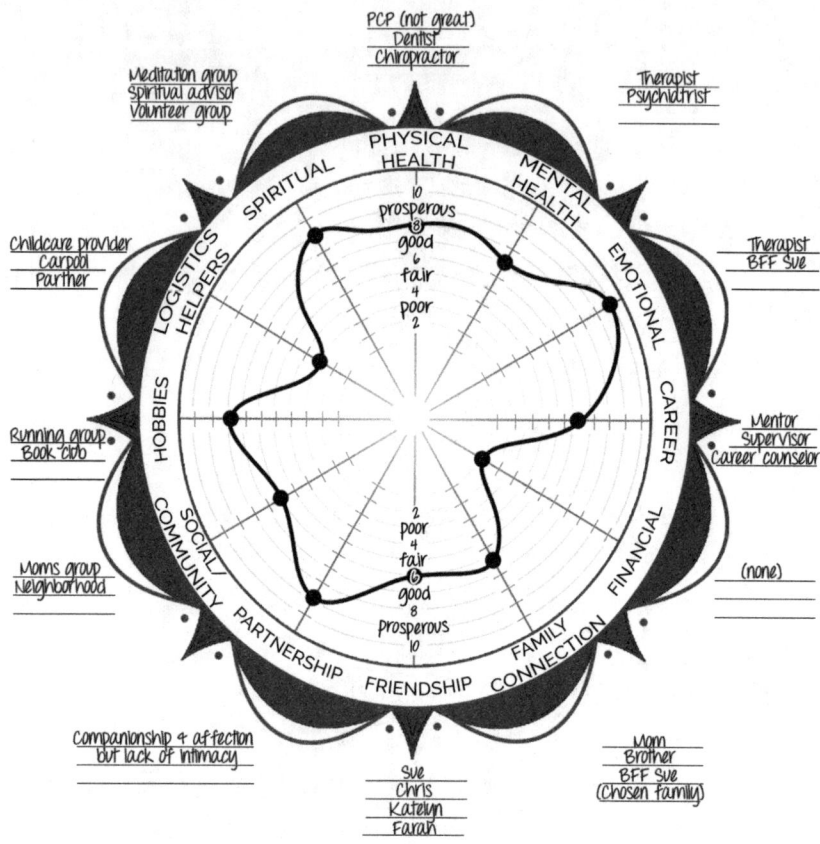

The Support Network Wheel Example

In this support wheel example, notice the two deepest dents in the wheel in the areas of Financial and Logistics Helpers. Also notice how few people have been identified to help with these areas.

In your journal, answer the following questions:

- Have you listed anyone in more than one area of support? This can be wonderful, but make sure you don't rely too heavily on one person. A client listed her husband in almost every area and didn't have too many other people in her close network. This exercise helped her realize that not having more friends or supporters was putting a strain on her relationship with her spouse.

- As you look at the dents in your wheel, are there sections where you have little or no support? Another client only had support in the career area, which helped to explain her workaholism.
- What three actions can you take to find more support in the areas where you are lacking (the biggest dents)?

Revisit this exercise quarterly to continue assessing your support network. Because support is reciprocal, consider completing this wheel a second time and focusing on the support you give others. This may provide insight into why your balance of give and take might not be optimal just yet.

...

Now that you've identified your support network, it's time to put them to good use. Sometimes this is easier said than done.

Utilize Your Network for Success

A couple of months ago, I was asked to give a presentation on a topic I had never spoken about before. I had procrastinated when it came to preparing and by the time I sat down at my computer to start working on it, a huge wave of panic and overwhelm hit me. That's when I decided to ask for help. I emailed three therapist friends and asked them if they had any resources to share. Within thirty minutes, each of them sent me a complete presentation on the topic and welcomed me to use their content. It saved me hours of work and reduced my stress level enormously. All I had to do was ask.

If your plate of responsibilities is full and you have a partner or kids at home, or interns or employees at work, you may be able to delegate. Before I do anything, I ask myself, "Am I the only person who can do this?" "Am I the best person to do this?" and "Do I enjoy doing this?"

If the answer is *no* to any of those, I consider delegating it. Delegating allows you to direct your time and energy to the tasks you must do or the meaningful work you feel called to do. This increases your productivity and also gives other people the opportunity to learn, participate, or earn a living.

Before you ask for help, think about each person in your support network as having a menu of support services that they are capable of providing you.

You want to go to the right person who's capable of providing you with the kind of support you need. You wouldn't go to a bakery and order a steak because you'd end up disappointed. When you're looking at your support network, know what's on the menu. So when you need a shoulder to cry on, don't ask the friend who's a blast to hang out with on a Saturday night or fun to go shopping with because you may not receive the emotional support you are seeking. Instead, ask the friends who have empathy and good listening skills on their menu.

You can ask for support when you need someone to:

- Listen when you just need to vent
- Help you think through planning and logistics
- Brainstorm solutions
- Provide advice, consultation, mentoring, or counsel
- Introduce you to others who can provide the support you need
- Recommend resources or services that could help you
- Keep you in their thoughts, send positive vibes, or say a prayer
- Be with you, keep you company, or do something fun with you
- Offer physical affection, closeness, and intimacy
- Help with a specific task
- Support your professional work on social media, endorse you, or attend an event
- Teach or train you on how to do something
- Provide mutual accountability, such as checking in with them regularly to report about health and fitness or financial goals.

You've done some incredible work in this chapter. Now it's time to assess your progress and see how you are doing with everything you've learned. The Support Wheel brings together all the skills you learned in this chapter and measures how well you are doing with support.

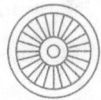

The Support Wheel
(20 minutes)

Date: _____

Rate your response after each question using a number from the following scale:

Poor (1–3), Fair (4–5), Good (6–7), Prosperous (8–10)

Poor			Fair		Good			Prosperous	
1	2	3	4	5	6	7	8	9	10

Plant Seeds: By planting seeds, I mean developing new connections through social activities, community events, professional networking, social media and online outreach, and marketing efforts such as e-blasts, newsletters, or mailings. When it comes to making new connections, how would you rate yourself? _____

Nurture Relationships: How would you rate yourself when it comes to regularly letting people know they are special to you? _____

End Toxic Relationships: By ending and "weeding out" toxic relationships you can empower yourself to set healthy boundaries in relationships you can't choose (like your sister or your boss) and terminate relationships that are truly unhealthy for you. How would you rate yourself when it comes to weeding out toxic relationships? _____

Ask for Help: How good are you at routinely asking for help with tasks as needed and as appropriate? _____

Seek Counsel: When it comes to regularly seeking advice, consultation, or wise counsel from people who are more knowledgeable or experienced in certain areas, how would you rate yourself? _____

Seek Care: How good are you at asking for support when it comes to your mental and physical health, including asking for affection? _____

Balance Giving & Receiving: How good are you at making sure you are striking a healthy balance between being supported and offering support to others? _____

Mentoring: This includes receiving support from others who have achieved what you would like to achieve and remembering to mentor others when appropriate. How good are you at asking for support from those you admire and then, on the flip side, giving that support to others? _____

Reciprocal Relationships: Reciprocating means striking a healthy balance of independence and dependence in your relationships so that you can experience the benefits of interdependence, including mutuality. How would you rate yourself at forming reciprocal relationships? _____

Permeable Boundaries: How would you rate yourself in ensuring that your emotional and relational boundaries are not too rigid or too loose so you can foster intimacy and connection? _____

Openly Receiving: When you are feeling the barriers of fear, shame, guilt, or pride, how open are you to receiving support? _____

Financial Support: This includes seeking help from a financial advisor or business consultant and applying for grants, loans, scholarships, loan forgiveness, and financial assistance programs that would support you. How well are you doing with asking and receiving financial support? _____

Chart your responses on The Support Wheel. (For a refresher on how to do this, see The Wheel Exercise Tutorial on page 11.) Start at the top: Are you Poor, Prosperous, or somewhere in between when it comes to being able to Plant Seeds for new relationships? Put a dot on the spoke next to the number that corresponds with your answer. Now continue going around the wheel, and after scoring yourself on every spoke, connect the dots to create a circle.

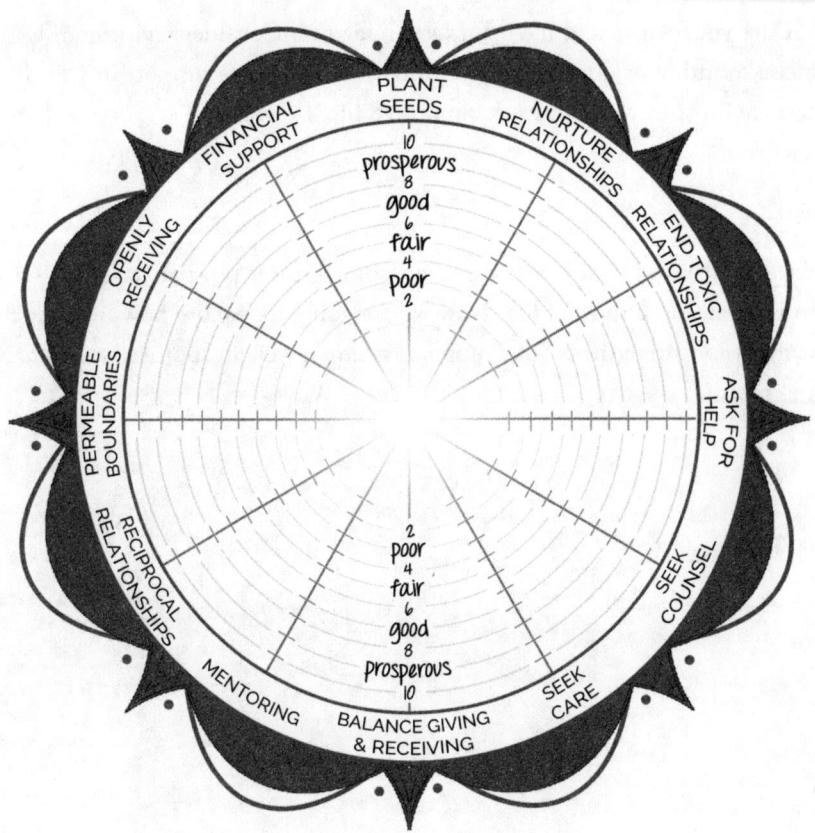

The Support Wheel

Don't worry if you scored poorly on this mindset. Asking for help is often one of the hardest things to do. Keep working on this mindset to see improvements.

In your journal, answer the following questions:

- As you look at the biggest dents in your wheel, do you know why you scored lowest in these areas?
- What three action steps can you take to improve in each area?

Date your wheel and file it for later reference. Consider revisiting this exercise monthly or quarterly to continue to create more support in your life. You are on your way to a more supported life. Bravo!

...

You will feel better and better and welcome greater prosperity as you start to live a more supported life. Now we are going to explore how living with compassion strengthens your support system as well as improves your financial health.

Chapter 9

COMPASSION

Explore the Spirituality of Business and Recognize That Love Is the Currency of Life

Thousands of candles can be lighted from a single candle, and the life of the candle will not be shortened.
   BUDDHA founder of Buddhism

A staff therapist knocked on my open office door when I was working at Urban Balance. She had been with our practice for under six months after working for a community mental health agency for over ten years. We didn't know each other very well. Normally impeccably dressed and well put together, she looked disheveled, worried, exhausted, and on the verge of tears. After shutting the door, we sat down together. She stammered a bit and seemed nervous about what she was about to say, but managed to share that she was experiencing a mental health crisis. She explained she was in the process of leaving a relationship that had recently become abusive and was experiencing significant anxiety and depression as a result of the trauma. While she couldn't afford to lose her job, she didn't feel she could do the work.

I commended her for her honesty and courage and thanked her for telling me. After asking what she needed, she suggested taking two weeks off and not taking any new referrals until she was feeling better. We discussed how she would make sure her clients had support and resources during her paid leave. She mentioned she was having difficulty securing an apartment because she had only had this job for a few months. I immediately hopped on the phone to verify her employment with the property manager, who agreed to let her sign the lease. For me, it was the ethical thing to do.

As she left my office, she asked if she could give me a hug and thanked me. I saw the relief on her face and we agreed to meet in two weeks. When she returned to work, she was back to her usual self and felt confident about working with her current caseload.

She ended up working at Urban Balance for the next seven years. Her clients loved her and gave her high reviews, with special comments about her deep capacity for compassion. She carried a full caseload, treating hundreds of clients during her time at the practice. Meanwhile, her colleagues respected her and she prospered financially, buying both her first car and first home. When she left Urban Balance, she gave me a card that said, "I will never ever forget all the ways you have supported me, both personally and professionally. I hope to pay that forward." Today she owns her own thriving practice and we are friends.

When we lean into relationships and life with love and compassion, we welcome greater prosperity into our lives.

Therapy Session Number 9
(20 minutes)

Welcome! In today's session, take some time to write about the following in your journal:

- Recall a time when you felt somebody was compassionate toward you. Maybe they were kind, thoughtful, or empathetic. How did that feel? Did their response change your situation?
- Recall an instance when you demonstrated compassion to somebody personally. How about professionally? Write about how this felt.
- Consider how demonstrating more compassion might improve your relationships at work and even your finances. Write a best-case scenario describing how this could play out.

- What's something you could do today to be more compassionate to the people in your life?

All this good karma will boomerang back at you, leading to true prosperity.

...

Now, let's explore how practicing empathy can lead to greater prosperity.

Empathy Is the Magic Wand That Can Create Transformative Change in Your Life

Empathy is the most essential quality of civilization.[1]
ROGER EBERT American film critic and author

According to Daniel Goleman, author of *Emotional Intelligence*, there are three levels of empathy: cognitive, emotional, and compassionate.[2] Cognitive empathy is when we understand the other person's perspective, emotional empathy is when you feel the other person's emotions along with them, and compassionate empathy is not only understanding a person's experience and feeling with them but also being moved to help if needed and welcomed. This is the level of empathy we should all work toward.

Empathy is perhaps the most important relational skill as it puts you in somebody else's shoes and reflects how they are feeling in a given situation. Listening empathetically allows you to relate to and understand their perspective, position, and feelings.

We don't need to have the exact same experience to empathize with somebody else. As human beings, we all experience similar feelings of joy, sadness, loss, love, fear, loneliness, pride, shame, guilt, relief, and elation. If we listen in a way that allows us to relate to that common feeling or human experience, we can improve our connection and shared understanding with others.

We cannot change or control other people's feelings. Instead, we can help them work through their feelings by letting them be heard and validating their emotional responses. Sometimes people appear to have a larger emotional response than is appropriate to the situation at hand because the event has tapped into a well of feelings from past similar experiences. Their response may seem excessive, but they are having normal responses to nature and nurture, so don't argue with them as it is a losing battle and can damage the relationship.

Verbalizing empathy allows the other person to feel heard, known, understood, and connected to us. It can diffuse conflict because once people feel heard, they may not feel the need to become increasingly defensive or aggressive to get their message across. Consciously stepping outside of ourselves and putting ourselves in the experiences of others can increase our awareness and improve our relationships.

GOOD FOR BUSINESS TOO

Empathy doesn't just help your personal relationships; it can improve your performance at work. Studies show that when people are compassionate, it can build up their self-efficacy, which leads to better job performance.[3] Furthermore, being compassionate can also cause people to be more positive, which has been positively correlated with job performance.[4]

I found empathy to be good for business when a well-known therapist in Chicago, whom I didn't know personally at the time, contacted me via email with a cease and desist note explaining that one of my staff therapists had plagiarized his book on Urban Balance's blog. I was horrified that this happened, took responsibility, and apologized, empathizing with how awful that must have felt to have his work reposted without proper attribution. To my surprise, he responded with a friendly note saying that he appreciated my kind response, noticed from my email signature that we had much in common professionally, and asked if I'd like to meet for coffee. We have referred countless clients to each other and have even presented together at conferences. We are still friends and colleagues ten years later.

Empathy is also good for business in the following ways:[5]

More sales, loyalty, and referrals. Every good salesperson knows that truly understanding your customers' needs and showing that you can meet those needs is good for business. Empathy strengthens relationships not only with customers but with referral sources, vendors, and more. Basically, when people like you, they want to do business with you.

Increased productivity and innovation. When people perceive your company as empathetic, sales increase because your employees are more productive and innovative. Employees who experience the most empathy tend to perform the best.[6]

Greater competitive advantage and financial value. According to the 2016 Empathy Index, the most empathetic companies were also some of the highest performing companies.[7]

Accelerated business engagement and collaboration. Business cultures that encourage empathy attract highly engaged individuals and have better retention and higher morale among employees.

GOOD AND BAD WAYS TO SHOW EMPATHY

Imagine your friend is crying and tells you she is upset that her boss reprimanded and criticized her in front of her peers. The following are ways to respond in both empathetic and non-empathetic ways.

Non-empathetic responses:

- "Don't let it get you that upset. You shouldn't feel that way." (Invalidating)
- "You just need to get a new job already. I keep telling you that." (Problem-solving, impatient)
- "Well, what did you do? Did you deserve it?" (Unsupportive, blaming)
- "It's not that big of a deal. At least you didn't get fired." (Minimizing)
- "I wouldn't care if that happened to me. I would just shake it off." (Comparing to oneself, not helpful)
- "You are too sensitive." (Critical)

Empathetic responses:

- "Gosh, I am so sorry that happened." (Sympathetic and caring)
- "That must have been embarrassing and uncomfortable. I imagine you feel frustrated, mad, and disempowered." (Empathetic, recognizing, and honoring the feelings)

- "I felt similarly when my mom used to criticize me in front of my brothers or friends. It was humiliating and enraging." (Relating and normalizing, as long as comments are kept brief)

Make sense?

To respond in a more empathetic way, become mindful of nonverbal communication and practice active listening. Be aware of your facial expressions, hand gestures, and body language. Learn to read others, because oftentimes people do not express what they actually feel. The body never lies, so notice nonverbals and ask some clarifying questions like, "You look upset, please tell me how I can help."

Instead of being closed off or inattentive, practice active listening, which involves being fully present to the person speaking to you, listening, making sure you clearly understand their message, responding thoughtfully, and remembering what was said. An additional bonus? Active listening is positively related to sales performance.[8]

Reading nonverbals and actively listening improve your capacity for empathy.

Increase Success Through Empathy
(15 minutes; lifetime practice)

In your journal, answer the following questions:

- What opportunities are there to show more empathy in your relationships? Scan through the list of non-empathetic and empathetic responses and write down any ideas on what you can say to be more empathetic.
- In what ways can you use nonverbal communication or active listening to express greater empathy?
- What might be the benefit of being more empathetic in a relationship you want to strengthen? How would this improved relationship improve your life?

. . .

The Transformative Power of Compassionate Connection: The Case of Suma

During our initial consultation, my prospective client looked at me with her intelligent eyes and beautiful young face, wrapped gracefully in a brown headscarf. When asked how familiar I was with her religion, I self-consciously and apologetically admitted I was not very familiar. I asked if she would be willing to teach me about her culture and her experience as a first-generation Muslim-American and gave her permission to call me out if I ever said anything from a place of ignorance and white privilege. I explained my belief that the therapeutic relationship is the foundation of therapy and it was essential that she felt safe, understood, and affirmed by me.

"I can see that you are kind, so I'd like to work with you," said Suma.

In the sessions to come, Suma shared a childhood where she was the only person of color at her school. She always felt different and never beautiful in a world of blonde and blue-eyed beauty ideals. Her parents were immigrants who made great sacrifices to move to the North Side of Chicago from East Africa in order to give Suma a better life. The great adversity and extensive trauma they dealt with themselves, paired with the stress of working multiple jobs to support their family in the US and overseas, made them prone to violent outbursts that included emotional and physical abuse. Their intention was for her to be a good person, but Suma grew up bombarded with unintentional messages that she was somehow never enough, wrong, or bad. She was left without a deeper experience of intrinsic value, inner peace, or interpersonal safety and respect.

Like many of us, her present life had striking similarities to her past. She married a well-respected and accomplished business consultant who, in so many words, repeatedly told her she was inadequate, flawed, and irrational if not downright "crazy." While he did not physically harm her, she did that for him. After their frequent unresolved arguments, she would harm herself by cutting her arms and legs where no one could see, trying to release the feelings of self-loathing, entrapment, and rage.

During our initial sessions together, we explored her experiences and feelings. In the beginning, when I would ask her how she felt about a memory she was sharing, often she would say "I don't know" or "Whatever, it happened. It's okay; it's fine." She looked deflated, sitting small with a flat expression and solemn face, disconnected from herself and her emotions. I told her that experiencing physical or emotional abuse was absolutely "not okay" and "not fine." I reflected how I imagined she might feel: "Gosh, I would imagine you would have felt really angry" or "It would seem understandable if you had felt very sad." Then her tears began to fall, melting her protective mask and opening her heart. Through our empathetic connection she learned to internalize my compassion and develop self-compassion, understanding that her feelings (like all of ours) are a normal response to our nature and our nurture.

As Suma developed compassion for herself, she tapped into feelings of sadness and anger. Instead of directing her negative feelings inward, as in the past, her anger empowered her to speak her truth and set healthy boundaries with others. She and her husband started couples counseling, which sounded like a frustrating process because her husband felt he was "right" and had limited willingness to change. However, she was standing up for herself and starting to understand more about their relational dynamics, his narcissism, his habit of "gaslighting," and the cycle of emotional abuse.

In her life outside of her marriage, Suma started advocating for herself and made advancements in her career by applying to law school. She prioritized self-care, spending time on hobbies such as painting and reading for fun. She freed herself from her Teflon mask and was bravely relating to others from a place of vulnerability and authenticity.

Throughout our relationship and during her journey, Suma taught me a tremendous amount about Islam. I saw its many commonalities with the other religions of the world; I believe these likenesses are universal truths interpreted through different lenses. I also learned about some Islamic beliefs that I found wise and compelling, such as financial debt is spiritually harmful, the importance of reverence for our mothers, and the concept of the "evil eye"—the negative impact of jealousy or envy of others. Like I aspire to do with all my clients, I honored and respected her cultural and religious belief systems and supported her with compassion in every way possible.

After nearly two years in therapy, she briefly removed her hijab during a session. She said that a safety pin was bothering her, but I felt there was a deeper meaning in this unveiling. We had reached a level of trust and intimacy and she was letting me really SEE her. I was overwhelmed by her beauty and this gift of truly seeing her, in every sense. So much so that my eyes brimmed with loving tears. Suma pretended not to notice, but I saw the corners of her mouth turn up slightly as she coolly kept sharing the week's events. She wasn't ready to discuss directly what was happening in the room or in our relationship, but this marked the start of her transformation.

It was about a year later that she made the brave decision to divorce her husband, who hadn't changed his emotionally abusive ways despite much therapy. This decision had once seemed impossible in the context of her family and her community, but Suma was at the point where she realized that in order to free herself, she would need to break any barriers that were causing her to be a lessened or muted version of herself.

Suma told her parents that she was in a marriage that recreated the abuse she experienced during childhood. She empowered herself and gave them a choice: they could get counseling to deal with their own trauma issues so they could stop the cycle of violence and they could support her in getting a divorce, or they could say goodbye to their relationship with her. They got help and supported her wholeheartedly. Even though their behavior had been abusive in the past, they were good people at the core who loved their daughter immensely and were doing the best they could under a variety of difficult circumstances.

The rest of Suma's life also underwent an incredible metamorphosis. She went on an adventure trip out of the country and took a trip to New York City with girlfriends. She began law school with the plan to advocate for others in a family law practice.

When Suma integrated my empathetic, compassionate, and affirming voice in therapy and reflected that in her own self-talk, our work was complete. We thoughtfully and successfully terminated our therapeutic relationship with much celebration and a few tears in that final session.

For a few years following our work together, Suma and I kept in touch. She is now a successful attorney and owner of a law practice, employing and empowering over twenty men and women. She also got remarried to a loving husband. She radiates positive self-esteem and lives a vibrant and bountiful life. She is one of the very best people I know—living life with kindness, reflection, integrity, and empowerment.

My relationship with Suma is a sacred relationship, and I will always hold her in my heart. I know we were brought into each other's lives to help one another learn and grow, and I am forever grateful for this blessing. As a woman who felt I had to swallow and mask my pain in the past, I'm sure I identified with Suma in some ways. But it was her willingness to be authentic and vulnerable with me that gave me the ability to foster an empathetic relationship with her.

Suma's story is a heroic tale of the awesome transformative change that occurs through compassionate connection. Like the phoenix rising from the ashes, she underwent a courageous metamorphosis, a shedding of the former self, and a rebirth into her greatest self.

Expand with Compassion
(10 minutes; lifetime practice)

In your journal, respond to the following questions:

- Reflect on a time in which you learned from a relationship or friendship with someone from a different background than you. What did you learn from this experience?
- When have you experienced a compassionate connection with somebody and how did that feel? How did it promote positive change in your life?
- How can you use what you've learned from these experiences to improve your relationships? How might this expand your life and success?

. . .

Fortify Relationships with Lovingkindness

Love is big. Love can hold anger; love can even hold hatred.[9]
ALICE WALKER American novelist and social activist

Sometimes empathy creates kindness. Kindness is the quality of being warm, friendly, caring, thoughtful, and considerate. While some might mistake kindness for weakness, kindness is an interpersonal skill involving effort, courage, and strength.[10]

Before speaking, spiritual master Shirdi Sai Baba suggests asking yourself, "Is it kind? Is it necessary? Is it true?" If the answer to even one of those questions is no, refrain from speaking. This can be extremely helpful in personal and professional relationships, but sometimes it is difficult to discern.

Early on in my clinical training, one of my clients reeked of body odor and had large yellow pit stains. Session after session he lamented about having no luck on the dating scene. My supervisor told me I had to tell him the truth in a way that was kind. (Oh no! really?) I managed to work it into the conversation by mentioning that persistent sweating was a side effect of his antidepressant. He said he noticed that and we talked about prescription deodorant, wearing an undershirt, and stain-treating his shirts. While it was a bit awkward, he was grateful. Two months later, we successfully terminated therapy and he was happy in a new relationship. Sometimes you have to care enough to tell the truth in a way that is kind.

Kindness involves patience: being gentle and understanding of others when they are causing you some delay or inconvenience. Other times kindness takes the form of encouragement: lifting others up with faith and confidence, and fostering hope. To nurture your relationships with lovingkindness, ask open-ended questions with an open heart. Remember, there are no conditions, no strings, no expectations, and no manipulations. Simply, love to love. Sprinkle your relationships with loving sentiments. Give compliments, love, affection, help, resources, time, consideration, thoughtfulness, respect, and empathy. Express love openly and freely with awesome vulnerability and joy and it will come back to you threefold.

Wield the Power of Lovingkindness
(15 minutes, lifetime practice)

In your journal:

- Choose a personal relationship you would like to strengthen. This could be a family member, your partner, or a close friend. Why is this person important to you?
- List ten attributes you like about this person.
- Circle three of these attributes and then find a way to communicate them to the person in the coming week. Notice the effects on your relationship and well-being.

...

Financial Health Boost: Pay It Forward

*Life's most persistent and urgent question is,
what are you doing for others?* [11]

MARTIN LUTHER KING JR. American Christian minister and civil rights activist

In previous chapters, you've learned how to continually recharge your battery by practicing self-care and receiving support. Now that you are supercharged, you can give and share what you can, whenever you can. Paying it forward through altruism, service, conscious capitalism, and charity can improve your mental wellness and even lead to unexpected rewards in prosperity.

Altruism is concern for the well-being of others and taking action at some cost to yourself—like giving time, money, information, or other resources. Research suggests altruism leads to mental health benefits that can help counter the negative effects of stressful life events.[12]

This was the case for my client Jenn, who was in therapy to help deal with multiple presenting problems, including a breakup that forced her to move, followed by job loss and significant financial stress. Even though she didn't have much savings, Jenn felt she wasn't in the mental state to conduct a job search. She decided she was going to use her gap in work to do something she always felt called to do: volunteer in Haiti. When she returned to therapy after three weeks of volunteering in Haiti, she said, "I have no problems." Being of service to people who had much greater problems and far fewer resources gave her the blessing of a larger perspective, including awareness of her privilege. Altruism shifted her thinking from a negative lens (seeing lack and problems) to a positive lens (seeing the blessings). This led to a significant boost in her mental health and reduced her depression and anxiety, which helped her have the wherewithal to obtain a sales job with a higher base salary and opportunity for greater commission.

Jenn's experience is consistent with research findings that show that volunteer activities help give meaning to people's lives and make people feel better. Studies show how participating in volunteer activities is positively correlated with well-being, life satisfaction, job satisfaction, and career satisfaction.[13]

While true altruism comes from the heart and is selfless in nature, it can lead to financial prosperity. When you put your heart into your work, it can improve your finances.

My marketing consultant, Julie, attracts clients who are doing good in the world and supports them in reaching their full potential through her company's services. She hires talented designers, writers, and SEO consultants. She builds community through ongoing interactive webinars and learning events for staff and clients. Julie is a fierce advocate for the fight against Alzheimer's, a disease that her grandmother suffered from. All of this makes me admire Julie, which then makes me a loyal consumer. It feels great to support businesses whose values are aligned with yours.

Being heartless and ruthless in order to succeed in business results in bad karma. To truly prosper in work and life, choose to be compassionate with your colleagues, boss, customers, competitors, staff, and clients. Choose to work for or create a compassionate business that benefits everyone who is connected to the organization. Instead of treating people like widgets, why not create compassionate, caring connections to boost morale, client and employee retention, and productivity? Being kind and authentic doesn't have to be costly.

Many successful companies, such as Salesforce, Warby Parker, Ivory Ella, Trader Joe's, The Container Store, and Patagonia, practice conscious capitalism, a philosophy that states that businesses should serve all principal stakeholders—including the environment. Conscious capitalism is based on four principles that mutually reinforce each other:[14]

Higher Purpose: Focusing on a purpose beyond pure profits.

Stakeholder Orientation: Realizing that when it comes to stakeholders in a business, there are many, including customers, employees, suppliers, investors, and others. It's not just the shareholders.

Conscious Leadership: A "we" rather than "me" mentality drives the business.

Conscious Culture: Fosters a spirit of trust and cooperation among all the stakeholders.

Conscious capitalism can also be a good press effort that can win over loyal customers who share the same values—such as when Patagonia donated $10 million to address climate change.[15] Part of being compassionate involves being a conscious consumer and supporting businesses that contribute to the greater good.

Generosity is another aspect of altruism and compassion. The more we value what we give, the more generous we are. Research supports that generosity can lead to success, which is important for achieving prosperity.[16] When you are generous, positive customer reviews can increase your financial performance.

My client Dale displays great generosity with his real estate clients. He helps sellers stage homes, gets professional photographs, and even arranges dog walkers during their showings. He is patient and willing to take buyers on endless showings until they find the home of their dreams. All of this has led to a successful business.

Finally, charity is an empathetic response, usually in the form of a donation, to an immediate crisis or need. Charity is how we express compassion for people impacted by natural disasters, acts of violence, and poverty. Charity can foster a sense of community and collaboration, which can promote mental health and wellness. On a larger scale, philanthropy involves generous donations of money to promote the welfare of others by supporting good causes. The financial upside to charitable and philanthropic donations is that they are tax deductible.

At Urban Balance, I started an initiative where the company donated one hundred dollars for every staff member to the charity of their choice. To educate our staff and clients about why that particular cause was important, each person wrote a short blog post about their chosen charity. This initiative promoted a sense of community within our organization.

Pay It Forward
(15 minutes; lifetime practice)

In your journal, answer the following questions:

- How are you already being of service, altruistic, and/or charitable? How has this improved your mental health?
- What keeps you from offering greater generosity in these areas? What needs to happen in order for you to expand your generosity?
- How might paying it forward also lead to true prosperity?

How compassionate are you? To help you answer that question, The Compassion Wheel brings together all the skills you learned in this chapter and measures how well you are living with compassion both at home and at work.

The Compassion Wheel
(20 minutes)

Date: _____

Rate your response after each question using a number from the following scale:

Poor (1–3), Fair (4–5), Good (6–7), Prosperous (8–10)

Poor			Fair		Good			Prosperous	
1	2	3	4	5	6	7	8	9	10

Active Listening: Being fully present to the person speaking to you, listening with all your awareness, making sure you clearly understand their message, responding thoughtfully, and remembering what has been said. How would you rate yourself when it comes to active listening? _____

Empathy: Understanding somebody's perspective and what they are feeling, sharing in that feeling, and having a desire to help them, if needed. When it comes to having empathy toward others, how would you rate yourself? _____

Kindness: How would you rate yourself when it comes to being friendly, warm, considerate, and thoughtful of others? _____

Encourage: Lifting others up by having faith and confidence in them and fostering hope is encouragement. How good are you at encouraging others? _____

Patience: Being gentle and understanding with others when they may be causing you some delay or inconvenience. How would you rate yourself when it comes to patience? _____

Generosity: Giving more than is required or expected in terms of time, information, assistance, services, money, or other resources. How generous are you? _____

Altruism: When it comes to selfless concern and devotion to the well-being of others, how would you rate yourself? _____

Open-Minded: When it comes to being open to different perspectives, thoughts, behaviors, and ideas without placing judgment, how would you rate yourself? _____

Accept Others: Multicultural awareness, acceptance, and affirmation. This includes acceptance of people from various races, cultures, ethnicities, religions, socioeconomic statuses, political orientation, sexual orientation, gender identity, and lifestyle. How would you rate yourself when it comes to accepting others? _____

Ethics: Upholding sound moral principles that govern your behavior both personally and professionally. Having mercy instead of displaying vengeance or litigiousness. How would you rate yourself when it comes to ethics? _____

Service: Being of service to a person, group, community, or cause through helpful behaviors, volunteer work, leadership, and other acts of contribution. When it comes to being of service to others, how would you rate yourself? _____

Charity: Note that this spoke refers to the Charity component on The Financial Health Wheel that you completed in the introduction. How would you rate yourself when it comes to donating money, food, or other resources to those in need? _____

Chart your responses on The Compassion Wheel. (For a refresher on how to do this, see The Wheel Exercise Tutorial on page 11.) Let's start at the top: Are you Poor, Prosperous, or somewhere in between when it comes to Active Listening? Put a dot on the spoke next to the number that corresponds with your answer. Now continue going around the wheel, and after scoring yourself on every spoke, connect the dots to create a circle. If you are having difficulty being honest with your responses, ask a trusted confidant to help you or imagine somebody close to you completing the wheel as if they were answering the questions about you.

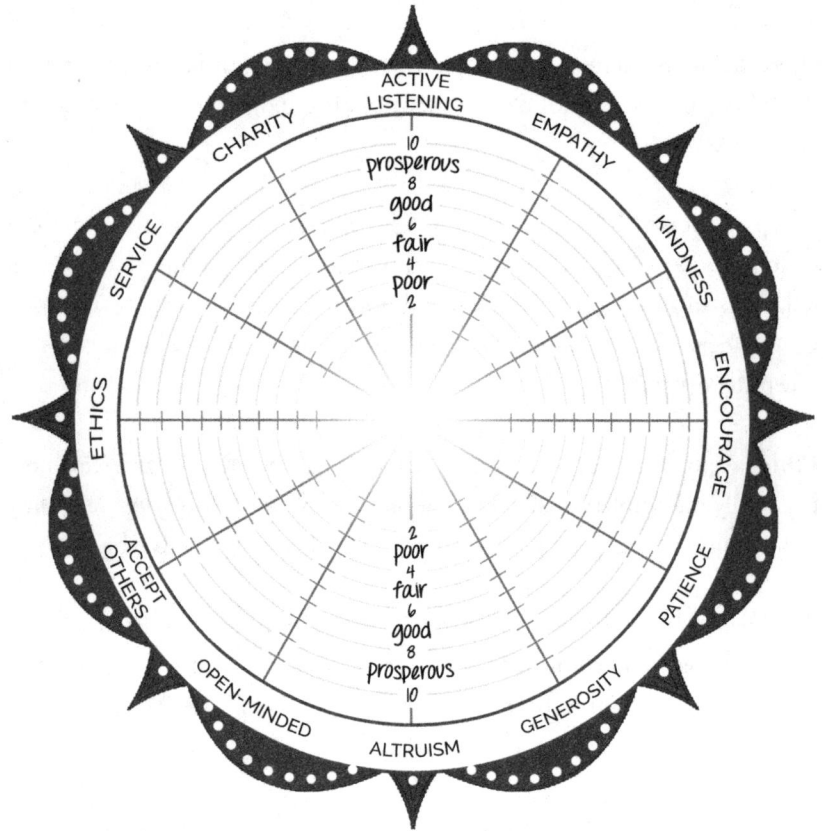

The Compassion Wheel

Don't worry about your scores. We are all works in progress and have room for improvement. Just be honest. In your journal, answer the following questions:

- As you look at the biggest dents in your wheel, ask yourself why you scored lowest in these areas.
- Do you value these traits or not? If not, how could this be limiting your prosperity?
- What three action steps can you take to improve in each of these areas?

Revisit this exercise monthly or quarterly to continue to cultivate compassion. Date your wheel and file it for later reference!

None of us are perfect and developing compassion takes time and attention, but it is an important factor that allows us to welcome true prosperity.

...

How much money we have, our titles, and our achievements don't define our worth; it's our ability to love ourselves and others that defines us and gives us a feeling of self-worth. Love is the currency of life. When our heart is full with loving compassion, financial reward is a natural by-product. Now that your heart is bursting with compassion, reach for higher heights and do greater good than you ever imagined. Detaching with love is key to making this happen.

Chapter 10

DETACHMENT

Disempower Fear, Negativity, and Financial Anxiety to Welcome Prosperity

Those who seek security in the exterior world chase it for a lifetime. By letting go of your attachment to the illusion of security, which is really an attachment to the known, you step into the field of all possibilities. This is where you will find true happiness, abundance, and fulfillment.
DEEPAK CHOPRA author of more than forty books, including *The Seven Spiritual Laws of Success*

When I took out a $50,000 business loan and put a lien on my house, I experienced crippling financial anxiety that came with insomnia and almost constant fears about money. When I shared this with my friend, Cherilynn, she said, "Would it help you if I told you that my husband currently has $200 million in loans?"

Wowza. This information did help, in a few ways. First, it made me laugh, which immediately separated me from fear and worry. Second, it gave me a larger perspective; Cherilynn's husband is an extremely successful commercial real estate developer. I realized it takes some serious risk tolerance to do big business while normalizing the experience of taking out loans. Taking risks and managing uncertainty is what people do on the road to success, so I needed to learn how to notice my emotions without judging them.

In therapy, my therapist, Arlene, said to me, "Your feelings are like waves, you can choose to surf rather than becoming engulfed by them." Arlene explained that through detachment I could learn how to separate myself from my emotions and observe them rather than being controlled by them. There's a big difference between feeling overcome with fear, judging my fear, and feeling shame versus noticing I am scared and coaching myself through that wave of emotion with self-compassion, positivity, and a long-term perspective.

The dictionary defines detachment as being aloof, distant, or uncaring. While some think of detachment as indifference, denial, or dissociation, this is not the kind of detachment Arlene was recommending. She was referring to the philosophical definition, which is a mindfulness technique where we don't attach our happiness to expectations, outcome, other people, possessions, or money.

Detachment from outcome doesn't mean we shouldn't set goals nor does detachment from money and possessions mean we shouldn't own anything. Rather, it means we shouldn't let material things or plans own us or impact our sense of worth and well-being. This allows us to persevere and bounce back quickly from setbacks, rejections, or negative feedback and continue to thrive. Detachment disempowers fear, facilitates freedom, and is one of the most powerful tools shared in this book. For me, it has been life changing.

Because of detachment, I was able to stay more neutral and balanced as we weathered the storm and continued to build the business into something larger than I ever imagined. I could better manage the not-so-pretty parts of owning a business, such as staff resignations, personality conflicts among staff, and financial worry about debts and liabilities.

Detachment also enabled me to network and market the business without attachment to outcome. Rather than focusing on expected results from a networking event or an outreach effort, I put all my effort into planting as many seeds as possible and nurturing them rather than worrying about whether they would grow into something or not. This helped me to avoid spinning my wheels while waiting for results and personalizing rejection, so I could forge ahead with determination. This strategy worked really well for me while I was growing my business, and I'm surprised by how often somebody I met years and years ago reaches out with a referral or a speaking request. We cannot control timing, so it's helpful to detach from expectations about when opportunities are going to sprout.

As Urban Balance grew, detachment helped me separate from fear of the uncontrollable and persevere. This became evident during the process of selling my business. At a meeting with four gray-haired prospective buyers, one of them asked me, "Doesn't it bother you that you have built your entire business based on accepting health insurance and the future of health insurance is a great uncertainty in our country?" My voice was steady with unwavering calm, and I replied simply, "No, it does not."

The group burst into laughter. They smiled and looked at one another, and I couldn't tell if they thought I was the biggest idiot ever or that I was kind of a badass—perhaps it was a little of both. I explained that I made the best decisions that I could for the company based on what is known in the here and now, that I refused to expend energy on fear of the unknown, and trusted all would be fine. They made me a full cash multimillion-dollar offer.

Therapy Session Number 10
(20 minutes)

I am excited to help you learn the art of detachment, an incredibly useful tool in work and in life. You can't detach if you are attached to expectations, outcomes, other people, money, or material possessions. In your journal, please answer the following questions:

- Which attachment—expectations, outcomes, other people, money, or material possessions—do you most relate to?
- How does this attachment affect you emotionally and/or financially?
- If you're attached to an expectation or outcome, why can't you let it go?
- How might detaching improve your well-being? How might it enhance your career or financial success?

You'll be amazed to see how living with healthy detachment changes your life.

. . .

In Times of Uncertainty, Detach from Fear and Anxiety to Welcome Prosperity

In detachment lies the wisdom of the uncertainty . . . in the wisdom of uncertainty lies the freedom from our past, from the known, which is the prison of past conditioning. And in our willingness to step into the unknown, the field of all possibilities, we surrender ourselves to the creative mind that orchestrates the dance of the universe.[1]
DEEPAK CHOPRA author of more than forty books, including *The Seven Spiritual Laws of Success*

Detachment can help us find peace and stop us from comparing the present with the past or future because we aren't attached to the way things were or the way they are supposed to be. Being curious about the endless possibilities of the unknown can foster spontaneity, creativity, discovery, and personal and financial growth. When it comes to embracing uncertainty, detachment can help when dealing with uncertain times at work. If you lost your job, are closing a business, retiring, or dealing with a corporate merger, detachment can help you peacefully ride the waves of change with acceptance. When we realize change is going to happen and we detach from it, we can begin to see positive aspects of change.

In addition to the inevitable changes in the workplace, there's also changing economic times or negative financial events to contend with. A climate of financial worry or poor economic change can trigger fear of the unknown, previous financial trauma, and financial anxiety. In my practice, I've seen people deal with the uncertainty, and subsequent financial anxiety, brought on by major world events, such as the Great Recession of 2008 and the more recent COVID-19 pandemic.

Traumatic financial losses can also result from a foreclosure, a stock market crash, a lawsuit or divorce, an unexpected tax bill, a business loss, or unemployment. The term *financial PTSD* is not an official psychiatric diagnosis but is often used to describe financially triggered PTSD. This includes different emotional, cognitive, and physical challenges people experience when they have difficulty coping with either an abrupt financial loss or the chronic stress of having inadequate financial resources. Physical symptoms include nervousness, jitters, insomnia, or a startle response to bank alerts or phone calls that could be from debt collectors. Emotionally we might not be able to feel close to others as we experience apathy, anxiety, depression, hopelessness, or despair. Meanwhile, persistent negative thoughts about finances may make it difficult to concentrate. These symptoms disrupt the home and/or work life and cause significant distress.[2]

According to research, 23 percent of adults and 36 percent of millennials experience financial stress at levels that qualify for a diagnosis of PTSD. This is of great concern because not having enough money keeps our physiology amped up practically all the time. Without the chance to recover, long-term stress releases hormones that can wear down the mind and body, causing psychiatric issues, diabetes, heart disease, and other health concerns.[3]

To recover from financial PTSD, we need to detach our worth from money. During the housing market crash of 2008, I conducted an emergency assessment for a business owner who had become suicidal because he had lost everything but hadn't yet told his wife and teenage children. Through therapy he learned how to detach his worth from money. He became closer to his family, and in time, he was able to rebuild his financial life.

Jim was a trader who had millions of dollars, yet was terrified about losing everything like he had done once before. He was incredibly miserly to the point that he would walk miles to work so he wouldn't have to pay to park his car. He would check his investments in the stock market every couple of hours. He was distant, irritable, and prone to angry outbursts. His girlfriend was both concerned and exasperated, so they came to me for couples therapy. I ended up working with Jim individually to help him find balance between saving and spending with trust and peace.

Claire dealt with crippling financial anxiety during the COVID-19 pandemic. Her husband lost his job, she was on disability for chronic PTSD and serious neurological issues, and they were living paycheck to paycheck. Like many Americans, they were facing retirement without any savings. Her catastrophic thinking brought fears of homelessness. She even made arrangements to have her beloved dog put down because they could no longer afford to feed her. After a few urgent sessions with me to foster detachment and referrals to organizations that could help, Claire found emotional peace and canceled the appointment to euthanize her dog. She said to me, "I realize I have been in bad financial states before and I have survived. I have a wealth of resources within me, including emotional intelligence that fosters self-compassion and loving compassion with my husband." This is something we all must remember.

Detachment allows us to zoom out and see the big picture, putting stressful events in a broader context with a long-term perspective. It's kind of like investing in the stock market in an intelligent way. If we were to obsess over the fluctuations in stock prices each day, we'd be riding an emotional roller coaster. With detachment, the financial dips or negative things happening in the market won't derail us. An added bonus of detaching from emotions is its power to facilitate equanimity: mental calmness and temperament even during challenging times.

Financial Health Boost:
Letting Go to Improve Financial Health

Many of us are constrained by the forces of fear and doubt. Ask yourself, "What would I do if I weren't afraid?" In my work coaching and counseling, I encourage people to take control of their work and financial life by having good accounting, financial, and legal practices. Since we can't predict what the financial future holds, having health, auto, home, and even life insurance is a good idea. Once we have taken control over what we can, we must let go and practice detachment so we can persevere with fearless courage. This includes detachment from money.

Attachment to money can cause fear that prevents people from pursuing endeavors that could improve their financial health. Risk tolerance is a financial aspect of detachment and is defined as the maximum degree of uncertainty someone is willing to accept when making a financial decision that entails the possibility of loss.[4] Did you know people with a lower level of negative emotion tend to make better financial decisions?[5] That's why it's a good idea for business owners, entrepreneurs, and investors to emotionally detach. Without detachment, our losses may cause anxiety and fear that

> cause us to lose focus on our vision and throw in the towel instead of persevering.
>
> For example, I have invested tens of thousands of dollars in preparing for the publication of this book and have had to detach from messages and fears that it may not be recouped. We should make investments wisely (considering factors such as our debt-to-income ratio), but also trust that the universe will return what we put out in the world in the form of some sort of reward whether it be personal, spiritual, or financial.

Mindfulness practices like the following help us detach.

Shelve Your Worries with "The Container"
(15 minutes; lifetime practice)

Eye Movement Desensitization and Reprocessing (EMDR) therapy and other trauma protocols use The Container technique to temporarily shelve distressing thoughts or feelings in order to decrease overwhelm and increase stability and coping. This is not denial, it is healthy compartmentalization. Are you ready to give it a try? Follow these five steps:

1. Connect with your breath and do a body scan. Notice where you are holding tension, fear, or negative feelings.
2. Imagine you now have a container that is big enough and strong enough to hold these negative feelings securely.
3. Imagine putting all of your negative feelings into this container, every last bit. When you are done, close the container tightly and lock it.
4. Imagine storing your container in a safe place. Visualize sinking it to the bottom of the sea, blasting it into outer space, or handing it over to a Higher Power.

5. Remember, you can open this container again when you are ready to deal with these feelings. This could be at your next therapy session or when you are with a close friend with whom you feel comfortable talking.

. . .

Recalibrate Expectations to Zero
(5 minutes; lifetime practice)

Before entering a meeting, going on a date, attending a family gathering, or investing in the stock market, check in with yourself about your expectations. While we want to be open to wonderful possibilities with abundant thinking, we can't attach our happiness to expectations or outcomes. So consciously recalibrate your expectations to zero and practice gratitude for any and all good that comes.

In other words, before heading out to an event or entering an interpersonal interaction of any kind, mentally scan for any expectations you may have, mindfully let them go, and cultivate an attitude of openness and receptivity. You might be surprised by the results. Many of my clients report significant improvements in their relationships when they recalibrate expectations to zero. Give it a try!

. . .

Now that you have learned how to detach from your own negative emotions, we are going to discuss how to detach from other people's negative emotions.

Disengage from Other People's Drama with Lovingkindness

Once when I was in the checkout line at Target, the woman in front of me was being completely rude to the cashier, loudly yelling at him about something that was beyond his control. She was totally disrespectful, even to the point of calling him names. He just looked at her kindly and nodded and empathized with her while continuing to check out her items. When her transaction was complete, he wished her well and she left, taking her negative energy out of the store.

As I approached him, I said, "I'm so sorry that woman was so rude to you! You remained so professional and calm. How'd you do that?" He replied casually, "Oh, I don't let anyone in my head who isn't paying rent."

Brilliant, right? This type of reaction is not typical. Many people struggle with detachment, causing billions of dollars in lost income for organizations throughout the US. There's a solution. Reducing negativity in the workplace can enhance creativity, motivation, and teamwork while reducing stress and turnover.[6] Through conflict detachment, we can mentally disconnect from the conflict and become more productive as opposed to engaging in fighting behaviors or excessive thinking about the conflict.[7]

My client Kristin, a single mom, increased the frequency of her sessions to twice a week after her micromanaging boss came down on her for low productivity and put her on probation. Kristin did a lot of work in therapy to make sure her anger and frustration with her boss wouldn't cost her the job. We worked on practicing some healthy detachment from his feedback and recognizing that much of his behavior was due to pressures in his own job. I guided her through some visualizations of surrounding herself with a protective bubble so she could visualize his criticism bouncing off the bubble while she remained safe and well inside. We worked on compartmentalizing some of her feelings about his behavior so that she could concentrate and do the work to keep the job she very much needed to support herself and her kids. When her performance improved and she passed her probation, she went on an intense job search. Today she is working at a different company with a very supportive team lead and is making more money.

Detaching from other people's stuff is a skill we can develop. My kids' elementary school counselor used to tell the children to "be a duck" and let stuff roll off their feathers. Doing this keeps other people from determining how we feel and disempowers bullies who want us to react. It's not intended to be used to endure abuse or harmful treatment; it is a technique to reduce harm. It's like dropping your end of the rope in a game of tug-of-war; it disables the conflict so you can make clearheaded decisions going forward. Detachment allows us to be less reactive while promoting good judgment during interpersonal conflict.

Detachment also keeps us from getting triggered so we can react in a way that is grounded and kind. We can't control other people's thoughts, behaviors, choices, and actions, or the outcome of any interpersonal situation. We can only control ourselves. You can never cause somebody to behave poorly—that's their choice. Wayne Dyer, author of *The Power of Intention*, said "How people treat you is their karma; how you react is yours."[8]

Detachment can also be invaluable in parenting. When my second daughter, Claudia, was born, my older sister, Paula, came to visit. Paula is nearly fourteen years older than me, has three lovely daughters, and is a wonderful mother. When it came time for me to put three-year-old Celeste to bed, I was nervous. I wanted things to go smoothly, but Celeste had a different plan. She exploded into a Level 10 Meltdown, rolling on the floor, wailing, and flailing. Embarrassed, I engaged in a ridiculous power struggle with my toddler that included threats of punishments and unsuccessful time-outs. Who do you think won? Celeste, of course. Forty-five minutes later, after reading several additional bedtime stories, I slinked down the stairs feeling humiliated. Paula said, "Oh honey, you locked horns with her. When she tantrums, you need to take a step back and detach."

Paula was right. I thought about cognitive behavioral therapy and realized that I was so reactive because I thought if my daughter was having a tantrum, then I must be a bad mom. Through the power of self-fulfilling prophecy, I became frustrated, impatient, and reactive—not the mom I wanted to be.

A couple weeks later, as I was entering Celeste's preschool, my friend Laura was coming out the door with her toddler, Lindsey, tucked gently under one arm like a bundle of sticks. Lindsey was freaking out, screaming and flailing her arms and kicking her legs because she didn't want to leave school. Laura chuckled and said with a smile, "Oh, hey, Joyce! How's it goin'?" She was totally calm and unphased by Lindsey's fit and was not personalizing her age-appropriate behavior like I had with Celeste. I needed to be like Laura and detach from my children's fits so that I could be an effective parent.

Today, when emotionally triggering events happen at home or at work, I try my best to bring my attention to my breath and detach from the drama. I try to observe from a place of neutrality, knowing that I am okay and this, too, shall pass. Practicing detachment allows me to stay more grounded and set healthy limits without letting emotions like guilt manipulate me. Now my daughters are teenagers, so I have loads of opportunities for detachment!

Separate from Negativity
(5 minutes; lifetime practice)

This is a visualization exercise. Close your eyes and spend a few minutes connecting to your breath and doing a body scan to notice where you are holding any tension or yuck. Breathe it out until you feel clear. Imagine being enveloped by a positive white light, enclosed in a safe bubble, or behind a protective, invisible shield that separates you from other people's negative feelings. When you are with others, remember this protective shield and envision their hurtful words or negative energy bouncing off the shield while you remain safe and well. This allows you to respond from a place of detachment.

...

Detach with Love in Your Relationships

You must love in such a way that the person you love feels free.[9]
THICH NHAT HANH global spiritual leader, author of *The Miracle of Mindfulness*

Detaching with love does not mean we are not connected to or care about our loved ones. Rather, it means having a healthy separation in relationships where you do not try to control another person while still loving them in a way that allows them to be free. When we are attached, we give away our power to others. We become clingy and needy in our relationships as we strive to get something from them to complete us or make us happy. Through healthy detachment, we shift our focus from the other person to ourselves. We engage in activities and self-care practices that strengthen our relationship with ourselves. When we do this, we become whole. We stop needing others, so we can start really loving them. By letting go of selfish attachments, we can give pure love. It's all about stopping being responsible *for* others and instead being responsible *to* them, as well as ourselves.

Beth had been trying to control and manage her husband's drinking for years by administering her own breathalyzers and calling bars to check up on him. After a few months of Al-Anon and therapy, she said, "I realized I don't have to ride this crazy train with him, so I'm hopping off." Instead of riding the emotional highs and lows of his cycle of recovery and relapse, she practiced detachment with love and took care of herself. This facilitated emotional stability for herself and their children and put an end to the nearly violent fights she and her husband would have from time to time. She encouraged her husband to stay in treatment and let him become responsible for his own sobriety, which was what needed to happen for him to get well.

This didn't mean that Beth didn't care about her husband. The lifeguard analogy is helpful in understanding why. Lifeguards are taught to only go into the water as a last resort because going into the water puts both the lifeguard and the drowning person at risk. It's better for both the drowning person and the lifeguard—if the lifeguard is safe on ground or in a boat—to throw a lifesaver. The phrase "reach or throw, don't go" is taught to lifeguard trainees to break the natural impulse to immediately jump into the water with the drowning person.

Detaching with love is an excellent antidote to helicopter parenting, where parents try to prevent their children from experiencing hardship. We must separate ourselves enough from our children to allow them to make their own mistakes so they can learn. Being responsible to them and not for them is the difference between making sure our kids have what they need to do their homework and making sure they experience consequences if they do not do it, versus doing the homework for them. In addition to giving our kids a strong foundation that includes support and limits, we also must give them wings so they can become their own person and live their own life. Our kids need to be free to be their authentic selves instead of living as we hope or expect them to be.

We can dramatically improve our relationships, partnerships, and friendships by practicing detachment with love. This means giving people the freedom to be who they are and loving them without trying to change or control them. I've learned so much from couples counseling. I've seen how trying to change or control somebody else stems from ego and can be very harmful to the relationship. Practicing acceptance and giving somebody the space to be themselves will both reduce conflict and deepen your relationship. Sometimes it's as simple as not commenting when your boyfriend wears his old jeans to visit your grandmother or not pointing out that your way of loading the dishwasher is better. And other times it's bigger things, like allowing your partner to practice their faith in the way they do or don't want to.

Detachment with love can also be used at work, where it has been shown to enhance productivity and performance.[10] Through detachment we can also learn to get along with coworkers who previously annoyed us.

The most important point to remember is that if we are trying to control another person, or are needing them to behave in a certain way in order for us to feel okay, it's time to practice detachment with love and focus on ourselves.

Practice Detachment with Love
(15 minutes; lifetime practice)

In your journal, answer the following questions:

- Name a person in your life whom you try to control. How is that working? How is that impacting your relationship? Your mental health?

- How would it feel to stop trying to control their behavior and focus on yourself? Is there something you would miss about the drama? If so, you need to take a deeper look and fill that void with activities and practices that are healthy for you.
- Name three specific controlling behaviors you are willing to let go of. Name three self-care practices you plan to increase. Try this for one week and see how detaching with love can facilitate peace and well-being with yourself and others.

...

Now it's time to see how well you do at detachment. The Detachment Wheel brings together all the skills you learned in this chapter and measures how well you are practicing detachment.

The Detachment Wheel
(20 minutes)

Date: _____

Rate your response after each question using a number from the following scale:

Poor (1–3), Fair (4–5), Good (6–7), Prosperous (8–10)

Poor			Fair		Good			Prosperous	
1	2	3	4	5	6	7	8	9	10

Internal Negativity: How well are you doing at unplugging from fear, anger, sadness, doubt, worry, and financial anxiety and observing them from a neutral place? _____

External Negativity: How good are you at observing other people's emotions and maintaining a healthy separation so you can stay calm and help as needed/desired? _____

Expectation & Outcome: How good are you at detaching from outcomes and being able to trust that the result will be fine regardless of how things play out? _____

Conflict: How good are you at unlocking horns and using detachment to react from a thoughtful, compassionate place? _____

Money: How successful are you at not attaching your sense of well-being to money or material possessions? _____

Embrace Uncertainty: How successful are you at welcoming endless possibilities and the curiosity of the unknown to foster spontaneity, creativity, growth, and discovery? _____

Accept Impermanence: How well do you embrace change in this constantly changing world? _____

Not Control Others: How good are you doing when it comes to realizing you don't have power over other people's health or happiness and not trying to control them? _____

Zooming Out: How good are you at taking a step back to see situations from a greater perspective instead of through your emotions? _____

Equanimity: How well are you doing when it comes to maintaining mental calmness and an even temper during challenging situations? _____

Emotional Intelligence: How compassionate and effective are you when it comes to managing your emotional process and disengaging from the emotional process of others? _____

Risk Tolerance: This spoke is related to The Financial Health Wheel you completed in the introduction. Are you able to accept uncertainty when making financial decisions that involve the possibility of loss? Having the proper amount of insurance may help ease some of your worries. _____

Chart your responses on The Detachment Wheel. (For a refresher on how to do this, see The Wheel Exercise Tutorial on page 11.) Let's start at the top: Are you Poor, Prosperous, or somewhere in between when it comes to Internal Negativity? Put a dot on the spoke next to the number that corresponds with your answer. Now continue going around the wheel, and after scoring yourself on every spoke, connect the dots to create a circle.

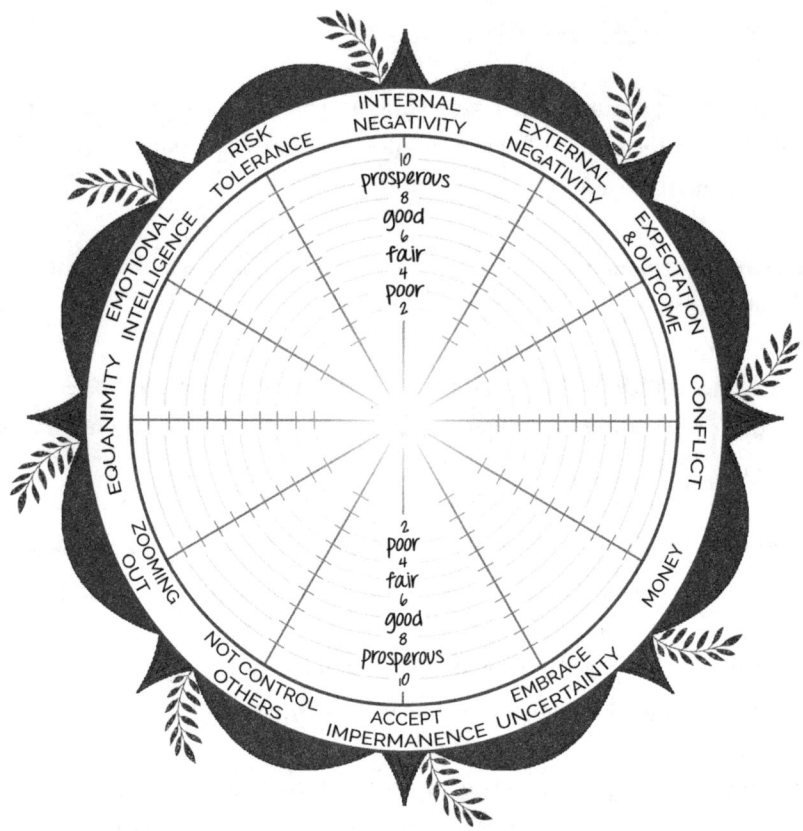

The Detachment Wheel

222   The Financial Mindset Fix

Don't worry about your scores. Just be honest. Review The Detachment Wheel and in your journal, answer the following questions:

- Look at the three spokes with the lowest scores and list two ways you can improve in each of those areas.
- What are two aspects of your life where you could most benefit from healthy detachment? For example, in your partnership, parenting, or your relationship with money?
- In what ways would your emotional suffering decrease if you increased detachment?

Consider revisiting this exercise monthly or quarterly to continue to practice the art of detachment. Date your wheel and file it for later reference! Nice work.

...

Practicing detachment is going to help you stay cool and resolve conflict along your path to success. Detachment builds resilience, the ability to move through challenges. In the next chapter, you will discover the difference positivity can make when it comes to your financial mindset.

Busted.

In the segment, I had a mock session with a fake client who was a friend of the producer. The idea was to provide this "client" tips on reducing stress—but he was an extremely relaxed and chill guy. When he asked me what else he could do, I panicked and said, "Well . . . even petting your dog or having sex can reduce stress . . ." The producer yelled, "Cut!" and we all doubled over in hysterics as the producer commented that while both of my suggestions had some merit, the combination of them was not great. This unleashed another round of laughter.

This event broke through my posturing and allowed me to be real. The producer took a liking to me and recommended me for future projects, including the opportunity to conduct group therapy for the roommates on MTV's *The Real World*.

A STANDING OVATION

It was the first week of my freshman year of high school. I'd forgotten my science homework and asked my teacher, Mr. Sneider, if I could turn it in the next day. "Only if you stand on my lab table in the front of the room and sing 'Joy to the World,'" he said. I looked him in the eye and smiled as I pushed back my chair. As I proceeded to the front of the silent room, I could feel twenty-five sets of eyes on my back, many of them belonging to students I had not yet met. I climbed on the high, black table and stood in my Madonna-inspired outfit, with a mesh bow in my badly permed hair (it was 1986 . . .). I took a deep breath and proceeded to belt out every verse of the "Jeremiah was a bullfrog . . ." version of "Joy to the World." My classmates gave me a standing ovation.

This silly display of bold behavior led to unexpected blessings in my life. Two girls whom I didn't know came up to me after class, said it was the bravest thing they ever saw, and asked me to be their friend (which I still am today). Mr. Sneider was dumbfounded, as he had apparently been saying that line for twenty years with no takers. He gave me credit for the homework and spread the story like wildfire amongst the teaching staff. When I went to my other classes, my teachers would say "Aren't you the girl who sang in Mr. Sneider's class?" This event resulted in the teachers taking notice of me, and they encouraged me to become involved in activities such as student government, cheerleading, and a capella choir.

Chapter 11

POSITIVITY

Harness the Power of Extreme Optimism to Manifest Success

We can change our lives. We can do, have, and be exactly what we wish. Be brave enough to live the life of your dreams according to your vision and purpose.
ROY BENNETT author and thought leader

At a neighborhood holiday party a couple years back, my friend Randy asked, "How's your book coming along?" I sighed and lamented that the book I had been aspiring to write for years still had not come to fruition. Being a therapist himself, I'm sure he recognized that my own issues were stopping the book from happening. He looked at me quite seriously and said, "Man, you really need to talk to my monk."

"Your monk?" I said in surprise. "Yes, my Buddhist monk. He will help you," Randy said confidently.

I'm open to all the help I can get, so I gave Randy's Buddhist monk a call and set up a consultation. He wasn't the Tibetan-looking, bald, robed monk in a monastery I was expecting. He was a regular guy, a Jewish man in his sixties wearing a black T-shirt who worked from his home office in Highland Park, an affluent suburb on the North Shore of Chicago.

During our initial banter, I quickly realized I was speaking to one of the most intelligent people I had ever met. As he was excitedly talking and drawing complex diagrams on small sheets of paper to illustrate his thoughts on science meeting spirituality, I was gaining hope and excitement that he could actually help me.

After he asked what brought me there, he listened as I shared all the reasons my book wasn't happening. After a while, he stopped me and said with a nod, "I have your answer."

He grabbed another little sheet of paper and wrote something on it. My heart raced; I hoped this would be the key to unlock my dream of having a book published.

Then he handed me the paper, which read, "WTF."

I thought, "Umm . . . excuse me?" I was kind of mad! I said incredulously, "Are you being serious right now?"

"Yes, I am. WTF stands for 'Weaken the Fiction.'"

He went on to explain that to succeed, I needed to weaken the negative narrative of excuses, rationalizations, and lack of action that was keeping me stuck.

That's when I committed to being passionate about shifting from a negative to a positive perspective. Positive psychology suggests we should act "as if" we have already accomplished something we desire. This is so we can try it on, see how it feels, and start to retrain our thinking to support the knowledge that this goal is possible.

So even though my book had been rejected by numerous publishers, I walked around my house saying "I am a successful author and speaker just like my hero, Brené Brown."

At first, my best friend, Cherilynn, accused me of "psychotic optimism." But then she joined in on the game. She left voicemails congratulating me on my book deal and asked if she could come to New York City on my book tour. As silly as this may sound, this kind of playful creativity changed the energy I was putting out in the world. This positive attitude opened doors and led to you reading these words right now.

Therapy Session Number 11
(20 minutes)

In today's session, we are turning up the volume on your positivity! In your journal, please answer the following questions:

- If you have a negative narrative in your head, how can you Weaken the Fiction?
- In what ways is negativity preventing your success?
- How might positivity open the doors to success in your life?

I am excited for you!

...

Now let's cultivate some positivity for greater prosperity.

Put on Your Rose-Colored Glasses to Greet Prosperity

Positive psychology focuses on the healthy strengths and skills that enable us to thrive and succeed. Therapists who embrace positive psychology focus on the client's strengths and avoid going overboard on discussing their problems. You can do this for yourself by focusing on the good.

Optimism involves being hopeful and confident about the future and expecting a favorable outcome. Being cheerful gives off a positive vibe that radiates happiness, good spirits, and a sense of humor. Studies show a positive outlook enables us to do the following:[1]

- Grow and flourish
- Cope with adversities, losses, and failures
- Improve job performance and team relationships, leading to greater financial success

According to neuroscience, the brain creates neural pathways based on our habits and behaviors. When negative thinking becomes the norm, it becomes our default pattern. With positive thinking and repeated new behaviors, we train our brains to create new neural pathways. As the pathways become stronger, positive thinking can become the new normal.[2]

Three ways you can shift your thinking from negative to positive are to: practice gratitude, act "as if," and focus on the positive to solve problems.

PRACTICE GRATITUDE

I got everything because I practiced being grateful.[3]
OPRAH WINFREY American media executive and North America's
first African American multibillionaire

My longtime client Brad arrived at a session with his head in a halo brace after breaking his neck in a car accident. I was quite taken aback by the large contraption he was wearing to immobilize his neck, a halo ring that looked like it was screwed into his skull with four large posts sticking out from his shoulders.

The first thing he said was "I am so grateful!" Rather than being upset that a driver had struck him, or focusing on his pain, Brad expressed profound thanks that his life was spared. This perspective allowed him to focus on the good while he was healing.

For some, gratitude comes more naturally than for others. When my daughter Celeste was around nine years old, I noticed she was starting to develop a "glass half empty" perspective. She'd say "We didn't go to the park today" instead of "I'm so glad that we went to the beach and I got to play with my friends." I bought her the positive thinking workbook *No More Stinking Thinking*, which included exercises to retrain her brain to look for the good in any situation. It definitely helped, and set a better example for her sister, Claudia, too. Just after their dad and I separated, Claudia wrote a school paper about gratitude and how fortunate she was to have two parents who love her and two homes with everything she needs.

We can retrain our minds by making a point to state the positive, keeping a gratitude journal, giving thanks during a mealtime blessing, or stating what we are grateful for at the end of a team meeting at work. Personally, as I lay down to sleep, I do a gratitude reflection and mentally give thanks for all the blessings of the day. It helps me feel more peaceful as I fall asleep.

Gratitude is a choice. I've seen unhappy people with great financial prosperity and happy people who practice gratitude with very little. For example, I had a client who lost almost everything to addiction. Her physician husband died of an opioid overdose and she lost her own liver from alcoholism (she underwent a transplant). She was once a wealthy socialite and highly accomplished journalist and was now permanently disabled and on public aid. During a session after Thanksgiving, her green eyes sparkled as she beamed with gratitude that both her grown children came for a simple dinner at her modest apartment. Her gratitude moved me to tears.

Gratitude can help positively reframe negative situations. For example, I am extremely grateful to a boss that wouldn't promote me. If it weren't for her, I never would have started my own business. Now, instead of being annoyed when somebody doesn't have confidence in me, I do a positive reframe of being underestimated! Gratitude helps you see the hidden blessings.

Studies show the following additional gratitude benefits:[4]

- Less depression and reduced negative emotions
- Increased positive emotions
- Greater sense of meaning in life
- Better strategies to cope with stress
- Healthier social relationships
- Increased job performance, which tends to lead to improved financial health

Now that you are sold on the power of giving thanks, let's practice some gratitude.

Reframe Positively to Become Grateful
(15 minutes; lifetime practice)

Positive reframing is a technique where you try to reconsider things in a positive light to help you practice gratitude. By doing so, it can powerfully transform your thinking.

Let's positively reframe some upcoming challenges for you. Here are a couple examples to get you started:

- An upcoming challenge could be a dreaded meeting with your counselor at the consumer credit agency to talk about your credit card balances, which have gotten much higher since your last meeting. A positive reframe could be being grateful for having dedicated time with a professional to help you improve your financial state.
- Another upcoming challenge could be a meeting with your boss about your low sales last month. A positive reframe could be being grateful for having a mentor and the opportunity to share and get feedback on your new sales strategy moving forward.

Now it's your turn. In your journal, do the following:

- List three upcoming challenges or obstacles. Make sure at least one pertains to your career or finances.
- What are the reasons why this is such a challenge?
- Now reframe the challenge in a positive way showing what blessings could result because of the situation.

. . .

ACT "AS IF"

Alfred Adler, the founder of Adlerian psychology, developed a therapeutic technique where clients would act "as if" they accomplished what they desired as a way of role-playing or "trying it on."[5] Social psychologist Daryl Bem said acting "as if" gives us the opportunity to create positive stories about our lives in order to enact the best possible outcomes.[6] Pretending can help us begin to get past any negative thinking that may be causing resistance.

At a recent pre-conference symposium, I asked around one hundred aspiring small business owners to introduce themselves to one another. They exchanged pleasantries and shared basic information about themselves, such as titles and workplaces.

After they developed their career and business vision, I asked them to reintroduce themselves to one another "as if" they already accomplished everything they dreamed.

At first there was some resistance and nervous laughs, and only a few people started to stand up hesitantly. Some asked for clarifying instruction, expressing concern that they might look like a fool if they admitted what they really wanted. I reminded them of abundant thinking and asked them to think as big as possible—the sky's the limit! Now that they were all on the same page, everyone stood up and participated. After a few minutes, they really got into it.

Suddenly the room was filled with internationally renowned, prize-winning inventors, authors, celebrities, and business leaders! They were standing taller, walking more confidently, smiling broadly, and soooo much *louder*! After twenty minutes, I struggled to regain the attention of the group; they didn't want to stop talking. It was as if they couldn't revert back to the more muted, self-constrained versions of themselves.

When we debriefed, the group said the exercise helped them move past the discomfort that was between them and what they wanted. In their evaluations, they praised the activity for being the absolute most powerful part of the day.

You can do this too! Your inner Doormat might feel uncomfortable at first, but your inner Diva will love it.

Act "As If"
(10 minutes; lifetime practice)

Give acting "as if" a try in whichever of the following ways works best for you:

- Record yourself (audio or video, but video is better because you can see your face when you replay it) telling a loved one of "recent accomplishments" that impacted your finances. The longer and more detailed, the better. Be sure to listen to it at least once or twice to retrain your neural pathways to think positively.

- Pick one trusted confidant (perhaps your partner, best friend, or therapist) and act "as if" you accomplished your goals for one to five minutes. Ask them for feedback, for example, if you seemed happy and excited.

Then write about what this assignment was like for you. How did it feel to speak as if you had achieved your dreams? Was it uncomfortable at first and then did it become easier?

...

Focus on the Positive to Solve Problems

Positive people look beyond problems to find solutions and focus on what's working. With solution-focused brief therapy (SFBT), the client and therapist focus on what is working well and build on that rather than being consumed with what is not working. "Problem-free talk" and "Look for the exceptions" are two popular SFBT techniques to help you become more positive and solution-focused.

Engaging in "problem-free talk" is a technique where the therapist and client spend time talking about aspects of the client's life that are not problematic. This approach can work well if you find yourself or others venting or complaining within a friendship, partnership, family, or work team. Give it a shot to see how it can make communication more positive and productive.

"Look for the exceptions" is a technique where therapists ask clients to think of exceptions to the problem they are having.[7] For example, if a couple frequently fights about money, the therapist encourages them to think of a time when they were able to discuss their finances without fighting. Instead of wasting time and energy focusing on everything that contributed to the problem, this helps clients realize they may already know a solution. Clients can then work on repeating the behaviors that led to positive results.

Now it's your turn.

Look for the Exceptions
(10 minutes; lifetime practice)

Answer the following questions in your journal:

- What's a current problem you are facing?
- Can you remember a time when this problem wasn't happening?
- What was different then?
- What were you *doing* differently?
- How were you *thinking* differently?
- What can you do differently *now* because of this exception?

...

Expand Your Comfort Zone with Positivity

Now that you are using positive talk, it's time to walk the walk and take action to create positive change in your life.

Whether it's speaking up at a meeting, asking for a raise, applying for your dream job, starting a business, or telling someone you love them, the only way to welcome greater prosperity is to do things that intimidate and scare you but move you in the direction of success.

Years ago, when I was contacted by ABC to shoot a national segment on stress management, I was terrified, but because I wanted to grow my business, I enthusiastically said *yes*. Ironically, I failed to follow any of my own stress management advice, barely sleeping a wink the night before, loading up on caffeine in the morning, and skipping my morning meditation.

When the producer and his crew arrived, the first thing they did was shove my perfectly staged furniture in a huge pile in the waiting room so they had room for lighting and sound equipment. When they were all set up, the producer asked if I was good to go. I said, "Absolutely!" trying to appear calm. The sound technician then chimed in, "Well, actually, I can hear your heart pounding through the microphone."

In my adult life, I continue to push myself toward these types of experiences, and like exposure therapy for phobias, each experience helps expand my comfort zone. As Brené Brown teaches, having the courage to show up and be seen, imperfections and all, brings many blessings. In the process, we gain confidence, experience, and become capable of more.[8]

Approaching new opportunities with positivity requires enthusiasm, courage, and action. We can't just hope and wish; we have to *do* something. Studies show that taking deliberate action to realize career goals results in greater career satisfaction and a higher salary.[9] Let's figure out what you are going to do to widen your world.

Do Some Exposure Therapy
(20 minutes; lifetime practice)

This exercise is based on systematic desensitization, a behavioral therapy technique used for treating phobias and anxiety. The idea is to expand your comfort zone by getting used to things that make you uncomfortable. Do the following:

- Name three activities outside your comfort zone that are important for your career success in the near future.
- Pick one of these activities that is particularly relevant and important. What resources and skills do you need to successfully accomplish this activity?
- Make a plan and set an intention for pursuing this activity in the near future. For example, if you have a fear of public speaking, join a Toastmasters group or take an improv comedy class.
- Set a target date for completing the activity and ask a trusted confidant to hold you accountable and support you in this endeavor.

...

Financial Health Boost:
The Power of Using Positivity in Negotiations

Believe in yourself and negotiate for yourself. Own your own success.[10]
SHERYL SANDBERG chief operating officer of Facebook,
billionaire, and founder of leanin.org

People are often surprised to hear how they can use positivity as a weapon during all kinds of negotiations. I'm constantly encouraging my clients and mentees to pursue opportunities for growth and to advocate for themselves through negotiation. When they tell me they are going for a promotion or new job, I ask, "Do you think you will get it?" If they reply with something like "Well, the competition is really tough, so I probably won't," then I'll say "Then you won't." They are often surprised and taken aback because they know I believe in them. However, I strongly believe in the power of self-fulfilling prophecy. If you are anticipating a negative result, you create that outcome through self-defeating behaviors. How is somebody else going to believe in you if you don't believe in yourself?

With the goal of selling my practice someday, I attended a negotiation seminar for women in business at the Kellogg School of Management at Northwestern University. The presenter encouraged us to move past our fears and negotiate everything from small purchases, buying or leasing vehicles, and our salaries to major business deals.

One of the speakers was the sociologist who conducted the research for Sheryl Sandberg's *New York Times* bestselling book *Lean In*. Her main message was that women don't negotiate and need to start. As somebody who has hired hundreds of people over my career, I sadly agreed with her. When offered a position and a salary, women often say "Thank you for the offer. I'll take it." Meanwhile, in my experience, men often say something like "Thank you. I would like to take a couple days to think about it. The compensation is lower than what I was hoping to receive." They will typically come back and negotiate a higher salary, better title, additional training, or better benefits.

> Men who assert themselves in the workplace are often perceived as confident and smart, while women who do the same are viewed as bitchy, aggressive, or difficult.[11] These cultural variables both cause and reinforce the gender gap in wages, but discrimination is the biggest reason why women only get paid seventy-eight cents on the dollar that men are paid for the same work.[12] The world needs more leaders such as the CEO of Salesforce, Marc Benioff, who dedicated $6 million to correct compensation differences by gender, race, and ethnicity across the company.[13]
>
> As a result of this seminar, I never paid for another filing cabinet. As Urban Balance expanded, I needed more filing cabinets that would've cost me $1,200 each. When negotiating office leases after the seminar, I would ask for any lockable file cabinets in good condition. It cost them nothing and saved me thousands of dollars. Whenever making a larger purchase, I ask the salesperson if it's the best they can do. I then read their body language. While purchasing patio furniture, I negotiated free delivery and got them to throw in the covers ($250 value). I began to share negotiation tactics with all of my student interns and coached them on advocating for themselves.

A TOUGH NEGOTIATOR

Before taking the negotiation seminar, I found myself on the other side of a good negotiator when meeting with Silvija, a young Serbian-American therapist I hired when she was still working on obtaining her clinical hours for licensure. Because Silvija was working an entry-level position that required supervision and training, her hourly rate was significantly lower than a fully licensed therapist, and she was struggling to make ends meet. At her one-year review, Silvija convinced me to pay her more than I had ever paid a therapist in that entry-level role, and I will never forget it. I'm sharing the five steps of negotiation she took to get the salary she wanted. I encourage you to do the same:

1. **Take action.** Silvija sent me a polite yet firm-sounding request for an in-person meeting with me as the owner of the company to discuss her one-year anniversary and possible raise. As a start-up, we weren't on

top of regular performance reviews and this wouldn't have happened without her prompt. I respected Silvija for this.

2. **Practice gratitude.** Silvija started our conversation by thanking me for hiring her and for all the learning opportunities. She gave heartfelt thanks for my willingness to hire an immigrant for whom English was a second language. I felt respected and valued by Silvija.

3. **Be prepared.** As we began our conversation about her compensation, it was clear Silvija had done her research. She showed me how many referrals she was given during the year and how many sessions she had, illustrating her wonderful client retention and productivity. Additionally, Silvija showed me how many new referrals she brought in by marketing herself to the Eastern European community of Chicago, reminding me that she is fluent in Serbian, Bosnian, and Croatian. Finally, she took the average fees paid by the insurance companies and subtracted her compensation, illustrating a wide gap. By doing so, it helped me respectfully see her work through her lens.

4. **Be aware.** With healthy self-esteem and in a matter-of-fact manner, Silvija demonstrated we could pay her more. As she clearly understood and was empathetic to our operating costs, I knew Silvija could see the situation from my lens as well. This diffused the defensiveness I was starting to feel.

5. **Be present.** This was the magic bullet. I gave Silvija the same explanation I had given dozens of therapists before about why the pay range was what it was and why the moderate increase I was offering her was appropriate. Whereas virtually everyone in the past would thank me at this point and we would be finished with the negotiations, Silvija stayed in that moment. It was as if time slowed down as we sat in the discomfort. I could hear the office clock ticking as she looked at me with her large, intelligent green eyes, and I knew that she knew I could pay her more considering how valuable she was to the organization. She held her head high, owning her worth while professionally holding her ground. Eventually I broke under pressure and offered her more than I had ever paid somebody in that position before. Sylvija thanked me profusely and we both left the meeting feeling fortunate.

Seven years later, Silvija became a clinical manager at one of Urban Balance's locations, earning far more than the salary she had negotiated with me years ago.

As I prepared to sell my business, I took some cues from Silvija. I also identified areas in which I was willing to compromise and where I was not. This helped me stay strong during the late stages of negotiation, when I was asked to maintain some liability. Even though it could have cost the deal, I held the line and my wish was granted.

Increase Your Work Satisfaction

The next exercise helps identify areas of needed improvement or negotiation in your work. Whether you work for somebody else, are self-employed, or own your own business, The Work Satisfaction Wheel assesses your satisfaction with your work and identifies any areas of needed improvement or negotiation.

While you might think negotiation primarily occurs around compensation, this wheel exercise encompasses all of the ways negotiation can benefit you. It comes in handy when you are preparing for a performance review or looking for a new job and comparing offers. If you are currently unemployed, complete this exercise based on your most recent job, or as a framework for negotiating future job offers. If you are self-employed or a business owner, this tool can help you identify and evaluate areas of low satisfaction that you can improve by negotiating higher fees, better deals with vendors or contractors, better benefit plans, and more.

The Work Satisfaction Wheel
(20 minutes)

Date: _____

Notice the lines at the end of each spoke, which provide space for you to jot notes about the pros and cons of your current work situation as related to each spoke. Then rate your response after each question using a number from the following scale:

Poor (1–3), Fair (4–5), Good (6–7), Prosperous (8–10)

Poor			Fair		Good			Prosperous	
1	2	3	4	5	6	7	8	9	10

Salary/Pay: Jot down the amount of compensation you receive including your salary or pay, plus any commissions or bonuses on the lines outside this spoke. How prosperous is your current compensation? _____

Health Benefits: List your current health-care benefits including medical, vision, and dental plans, a health savings account, or other perks like gym access. How prosperous are you in health-care benefits? _____

Retirement Benefits: Write down your current retirement benefits including your ability to invest (not how much you have invested) in pre-tax earnings into a 401(k) plan (in for-profit settings), 403(b) plan (in nonprofit or government settings), or Roth IRA (self-employed settings). How prosperous are you in accessing retirement benefits? _____

Time Off: Jot down how much flexibility you have to take time off, whether or not it is paid time off, and how much time you can take off for vacations, sick days, and other leaves of absence. How prosperous are you when it comes to taking time off? _____

Ownership/Interest: Write down notes about your ability to become a partner or owner, obtain stock options, or have a vested interest in your place of work. How prosperous are you in your ability to have ownership or a vested interest? _____

Enjoyment: Jot down the aspects of your job you enjoy or don't enjoy. How prosperous are you in terms of deriving pleasure and enjoyment from your work? _____

Meaning: List which aspects of your work are meaningful and rewarding to you on a deeper level. How prosperous are you when it comes to finding meaning in your work? _____

Self-Alignment: Mark down your unique gifts and talents, core values, and mission in the world. How prosperous are you in your work aligning with your true self? _____

Work-Life Balance: Write down the aspects of flexibility or lack thereof in your current work situation. This includes the ability to work from home, flexible hours, work-life balance, commute time, or required travel. _____

Appreciation: List the ways you are acknowledged for your efforts and achievements, including words of affirmation, appropriate title, awards, or special perks. How prosperous are you in appreciation and recognition at work? _____

Professional Growth: Jot down your current opportunities for professional growth including mentoring, continuing education, or other alternative opportunities for learning. How prosperous are you in opportunities for professional development? _____

Connect to Colleagues: Write notes about how your work does or does not foster collaboration, social support, and a sense of belonging. How prosperous are you in connection to colleagues? _____

Chart your numbered responses and then connect the dots. (For a refresher, see The Wheel Exercise Tutorial on page 11.) Start at the top: Are you Poor, Prosperous, or somewhere in between when it comes to negotiating Salary/Pay? Put a dot on the spoke next to the number that corresponds with your answer. Now continue going around the wheel, and after scoring yourself on every spoke, connect the dots to create a circle.

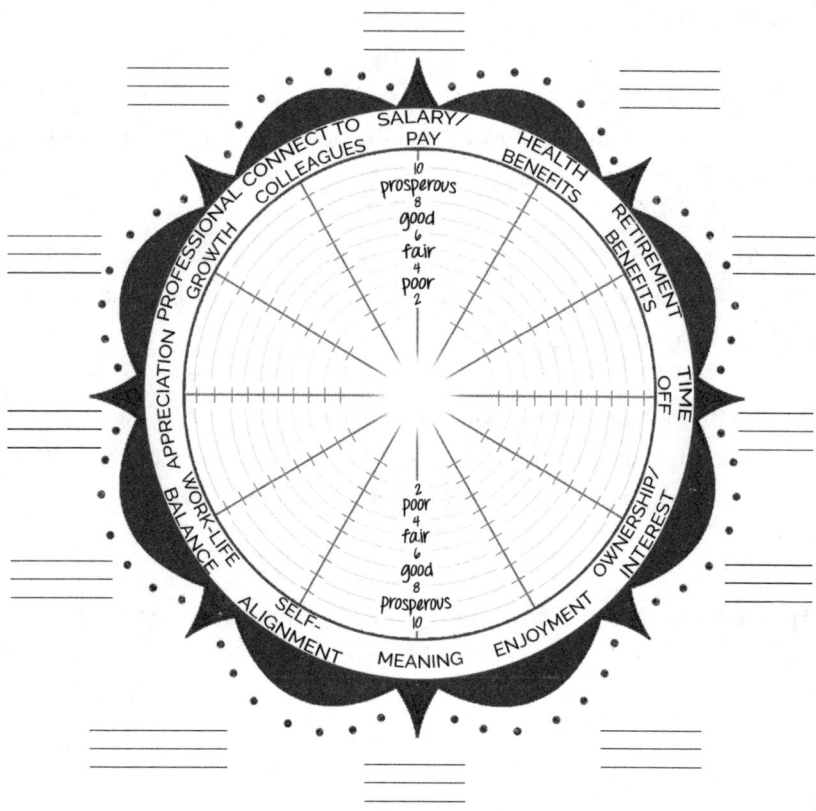

The Work Satisfaction Wheel

At the end of each spoke, list what's important to you under each of the categories. To get you started with ideas, see The Work Satisfaction Wheel Example.

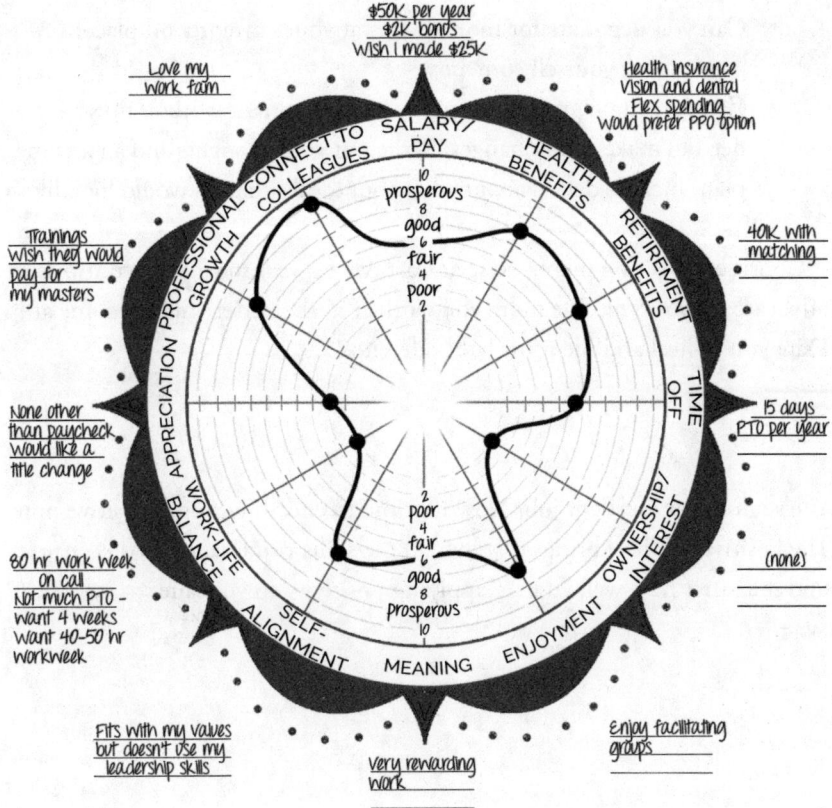

The Work Satisfaction Wheel Example

In The Work Satisfaction Wheel Example, notice the two deepest dents in the wheel are in the areas of Work-Life Balance and Ownership/Interest. These would be the areas of needed improvement or negotiation.

After filling in your wheel completely, answer the following questions in your journal:

- To see your overall satisfaction with your work, add up your total spoke scores and divide the total by twelve. Is it closer to the Poor or the Prosperous range?
- What are your three lowest ratings or dents on the wheel?

- Can you negotiate for more of this at your current workplace? Or create it for yourself somehow?
- Can you attain greater prosperity in your current work or do you need to make some changes? Write out your thoughts and an action plan. Include details about what your ideal situation would look like.

Consider revisiting this exercise at least twice a year so you can continue to advocate for yourself. The more you work at it, the better you'll become at it. Date your wheel and file it for later reference!

...

You've done an excellent job. Now it's time to end things on a positive note. The Positivity Wheel brings together all the skills you learned in this chapter and measures how well you are applying positivity to your life.

The Positivity Wheel
(20 minutes)

Date: _____

Rate your response after each question using a number from the following scale:

Poor (1–3), Fair (4–5), Good (6–7), Prosperous (8–10)

Poor			Fair		Good			Prosperous	
1	2	3	4	5	6	7	8	9	10

Positive Psychology: Focusing on the strengths and gifts that enable you and others to thrive and succeed. When it comes to answering the proverbial question "Is your glass half empty or half full?" how would you rate yourself at being half full? _____

Weaken the Fiction: Identifying and overcoming excuses or negative narratives you tell yourself that are between you and the success you deserve. How successful are you at WTF? _____

Gratitude: Expressing thanks and appreciation. How successful are you at taking the time to reflect on what you are grateful for? _____

Positive Reframing: How would you rate yourself when it comes to looking at the good parts of any situation? _____

Cheerful: Expressing happiness, joy, humor, and good spirits. When it comes to expressing cheerful vibes, how would you rate yourself? _____

Optimism: Being hopeful and confident about the future; expecting a favorable outcome. How optimistic are you about the future? _____

Passion: Bringing excited energy to what you do. How passionate are you about being positive? _____

Courage: Doing something that frightens you; expanding your comfort zone. When it comes to being courageous, how would you rate yourself? _____

Action: Identifying opportunities and taking steps to achieve them. How would you rate yourself when it comes to taking action? _____

Creativity: Utilizing positive energy to develop original thoughts, ideas, or innovations. How would you rate yourself when it comes to creativity? _____

Solution-Focused: Focusing on building strengths and finding solutions rather than just discussing problems. How would you rate yourself at being solution focused? _____

Negotiate: How good are you at advocating for yourself in your work and financial life to arrive at win-win agreements? _____

Chart your responses on The Positivity Wheel. (For a refresher on how to do this, see The Wheel Exercise Tutorial on page 11.) Start at the top: Are you Poor, Prosperous, or somewhere in between when it comes to embracing Positive Psychology? Put a dot on the spoke next to the number that corresponds with your answer. Now continue going around the wheel, and after scoring yourself on every spoke, connect the dots to create a circle.

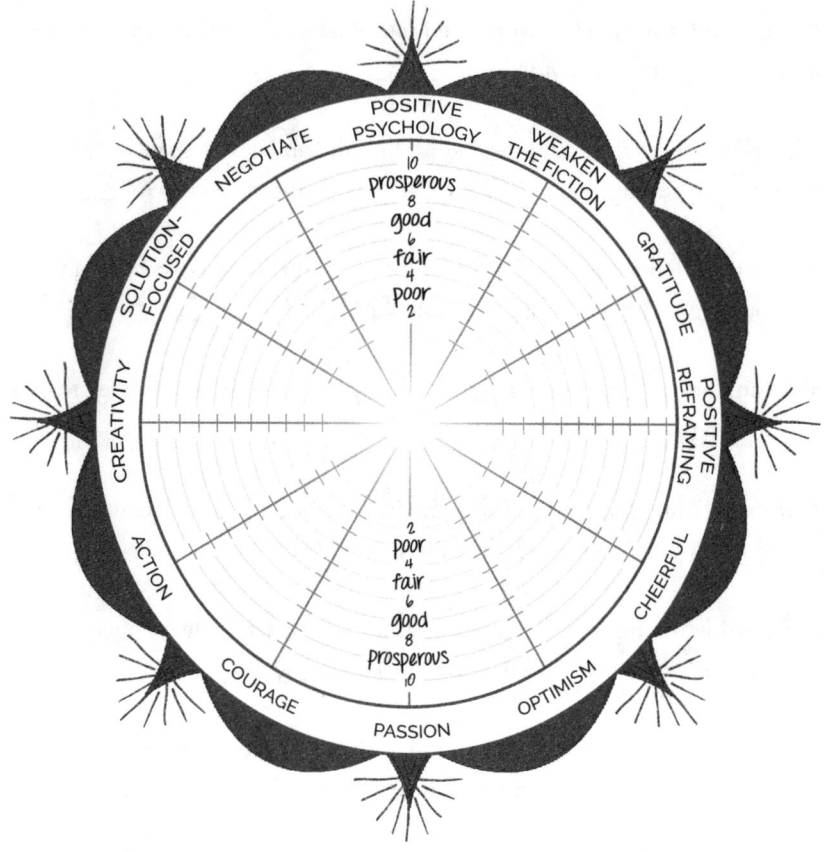

The Positivity Wheel

We all can use a little more positivity in our lives. Consider revisiting this exercise monthly or quarterly to continue to keep increasing your positivity. Date your wheel and file it for later reference!

In your journal, answer the following questions:

- As you look at the biggest dents in your wheel, notice which areas you scored yourself the lowest. Why do you think this is so?
- How might working on these areas improve your personal life? Professional life? Financial life?
- What three action steps can you take to improve in each of these three areas?

You got this! Yippee! Hurray! (Can you tell I was a high school cheerleader?)

...

Now that you are grooving with positivity, I'm going to show you how *not* to let anyone or anything slow you down.

Chapter 12

RESILIENCE

Convert Adversity into Opulent Opportunity

*Our greatest glory consists not in never falling,
but in rising every time we fall.*
RALPH WALDO EMERSON nineteenth-century poet and philosopher

The words from my former boss, Bill Heffernan, brought me some peace after my business partner left abruptly: "You have just been given a tremendous gift." I didn't exactly understand what Bill meant, but was hopeful some blessings would come from this loss and hardship.

The next few months were some of the hardest in my life. I felt the weight of the world on my shoulders, but each day I got up and put one foot in front of the other as I faced debt collectors and worried staff. As each day passed, I stood taller, became more confident in my decisions, and reflected strength and hope to my staff. This felt like a metamorphosis; I shed the skin of a smaller version of myself and unfolded into my greatest potential. While I had previously felt like I needed the security of a copilot to operate, I was learning that I could fly solo, and with that came new freedom and confidence.

From the outside, my life was still not ideal, but I felt so much more capable inside. Author Rita Mae Brown said, "People are like tea bags, you never know how strong they'll be until they're in hot water."[1] Overcoming this business challenge gave me the confidence that I could handle whatever comes my way.

I finally understood what Bill meant when he said I had been given a gift. He overcame four different episodes of cancer treatment despite being told after the third treatment failed that maybe it was time to stop trying for a cure and move to palliative care. Because of this experience, he has amazing clarity on what matters in life and what does not. He spends much of his time cherishing his family and inspiring others to persevere through challenges. He is one of the most resilient people I know.

I have continued to work on my resilience through mindfulness. The practice of yoga has taught me that if I am experiencing the discomfort of a pose, I can breathe through it and it will pass. As a result, I will come out more flexible, balanced, strong, and capable of enduring the pose the next time.

One day, a naval officer walked into the yoga studio and said, "We do yoga in the military but they don't call it yoga. They call it resilience training." After hearing this, I started to pay even more attention to how I could use yoga to build resilience, pushing past the voices of self-limitation and being willing to fall again and again before achieving something I could never do before.

Do you know what crow pose is in yoga? It's an arm balance pose where you squat down and place your hands on your mat shoulder-width apart. You then press your knees into your triceps, shift your weight into your fingertips, lift your hips, bend your knees, and lift your feet off the floor.

Crow Pose

It's a challenging pose that requires a lot of strength and balance. When I first tried it, it seemed impossible. So for years, whenever it came up in a class, I would think to myself, "I can't do crow pose," and would regress into child's pose—essentially giving up and resting in a fetal position face down on my mat.

Then one day I asked myself, "Am I setting my own ceilings? I need to practice what I preach."

So I tried it—putting one leg on one arm at a time. Then I faked it by leaning forward with my knees on my arms while keeping my feet on the ground. Then I tried it for real and face planted a hundred times. After a couple months, I did it. Albeit I do it very briefly, but I can do it!

This practice taught me to try, let myself fail and fall, get up, and try until I pushed through my self-imposed limitations. The falling is a necessary part of the learning and the accomplishment feels great! Today I am stronger because of what I've been through and ready for the next challenge.

Therapy Session Number 12
(20 minutes)

This is our final session! All the skills you have learned in our work together foster resilience. Today I'd like you to think of a significant challenge from the past that you overcame and then answer the following questions in your journal:

- How did you get through it?
- What lessons did you learn?
- How might these lessons help you develop financial resilience?

You're doing such important self-reflection! Wonderful work.

. . .

Resilience Is Essential for Success and You've Got the Building Blocks

> *More than education, more than experience, more than training, an individual's level of resilience will define who succeeds and who fails.*[2]
> DIANA COUTU, *Harvard Business Review*

Resilience is the ability to fully engage in life, recover from challenges, and increase your capacity to thrive in the future. Resilience allows us to bounce back after experiencing difficulty and come out stronger.

Without resilience, a person can claim defeat and halt progress. In my practice, these are the clients who say "There's nothing I can do," "I tried that once and it didn't work," "I guess I'm destined to be alone forever," or "My business idea failed so I am stuck at the job I hate." Unless we examine and change these false belief systems, we will fail in our endeavors.

Resilience is a critical component of succeeding in work and life. Resilience training seminars are some of my most requested corporate trainings. Studies have found positive relationships between resilience and the following outcomes:

- Job performance (which impacts your financial health)[3]
- Positive mental health[4]
- Greater satisfaction with life[5]
- Longevity[6]

In my practice, I've discovered that one of the most resilient groups of people are recovering addicts. I love working with them because I never cease to be awed and inspired by their resilience. I've seen clients who lost marriages, jobs, money, health, and virtually everything to addiction and then bounced back to live a life filled with health, love, and prosperity. They did this by utilizing all the skills you've already learned in this program, which are empirically proven to facilitate resilience:

ABUNDANCE

Abundant thinking opens you up to seeing possibilities and solutions when experiencing challenges. It helps you embrace a spirit of collaboration and teamwork, which fosters resilience.[7] Having greater self-worth reminds you that you deserve greatness.

AWARENESS
Greater awareness of yourself and others allows you to better adapt to and move through stressful situations.[8]

RESPONSIBILITY
Taking responsibility for your role in any negative life events, practicing forgiveness, and letting go when events are outside of your control helps you move forward with resilience.[9]

PRESENCE
Staying present with mindfulness reduces negative thoughts and rumination, enhancing your ability to recover and bounce back from stressors.[10]

ESSENCE
Healthy self-esteem allows you to assertively navigate through challenges. Humility makes you more resilient after receiving negative feedback. Having a spiritual outlook that includes a sense of greater meaning or deeper purpose in life fosters resilience.[11]

SELF-LOVE
By practicing self-compassion, you won't feel shame even in the face of failure.[12] Self-care includes proper sleep, nutrition, and exercise, which foster your emotional and physical resilience.[13]

VISION
Planning (including financial) helps you successfully navigate through challenges because you are better prepared.[14]

SUPPORT
Social support boosts your psychological health, allowing you to become more resilient.[15]

COMPASSION

Compassion allows you to feel positive emotions even during difficult circumstances.[16]

DETACHMENT

Detachment conserves your energy for when you need it, often during challenges.[17] Through emotional intelligence, you respond better to stressful conditions and deal with emotions in a healthy way.[18]

POSITIVITY

Positive emotions contribute to creative thoughts, strong relationships, and flexible mindsets that all build resilience.[19] Having gratitude helps you in adapting to situations and coping with times of stress.[20] Thinking positively and taking action helps you persevere and continue to forge ahead.

Now that you are equipped to be resilient, let's explore how resilience can transcend any situation life throws you.

When Frightening Obstacles Appear, Move Through Fear with Resilience

> *You gain strength, courage and confidence by every experience in which you really stop to look fear in the face. You are able to say to yourself, "I have lived through this horror. I can take the next thing that comes along."*[21]
> ELEANOR ROOSEVELT diplomat, activist, and former First Lady of the United States

A few years ago, my husband, Jason, took me camping at the Theodore Roosevelt National Park in western North Dakota. I got up in the middle of the night to go to the campsite restrooms, which were located across an open field about one hundred yards away. As I was walking, I noticed what looked to be a shrub in the shadows near me. Then suddenly the shrub stood up. It was a bison. It was about twenty feet away from me and was kicking dust and snorting.

Throughout the park there are signs that warn against approaching the bison because they weigh between one and two thousand pounds and can run as fast as forty miles an hour. What they don't tell you is what to do when one is standing in front of you and mad because you woke it up!

I went from half asleep to high alert in a split second. Every hair on my body was standing on end. I froze and stopped breathing. I wasn't sure if I should stay still or make a run for the restroom building, which was still fifty feet away.

When I noticed he had a friend standing up behind him, I realized that I was in great danger. I remained still, afraid that if I bolted, they would be startled and charge after me. So I took a deep breath, focused on being present, and tapped into my intuition. I maintained eye contact with them and slowly moonwalked backward, gently gliding to the restroom building but prepared to run like hell if needed. They seemed pleased that I was leaving and watched me until I was inside the building.

Once safe, I let out a huge sigh of relief. Before I left the restroom, I looked out and saw that they were still standing there in the moonlight. I made sure to stay as far away from them as possible, making my way back to the tent on a paved road, where I hoped it would be less likely to find bison sleeping . . .

When I got back to the tent, I woke Jason up and told him what happened. His eyes bugged as he looked at me with an expression that revealed that I could have been killed. But since I survived, it was a cool experience! And one that made me think about fight, flight, or freeze.

As human beings, we are primed to respond to stressors with either a fight, flight, or freeze response. These reactions are unconscious and rigid responses to fear that are usually not optimal, nor do they result in positive growth or evolution. We can use internal resources such as presence, detachment from fear, and positive thinking to tap into our intuition and enable conscious problem-solving and decision-making to choose responses that are more adaptive—making us more resilient when going through stressful events.

Cognitive flexibility is the ability to consider other options; it is the opposite of rigid thinking that believes you only have one or two choices, and it promotes resilience under high-stress conditions.[22] High-rise buildings are built so they can sway in the wind; they are made to be flexible so they don't break under pressure. We can also choose to be flexible, fluid, open, and creative as we adapt and respond to life's challenges.

Facing your fears with resilience can result in positive outcomes. Studies show that individuals who face their fears and stressors and are motivated to put forth more effort to resolve problems and grow tend to have greater performance.[23] Challenges also foster personal self-discovery and growth.

BISON IN THE PROFESSIONAL WORLD

On a personal note, I applied what I learned from the bison experience to one of my scariest moments as a business owner. For many years, Urban Balance had a credentialing issue with a major insurance company. When we applied for a group contract, they incorrectly linked Urban Balance's name and tax ID with my individual contract. After two years of phone calls, letters, and emails, it was still not corrected. Foolishly, I gave up, even though I knew the contracting wasn't exactly right. I did this out of some level of desperation because their members represented 20 percent of our business.

Then I received the dreaded call from their risk management team. They said, "Joyce, according to our records you saw forty-eight clients on Monday. We need to have a call." My blood went cold with fear. Even though these sessions had legitimately taken place with licensed therapists, it appeared in their system that all the clients were meeting directly with me. I imagined being charged with fraud, kicked off the panel, and watching my business go down the drain. I was paralyzed with fear and shame, which was a freeze response.

I thought about resigning from the panel in order to make the problem go away. But then we would have hundreds of clients who would have to pay out-of-network to see their therapists and the business would suffer when it was already challenged. This would have been a flight response.

I also thought about lawyering up and having my attorney join the call. This would have been a fight response, and fighting a major insurance company would be like trying to fight the bison.

So instead, I chose to ground myself through presence, detach from fear, seek support from my practice manager and biller, and face the situation.

Before the call, I laid on the couch in my office in a fetal position attempting to meditate. While preparing for the worst, I was trying to get myself in a neutral space so I wouldn't become defensive. On the call, I explained honestly what had occurred. My practice manager was extremely helpful in mediating the discussion that followed. I was shocked when they responded with, "Your practice has provided excellent service to many of our members who wanted to be seen in-network. Thank you. We're going to get the credentialing fixed for you."

Wow. What an enormous relief! This experience also resulted in personal growth because I learned that I will never, ever conduct any business that isn't absolutely compliant with contracting or any other regulations, ever. It also provided me with a template for how to deal with challenging situations in the future:

- Resist the immediate fight/flight/freeze response.
- Look to your network for consultation and support.
- Use mindfulness strategies to calm your mind and promote a relaxed and collaborative atmosphere for resolving problems.

You can do this too!

Flagging the Minefield
(10 minutes; lifetime practice)

To get started, consider a time when you faced a big challenge and were able to manage it successfully because you planned for it. You used a technique used in solution-focused brief therapy called Flagging the Minefield.

Want to give it a try? You can practice this by identifying any upcoming stressful situations and proactively thinking about which coping strategies you can use to move through them successfully.

I've done this by going as far as to flag certain times of the year that may be more stressful for me. For example, as a mom of school-aged children, September, December, and May seem to be the busiest times of year, so I plan to not overextend myself with work and to build in extra time for self-care. From a financial perspective, my therapy practice is the slowest during December and August, which used to cause me financial anxiety until I flagged it and planned for it, by using that time of year for my own vacations as my clients weren't coming in then anyway.

In your journal, please do the following:

- In looking at the week or month ahead, write down three upcoming events that you anticipate will be stressful. Make sure at least one is financial, such as paying your bills or reviewing your budget.
- For each upcoming event that you have flagged, write down three strategies that have helped you successfully cope with these types of situations in the past. For example, you went for a run before doing your bills or rewarded yourself by meeting up with friends afterward.
- Now, schedule in time for your coping strategies before or after the stressful event.

Congratulations on having prepared to be resilient!

...

Financial Health Boost: Build Your Financial Resilience

Financial resilience refers to your ability to bounce back from adverse financial events, like losing your job, absorbing unexpected expenses, experiencing a decrease in work or business, a recession, a pandemic, or losing money in an investment. According to financial expert Dave Ramsey, having good finances is like building a house. You need the right foundation in place (e.g., emergency fund, low or no debt), otherwise any sort of storm (adverse financial event) will knock it down.[24]

The ability to rebound from a financial setback is directly proportionate to your financial health before the event. According to a 2017 report, 39 percent of Americans have zero money set aside and 57 percent have savings of less than $1,000.[25] Therefore, two-thirds of Americans do not have financial resilience and could not withstand a major money challenge like what occurred for many during the COVID-19 pandemic. If you have little money saved, have lots of debt, and do not live by a budget, your recovery time from such an event is significantly extended. To become financially resilient, follow these best practices:

- Budget
- Keep your debt-to-income ratio low
- Live below your means by limiting your discretionary spending so you can save money
- Establish an emergency fund
- Pay down outstanding debt
- Stay the course with your investment strategy (not pulling funds when a recession hits)[26]

Financial planners often recommend having enough savings to cover three to six months of expenses so that you can successfully move through hard times. Again, this can be established by reducing your variable, nonessential expenses. Consider having funds automatically transferred to your savings account or contributed to your investments on a monthly basis. Consider reading books such as *The Latte Factor* by David Bach and John David Mann or *Financial Peace* by Dave Ramsey to see how saving small amounts, like the price of a latte, can create significant financial improvement over time.

Savings should be kept liquid in a savings account, money market, or short-term CD where you have easy access to it if and when you need it. Once you have that in place, you may look at investing more in your future through retirement plans, college funds, or buying a home and paying down the mortgage. You might consider diversifying your investments to increase your financial resilience. For example, if all your savings are invested in your house, you may not be financially resilient if the housing market crashes. However, if you have invested in your home as well as mutual funds or CDs, you will have financial resources available during a housing market downturn. It's a good idea to make sure your investments align with your values, so consider socially responsible investing—for example, in companies that are focusing on creating environmental sustainability. Doing so contributes to the resilience of our global community.

Another way to foster your financial resilience is to cultivate your human and social capital.[27] Your human capital is all of the knowledge, skills, experiences, and other qualities you have to offer potential employers. This includes your health, because it affects your ability to work, be productive, and maintain a high job performance. Your social capital includes a support network that can provide financial assistance and/or emotional or logistical support during difficult times. This might include people who could provide you with rides if you no longer could afford transportation.

Increasing your financial best practices and human and social capital fosters financial resilience. In my practice, I've counseled both the financially resilient and those who weren't during challenges such as the housing market crash of 2008 and the COVID-19 pandemic. Let me tell you, the difference in stress, relationship strain, and financial trauma is marked. My client Amber was barely able to pay her bills and was always on the cusp of being entirely broke. The more we worked on her self-esteem and self-care, the more she prioritized having more of a financial cushion in the event of an emergency. She increased her freelance graphic design fees and dramatically grew her marketing efforts to generate more business for her side hustle. Within six months, she had a couple thousand dollars saved and was also approved for a credit card to use in emergencies only. When she was laid off from her nine-to-five job during a recession, she was able to cover her rent for a couple months and continue to generate graphic design work until she landed a new day job.

I want you to be safe in the event of an unexpected financial challenge, so let's do an exercise.

Create a Financial Resilience Plan
(20 minutes; lifetime practice)

In your journal, answer the following questions:

- In what ways might financial resilience improve your situation?
- How well are you doing at following the budget you created in chapter 2? Are there any changes you need to make to help you live below your means so you can save more money?
- Do you have an emergency fund? If so, is it enough to pay three to six months' worth of expenses? If not, what is a realistic goal for bolstering your emergency fund? What are two concrete steps you can take to achieve this goal?
- In the case of an adverse financial event, who would you turn to for emotional, financial, or logistical support? What can you do now to strengthen your social capital to prepare for hard times?

...

Progress Isn't Linear: View Setbacks as Opportunities for Learning and Growth

We may encounter many defeats, but we must not be defeated.[28]
 MAYA ANGELOU American poet and civil rights activist

Setbacks are a normal part of life. It is how we respond to those challenges that determines if we are going to spiral downward, stagnate, or grow and develop. We must proceed with resilience.

In my practice, clients often initiate therapy during some setback, such as a job or business loss, professional disappointment, a breakup, a relapse, a depressive episode, or a mistake or failure in some endeavor. When stressors like these occur, it's normal for us to experience a regression—a fallback to self-destructive behaviors or negative ways of thinking. Part of resilience is to recognize these setbacks and implement strategies to recover and get back on course.

At first, many of my clients expect their progress to be linear—they think that they should continue to feel better and better each day in a straight, upward path. But personal and professional progress is not linear. The figure below illustrates what we expect versus the real nature of progress. It is more common for people to make progress, experience another setback, learn from it, recover, and then make progress again. This is the way people heal and evolve. The goal is to have the setbacks be fewer, less frequent, and less intense as you build resilience.

What We Expect Versus Reality

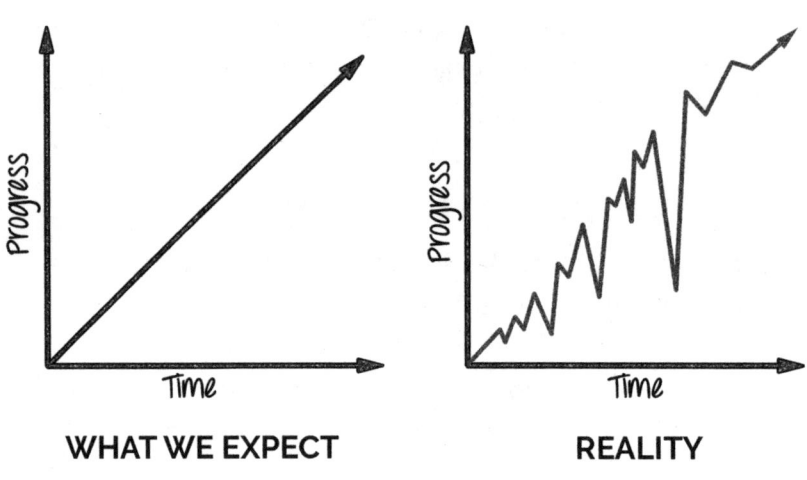

APEX OF THE MOUNTAIN SYNDROME

In my practice, I've noticed that just before people achieve a long-anticipated goal, they have a significant setback. I call it the Apex of the Mountain Syndrome. Right before they reach a high point they have never before achieved, they have a crisis of confidence and come crashing down mentally. Researchers in sports psychology have found that self-efficacy (one's belief about their ability to succeed) is negatively related to effort over time.[29] This means that people often experience a crisis of self-doubt prior to accomplishing a major goal. The self-doubt helps people realize that they need to put in incredible effort to accomplish their goal. A final push is what helps them get over the hump and make the incredible accomplishment.

I've seen the Apex of the Mountain Syndrome in clients who are about to reach milestones in their recovery from addiction, in clients who have identified so long with their depression that they are scared to be free of it entirely, and in clients who are just about to achieve career milestones. Ironically, I am experiencing this phenomenon right now as I write this last chapter of the book. There is a Chinese proverb that speaks to this: "The temptation to quit will be greatest just before you are about to succeed."

The Apex of the Mountain Syndrome might be the result of:

- Fear of failure after working so hard
- Fatigue or burnout from putting forth great effort for a long period of time
- Fear that the success will not feel like you hoped
- Fear of success and all the expectations and responsibilities that come with success

GROWTH MINDSET

One way to better manage setbacks, including big ones, is to develop a growth mindset to foster resilience. Research shows that:

- Hard work, good strategies, and input from others help you put in extra time and effort, which ultimately leads to higher achievement.[30]
- Setting learning goals rather than performance goals allows you to not get discouraged by negative feedback or setbacks. Reframing a negative

challenge or setback as a positive learning experience keeps you motivated to stay the course and on task while striving for greatness.[31]
- Having a growth mindset at work improves job performance and subsequently financial health.[32]

For the past several years, I've been invited to serve on a panel of therapists who have been successful in private practice. The common thread in all of us is that we made mistakes that nearly sunk our business, yet we all got up and tried again. Paulo Coelho, author of *The Alchemist* said, "The secret of life, though, is to fall seven times and to get up eight times."[33] You can do this!

Focus on Growth
(15 minutes; lifetime practice)

Please answer the following questions in your journal:

- What are your expectations for making progress in your career, business, or finances? Do you expect your progress to be linear or do you envision many ups and downs on the road to success?
- Have you ever experienced Apex of the Mountain Syndrome (i.e., self-doubt prior to a major accomplishment)?
- Do you tend to frame major setbacks as a learning experience? What might be the value of developing a growth mindset in response to setbacks you may face in the future?

...

Transform into Your Best Self Through Resilience

Our challenges carve deep wisdom into our being. Moving through them with resilience can be transformative; we can shed former self-limitations and unfold into our greatest self, a self that is a more evolved, conscious, and prosperous being.

In my work with clients, I have noticed that overcoming challenges with resilience has brought them the following blessings:[34]

- Greater self-compassion and empathy for others; less judgment
- Increased awareness and perspective of the value of life, what is important, and how we are all interconnected
- Higher self-worth, self-confidence, and self-esteem
- Greater confidence in handling challenges life throws at them
- Less worrying about the little things and accepting what is out of their control
- Motivation to apply what they've learned to help and support others
- Building character
- Realizing their true strength
- Finding and relating to friends who have had similar experiences of adversity and expanding their social network

During my final sessions with clients, I reflect to them all the positive change and growth I see in them and how they are forever transformed. It is a bittersweet honoring of the tremendous and powerful work they did in therapy and an ending of our work together.

Imagine how the world might be different if we all worked to become more resilient. There would be a ripple effect of healing and positive change in the world. Thank you for your dedication to becoming your best and most prosperous self.

The following tips will help you stay motivated on your journey:

- **Don't compare your progress to others along the way.** Recognize that everyone has different blessings and challenges, so your road to success might look different than other peoples. Avoid creating performance goals that involve comparing your performance to others,

as that can decrease motivation.[35] Put on your blinders and measure your progress against yourself only.
- **Have faith in a positive outcome.** Keep your eye on the prize and maintain hope in achieving your goals. Trust in the process.
- **Appreciate the power of divine timing.**[36] Divine timing is the belief that there is a universal plan and that all events happen as they should. While success happens when it is supposed to, failure is simply delayed success.

Practice Affirmations for Resilience[37]
(10 minutes; lifetime practice)

Practice some affirmations to continue to foster resilience:

- I made it through challenges in the past and I trust that I will again.
- I am bendable and flexible like a reed in the wind. (This is my husband's favorite affirmation, which he created!)
- I am open and adaptable.
- I am growing, evolving, and thriving.
- I will persevere and prosper.
- I claim my personal power and refuse to give it away to others.
- I share my talents and gifts openly and brightly. I refuse to make myself small or less-than for the sake of not threatening others.
- I shine the unique light of my spirit with brilliance and magnificence.
- I use my voice to speak honestly and directly for my mind, my heart, and my gut.
- Because I love myself, I regularly ask for what I want, need, hope, desire, and dream.
- I trust that I will survive and manage all that comes and refuse to succumb to the fear of rejection or failure.
- I express love openly and freely with awesome vulnerability and joy.

- I set healthy boundaries personally and professionally and say no as needed.
- I actively seek work, hobbies, and relationships that are meaningful to me and nurturing to my soul, and free myself from commitments that bind my spirit.
- I welcome new experiences, relationships, and opportunities that will expand my comfort zone.
- I practice self-compassion and self-acceptance and lovingly melt away any shame, embarrassment, or insecurity to prevent me from being my highest and best self.
- I free myself from the powers of fear and doubt. I choose love, faith, and courage as my guides.

...

The Resilience Wheel brings together all the skills you learned in this chapter to assess your increased resilience.

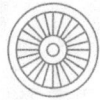

The Resilience Wheel
(20 minutes)

Date: _____

Rate your response after each question using a number from the following scale:

Poor (1–3), Fair (4–5), Good (6–7), Prosperous (8–10)

Poor			Fair		Good			Prosperous	
1	2	3	4	5	6	7	8	9	10

Challenges as Opportunities: How well are you able to look at the upsides and blessings that come with adversity? _____

Trust the Process: How well are you doing with maintaining faith in a positive outcome while navigating challenges and inevitable delays throughout the process? _____

Adaptable: How well are you able to internally adjust to any new conditions in your life or work so you can continue to thrive? _____

Flexible: How open-minded and willing to compromise with others are you while on the road to success? Are you willing to make necessary changes to your initial plan without giving up? _____

Strength: How strong do you feel in mind, body, and spirit? How much grit do you possess? _____

Motivation: How driven and determined are you in your mission to achieve your goals? _____

Growth Mindset: How well do you frame setbacks and failures as normal aspects of growth? _____

Financial Resilience: How well have you done at creating an emergency fund and diversifying investments and personal and social capital so you can move through financial challenges and continue to thrive? _____

Avoid Comparing: How well do you avoid comparing yourself to others as you pursue your goals? _____

Bounce Back: How easily do you typically return to your usual functioning after a challenging event or experience? How well do you get back up after setbacks such as a job loss, a breakup, an illness, or other life challenge? _____

Persevere: Perseverance is the determination to stick to something and stay on course in spite of obstacles. How likely are you to continue to strive to achieve your goals despite difficulties or delays? _____

Transform: How good are you at using your resilience to create personal, professional, and financial growth and evolution in your life? _____

Chart your responses on The Resilience Wheel. (For a refresher on how to do this, see The Wheel Exercise Tutorial on page 11.) Let's start at the top: Are you Poor, Prosperous, or somewhere in between when it comes to viewing Challenges as Opportunities? Put a dot on the spoke next to the number that corresponds with your answer. Now continue going around the wheel, and after scoring yourself on every spoke, connect the dots to create a circle.

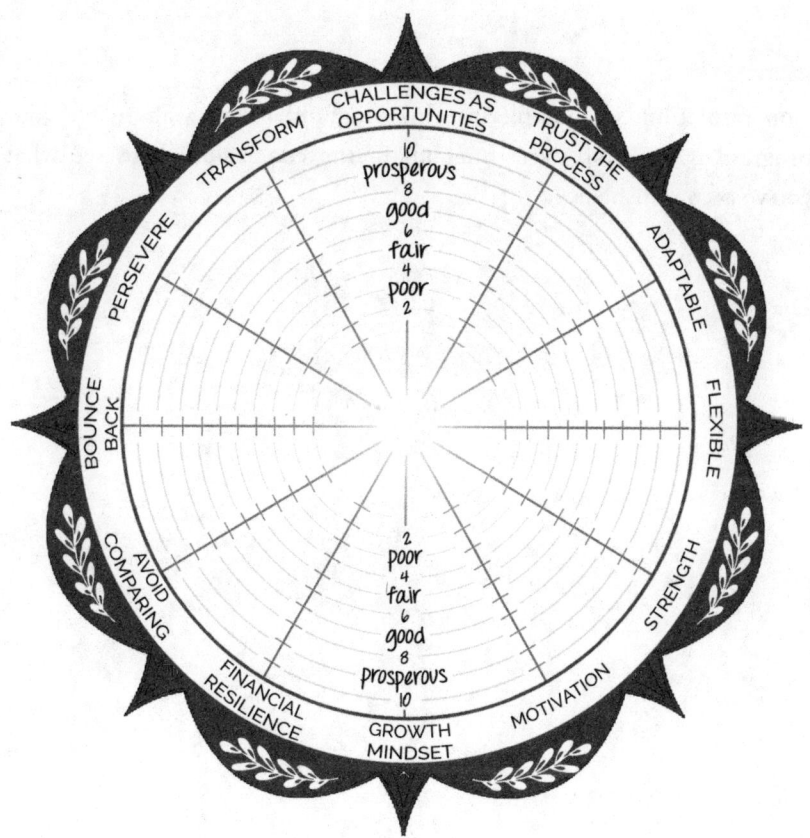

The Resilience Wheel

In your journal, answer the following questions:

- Look at the dents in your wheel—in which three areas do you need the most improvement when it comes to resilience?
- How have you improved your resilience since you started this program?
- In what ways do you plan to continue to foster resilience in your life?

Date your wheel and file it for later reference. Consider revisiting this exercise monthly or quarterly to keep building your resilience. Soon you will be a resilience rock star!

...

Congratulations on completing this program! I can't wait to see your progress as we wrap everything up in the conclusion. Let's see what you've accomplished!

Conclusion

FINANCIAL MINDSET WISDOM

Bringing It All Together for Complete Prosperity

For me, becoming isn't about arriving somewhere or achieving a certain aim. I see it instead as forward motion, a means of evolving, a way to reach continuously toward a better self. The journey doesn't end.
MICHELLE OBAMA lawyer, author, and former First Lady
quoting her *New York Times* bestselling memoir, *Becoming*

Congratulations for making this commitment to your financial mindset. By working through this program, you've got everything you need to be successful in work and life. What have you learned? Are you walking the walk as well as talking the talk? It's time to see how far you've come!

The Mindset Fix Wheel
(20 minutes)

Date: _____

Rate your response after each question using a number from the following scale:

Poor (1–3), Fair (4–5), Good (6–7), Prosperous (8–10)

Poor			Fair		Good			Prosperous	
1	2	3	4	5	6	7	8	9	10

Consider each of the chapter's mindsets in this book as one small slice of The Mindset Fix Wheel:

Abundance: How successful have you been at shifting your thoughts of scarcity to abundance? _____

Awareness: How successful have you been at consciously breaking habit and thought patterns and choosing a more prosperous path? How are you doing with being aware of your mental health? How are you doing at breaking through defenses and denial? _____

Responsibility: How successful have you been at freeing yourself of resentment and anger by taking responsibility and granting forgiveness? _____

Presence: How good are you at giving yourself the present of presence to experience the riches only available in the here and now? _____

Essence: How connected do you feel with your inner light and highest self? _____

Self-Love: How good are you at practicing self-care, self-affirmation, and self-compassion? How well are you silencing your Inner Saboteur? _____

Vision: How successful have you been at recreating your life in new and magical ways by envisioning the streets paved with gold? _____

Support: How successful have you been at opening yourself up to receiving support, weeding out toxic relationships, and welcoming supportive people into your life to do more good in the world? _____

Compassion: How good have you been at opening your mind, encouraging others, and paying it forward with generosity? _____

Detachment: How good are you at detaching from drama and negativity and staying on course? _____

Positivity: How good have you been at spinning straw into gold by practicing gratitude in order to attract greater prosperity? _____

Resilience: How are you doing when it comes to resilience? Are you better able to bounce back from challenges and thrive? Are you transforming into your best self in the process? _____

Chart your responses on The Mindset Fix Wheel. (For a refresher on how to do this, see The Wheel Exercise Tutorial on page 11.) Start at the top: Are you Poor, Prosperous, or somewhere in between when it comes to Abundance? Put a dot on the spoke next to the number that corresponds with your answer. Now continue going around the wheel, and after scoring yourself on every spoke, connect the dots to create a circle.

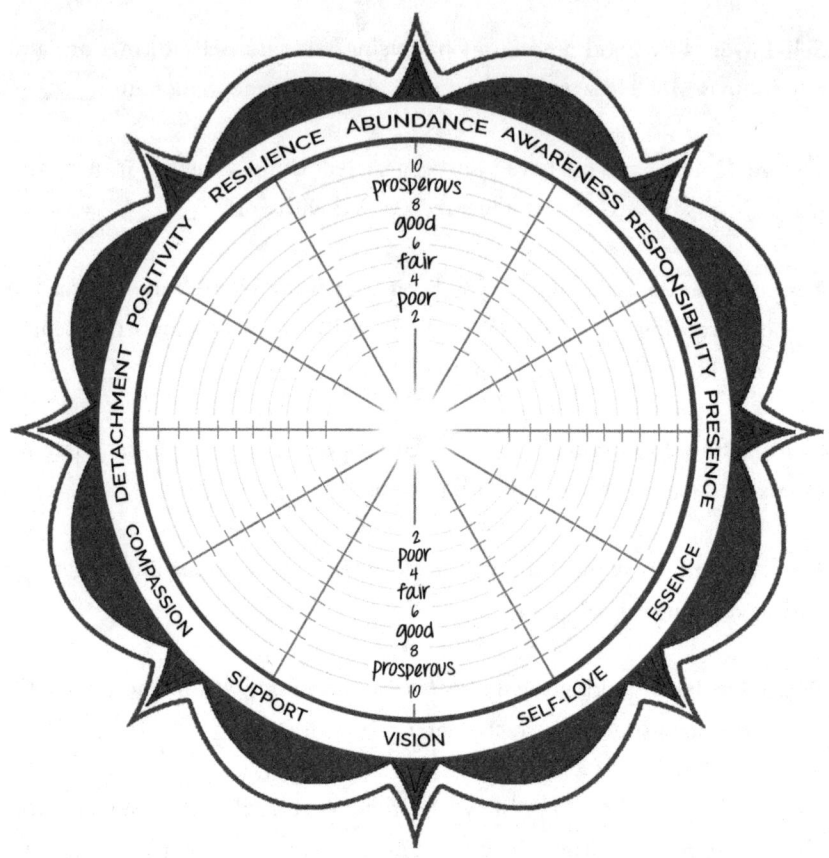

The Mindset Fix Wheel

Look at your wheel and think about how much you have improved in each area since starting this program. To keep yourself on track, consider completing this exercise once a quarter so you can live more consciously.

Your journey doesn't end here. A financial mindset fix is not a finite accomplishment, it is a way of living. As life throws you challenges, there will be dents in your wheel—that's okay and natural. You've got all the tools you need to keep working as you continue to strive for balance, wholeness, and greater prosperity. We are all works in progress striving toward greater mental and financial health.

In your journal, answer the following questions:

- Which three mindsets are the strongest for you and why? How can those strengths help bolster less strong areas?
- What are your lowest-scoring spokes (the biggest dents in your wheel)? Why do you think this is? What are you going to do to continue to build these mindsets?
- What would be most helpful to you while you continue to work through the program? Do you need an accountability partner or a small group to work through the program together?

...

Wherever you are in your journey, you are exactly where you are supposed to be right now. Remember when I told you how my clients who were working on their mental health were surprised at how their bank accounts improved as well? I suspect the same is true for you. Let's see how this program has improved your financial health.

At the beginning of this program, you completed your Financial Health Wheel; pull it out for reference. Each spoke of The Financial Health Wheel applies to a spoke in each of the chapter's wheels. To refresh your memory, I've included the chapter in which you worked on this skill. Let's look at how your financial health has improved since you started working through the program.

The Financial Health Wheel
(20 minutes)

Date: _____

Rate your response after each question using a number from the following scale:

Poor (1–3), Fair (4–5), Good (6–7), Prosperous (8–10)

Poor			Fair		Good			Prosperous	
1	2	3	4	5	6	7	8	9	10

Own Your Worth: How deserving do you feel of achieving greater financial prosperity? (Abundance) _____

Budget: How aware are you of your spending versus your budget? How successful are you at avoiding financial denial? (Awareness) _____

Timely Bill Pay: How good are you at taking responsibility for organizing and paying your bills on time? (Responsibility) _____

Spend Within Means: How mindful are you of your spending habits and spending within your limits so that you do not accrue debt? (Presence) _____

Know Your Net Worth: How aware are you of your approximate net worth at any given time? Net worth is the calculation of all your assets (bank account balances, value investments, property, etc.) minus your liabilities (credit card balances, loans, mortgages, etc.). (Essence, Not Ego) _____

Treat Yourself: How good are you treating yourself within your means? Just like a healthy diet allows for the occasional cheat day (which actually keeps you satisfied and sticking to the overall plan), it's okay to treat yourself. (Self-Love) _____

Financial Planning: How are you doing with planning for your financial health, including paying off student loans or credit card debt and saving to buy a home, kids' college, or retirement? (Vision) _____

Financial Advisor Check-Ins: How are you doing with making an appointment with your financial advisor once or twice a year to keep you on track? (Support) _____

Charity: How are you doing when it comes to supporting causes that are meaningful to you in a doable way? If your finances are tight, are you giving in other ways such as volunteering your time, donating unneeded items, or promoting awareness of these causes through social media or other formats? (Compassion) _____

Negotiate: How good are you at negotiating better pay or benefits, major purchases, or bartering services to get deals? (Positivity) _____

Risk Tolerance: How close are you to having the proper amount of insurance for your health, car, house or apartment, business, and even your life? (Detachment) _____

Save & Invest: How close are you to having three to six months of emergency savings and are you investing money for your future? Remember, having savings allows you to persevere through unexpected challenges, such as a job loss. (Resilience) _____

Chart your responses on The Financial Health Wheel. (For a refresher on how to do this, see The Wheel Exercise Tutorial on page 11.) Start at the top: Are you Poor, Prosperous, or somewhere in between when it comes to being able to Own Your Worth? Put a dot on the spoke next to the number that corresponds with your answer. Now continue going around the wheel, and after scoring yourself on every spoke, connect the dots to create a circle.

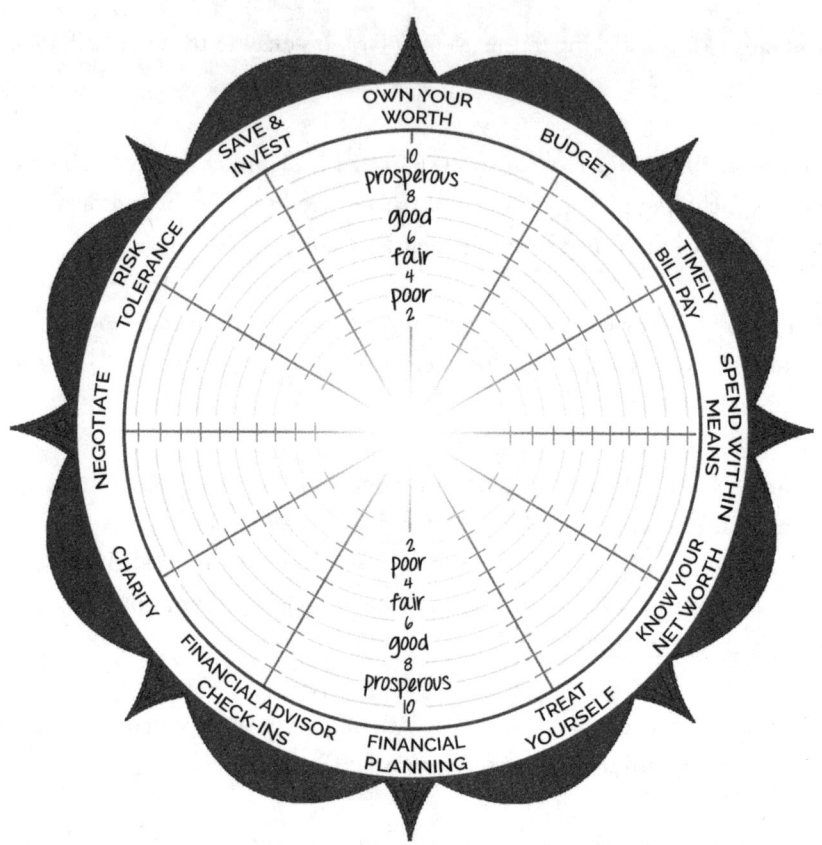

The Financial Health Wheel

Compare The Financial Health Wheel you completed at the beginning of the program to see your progress. Write your responses to the following questions in your journal:

- In which three areas did you most improve? How does that feel?
- What would you like to do to build on or celebrate this improvement?
- Which three areas need ongoing attention (the biggest dents in the wheel)?
- What is your action plan for continued improvement?

Date your wheel and file it for later reference as you witness how your financial mindset continues to increase your financial health. Congratulations! You have now completed your final activity in this program!

...

Keep working on The Financial Health Wheel, developing, evolving, and expanding yourself into the abundant flow of life, love, and prosperity. You are now well equipped to handle anything life throws at you because you have all these tools to prosper while maintaining work-life balance and personal well-being. I encourage you to share your progress with others and invite them to join The Financial Mindset Fix program. By continuing to work on ourselves, we can leave the world better for the generations to come.

Success is to live life openly, authentically, and lovingly in alignment with the highest good of self and others and to the highest extent possible. This is my wish for you. May our minds be conscious, our hearts be open, and our spirits dance with joy as we thrive and prosper together!

ACKNOWLEDGMENTS

Eternal thanks to Joy Tutela, my literary agent, for your belief in me and my work, your wisdom, guidance, and advocacy in making my dream of this book come to fruition. This would never have happened without you. I thank you for your diligence, kindness, and patience from the bottom of my heart.

Many thanks to the dream team at Sounds True, including Jennifer Brown, Gretel Hakanson, and Leslie Brown, that made this book the best it could be. Your expert counsel and input has been invaluable and so appreciated. It has been a true pleasure working with you.

Never-ending gratitude to Corrine Casanova of Daily House, my developmental editor. You are a true book whisperer and helped pull this book out of me from the early stages of its proposal. You have been a writing coach, cheerleader, and honorary therapist to me as a first-time author. I've so appreciated your gifts of providing clarity and structure to what was a pretty abstract group of thoughts not so long ago. Your positivity, confidence, and easy-breezy personality has made you an absolute delight to work with and made this process both manageable and enjoyable. I have great respect and admiration for you.

A huge shout out to Simon Golden, PhD, my researcher and content consultant—you have been enormously instrumental in making this book better than I could have ever hoped by sharing your invaluable feedback and suggestions. You are one of the most intelligent, kind, and reliable professionals I know. I believe in synchronicity and a spiritual web of people and am so grateful to your aunt, Gail Golden, PhD, for introducing us.

Many thanks to Alexis Neumann for your beautiful illustrations and all your creativity, flexibility, and patience during the design process. Thank you to Julie Holton of mConnexions for your branding consultation and endless support in my marketing endeavors. You are both talented, kind professionals who have put your heart and soul in your work with me. Thank you.

Thank you to others who have contributed along the way, especially developmental editor Cindy Tschosik, who helped make the book proposal material more digestible. I truly believe you helped me land the book deal of my dreams with Sounds True. I so appreciate you, your humor, and passion as a mental health advocate.

I sincerely thank the reviewers of this manuscript for your honest and insightful feedback that helped to strengthen this book, especially Farah Hussain Baig, LCSW; Leslie Baker Kimmons, PhD; Lisa Lackey, LCPC, CSAT; Dr. Michele Kerulis, LCPC; Ann Petrus Baker, BSN, MPH, WHE; Laura Tanner, MA; Laura Connor, LPC; Bill Laipple, CFP; and Helen McKean, MSN, RN. I selected you for your wisdom and am honored and grateful for your friendship, time, and input.

Deep heartfelt thanks to Staci Page Oien, CST, my integrated healer and coach; there really are no words to describe the profound ways you've nurtured my mind, body, and soul. You have coached me through my healing and throughout the development of this book, which I believe is a large part of my soul's purpose. I love you and thank God for you.

Infinite thanks to the leadership team, staff, consultants, and clients for making Urban Balance successful, especially Shelly Vanover; Alison Thayer, LCPC, CEAP; Luann Toy; John Vanover; Andria Emerick Brown; Alyssa Yeo Jones, LPC; Leslie Holley, LCPC; Taejah Vemuri, LPC, MPH; Bridget Levy, LCPC; and many, many more. Many thanks to Tim Kenny, CPA; Mike Adhikari, MBA, CMAA; and Steve Gold and the team at Refresh Mental Health. My career would not be what it is without you.

I have much appreciation for my mentors and consultants, including Mark Samuelson, LCSW; Bill Heffernan, LCPC; Lisa Faremouth Weber, E-YRT; Kathryn Janicek; Nancy Vogl; Dr. Sandy Kakacek, LCPC; and more for believing in me and supporting me in becoming better as a therapist, speaker, and professional. You changed the trajectory of my life and inspired me to mentor and support others. Thank you.

Heartfelt thanks to Arlene Englander, LCSW, my therapist for many years. I credit you and have deep gratitude for the powerful healing and positive change you created within me. None of the radical transformations that have taken place in my life over the past ten years would have happened if it weren't for our work together.

I have much love and appreciation for my siblings, Teresa Costantini Levin (and her husband, Steve Levin), Paula Belanger (and her husband, Leo Belanger), and Robert Brinkman for all your love, encouragement, and support. T, you have always believed in me and supported me in becoming my best. I'm grateful for so many happy and fun times together as sister-friends. Paula, you've always served as a mentor in everything from faith to motherhood, and I greatly value the depth of our connection and the three beautiful nieces (Lucia, Madelyn, and Rachel) you brought into my life. Rob, you are the epitome of work-life balance and showed me that it's possible. I love you all, and know Mom and Dad are proud of each of us in many different ways.

I have total love and appreciation for my dearest friend, Cherilynn Veland, LCSW. You have been my rock for over twenty years and make me laugh and feel supported. I treasure our friendship every single day. You are an enormous gift in my life.

Big hugs and thanks to all my strong women friends not yet mentioned, including Shelly Greco, Nicole Laipple, Charlotte Morris, Debi Ardern, Jennifer Jacque, Jennifer Froemel, Carrie Swearingen, and all my other mom friends, work friends, yoga friends, childhood friends, and more. You each inspire me.

All my love to my husband, Jason Marotzke, and our children. Jason, your gentle spirit has soothed my soul, and I love you to the moon and back. You are the best friend and partner anyone could ever ask for, and I so appreciate your wisdom, kindness, generosity, and strength. Celeste and Claudia, being your mom is my highest honor and greatest joy, and I thank God for you every single day. You are my lights and loves and I am blown away by your wide array of talents, hard work, humor, athleticism, and strength of character. My heart bursts with love and pride for you. Katelyn and Nicholas, having you as bonus children is one of the most amazing gifts. You are two of the most kind, gracious, grateful, funny, creative, and talented young people I know. I love you tons and tons. I absolutely love our family and am grateful for all the blessings we bring to one another. A big thanks to Jason's family, my in-laws, for welcoming my girls and me into your fun and close-knit family.

Last but certainly not least, to all my clients, supervisees, and students who gave me the profound privilege and honor to work with you. You have taught me a lifetime of lessons and made my life a rich tapestry of experiences. I thank you for causing me to grow and inspiring me to write what I learned from you in this book, with the intent of helping many others. Thank you.

Namaste,

Joyce

NOTES

INTRODUCTION: WAKE UP! YOU DESERVE A GREATER LIFE
1. Suze Orman, *Women & Money: Owning the Power to Control Your Destiny* (New York: Spiegel & Grau, 2010), 16.
2. Pierre-Carl Michaud and Arthur van Soest, "Health and Wealth of Elderly Couples: Causality Tests Using Dynamic Panel Data Models," *Journal of Health Economics* 27, no. 5 (September 2008): 1312–1325, doi.org/10.1016/j.jhealeco.2008.04.002.
3. Dave Ramsey, *The Total Money Makeover: A Proven Plan for Financial Fitness* (Nashville, TN: Thomas Nelson, 2009).
4. "What is Stress?" American Institute of Stress, last modified December 18, 2019, stress.org/daily-life.
5. "Key Substance Use and Mental Health Indicators in the United States: Results from the 2018 National Survey on Drug Use and Health," Substance Abuse and Mental Health Services Administration, August 2019, samhsa.gov/data/sites/default/files/cbhsq-reports/NSDUHNationalFindingsReport2018/NSDUHNationalFindingsReport2018.pdf.
6. "5 Surprising Mental Health Statistics," Mental Health First Aid, last modified February 6, 2019, mentalhealthfirstaid.org/2019/02/5-surprising-mental-health-statistics.
7. "Our Mission," Hope for the Day, accessed January 5, 2020, hftd.org/about-hftd.
8. "Mental Health by the Numbers," NAMI: National Alliance on Mental Illness, accessed January 5, 2020, nami.org/learn-more/mental-health-by-the-numbers.
9. "Mental Health by the Numbers" Philip S. Wang et al., "Delays in Initial Treatment Contact After First Onset of a Mental Disorder," *Health Services Research* 39, no. 2 (April 2004): 393–416.
10. "Projected Deaths of Despair from COVID-19," Well Being Trust, May 2020, wellbeingtrust.org/areas-of-focus/policy-and-advocacy/reports/projected-deaths-of-despair-during-covid-19.
11. Mark É. Czeisler et al., "Mental Health, Substance Use, and Suicidal Ideation During the COVID-19 Pandemic—United States, June 24–30, 2020," *Morbidity and Mortality Weekly Report* 69, no. 32 (August 2020): 1049–1057, dx.doi.org/10.15585/mmwr.mm6932a1.
12. Selcuk Özdin and Sükriye Bayrak Özdin, "Levels and Predictors of Anxiety, Depression and Health Anxiety During COVID-19 Pandemic in Turkish Society: The Importance of Gender," *International Journal of Social Psychiatry* (May 2020): 1-8, doi.org/10.1177/0020764020927051.

13. Feten Fekih-Romdhane et al., "Prevalence and Predictors of PTSD During the COVID-19 Pandemic: Findings from a Tunisian Community Sample," *Psychiatry Research* 29 (August 2020): 113131, doi.org/10.1016/j.psychres.2020.113131.
14. Prestia Davide et al., "The Impact of the COVID-19 Pandemic on Patients with OCD: Effects of Contamination Symptoms and Remission State Before the Quarantine in a Preliminary Naturalistic Study," *Psychiatry Research* 291 (September 2020): 113213, doi.org/10.1016/j.psychres.2020.113213.
15. "Impact of the COVID-19 Pandemic on Family Planning and Ending Gender-Based Violence, Female Genital Mutilation and Child Marriage," UNFPA, April 2020, unfpa.org/sites/default/files/resource-pdf/COVID-19_impact_brief_for_UNFPA_24_April_2020_1.pdf.
16. Louise Brådvik, "Suicide Risk and Mental Disorders," *International Journal of Environmental Research and Public Health* 15, no. 9 (September 2018): 10.3390, doi.org/10.3390/ijerph15092028.

CHAPTER 1: ABUNDANCE

1. Amy Morin, "5 Things That Shouldn't Determine Your Self-Worth (but Probably Do)," Inc., February 6, 2020, inc.com/amy-morin/how-do-you-measure-your-self-worth.html.
2. Michelle Obama, *Becoming* (New York: Crown, 2018).
3. Yilmaz Akgunduz, "The Influence of Self-Esteem and Role Stress on Job Performance in Hotel Businesses," *International Journal of Contemporary Hospitality Management* 27, no. 6 (October 2015): 1082–1099, doi.org/10.1108/ijchm-09-2013-0421.
4. Bryant McGill, *Simple Reminders: Inspiration for Living Your Best Life* (self-pub., 2018).
5. Sara Kafashan et al., "Prosocial Behavior and Social Status," *The Psychology of Social Status*, ed. Joey T. Cheng and Jessica L. Tracy (New York: Springer, 2014), 139–158.
6. Audrey Freshman, "Financial Disaster as a Risk Factor for Posttraumatic Stress Disorder: Internet Survey of Trauma in Victims of the Madoff Ponzi Scheme," *Health & Social Work* 37, no. 1 (February 2012): 39–48, doi.org/10.1093/hsw/hls002.
7. Anthony Canale and Bradley Klontz, "Hoarding Disorder: It's More Than Just an Obsession—Implications for Financial Therapists and Planners," *Journal of Financial Therapy* 4, no. 2 (December 2013): 42–63, doi.org/10.4148/1944-9771.1053.
8. Katalin Takacs Haynes, Matthew Josefy, and Michael A. Hitt, "Tipping Point: Managers' Self-Interest, Greed, and Altruism," *Journal of Leadership & Organizational Studies* 22, no. 3 (May 2015): 265–279, doi.org/10.1177/1548051815585171.
9. Mahatma K. Gandhi, *Ethical Religion* (Madras: S. Ganesan, 1922), 61.
10. Chris Gardner, *The Pursuit of Happyness* (New York: Amistad, 2006).

CHAPTER 2: AWARENESS

1. Tanya Ghahremani, "Will Smith Feels That He Is, at Heart, a Physicist," Complex, June 1, 2018, complex.com/pop-culture/2013/05/will-smith-feels-that-he-is-at-heart-a-physicist.
2. R. Skip Johnson, "Escaping Conflict and the Karpman Drama Triangle," Borderline Personality Disorder, last modified January 4, 2018, bpdfamily.com/content/karpman-drama-triangle.
3. Marguerite Ohrtman and Erika Heitner, "Part IV: Family Systems Theory," *Contemporary Case Studies in School Counseling* (Lanham, MD: Rowman & Littlefield, 2019), 115–142.
4. Jill Zimmerman and Larry Cochran, "Alignment of Family and Work Roles," *Career Development Quarterly* 41, no. 4 (June 1993): 344–349, doi.org/10.1002/j.2161-0045.1993.tb00408.x.
5. Rebecca Allison Peeler, "Perceptions of Professional and Financial Worth Among Master of Social Work Students" (master's thesis, University of Texas at Arlington, 2015), rc.library.uta.edu/uta-ir/bitstream/handle/10106/25363/Peeler_uta_2502M_13289.pdf?sequence=1&isAllowed=y.
6. Brennan Manning, *All Is Grace: A Ragamuffin Memoir* (Colorado Springs, CO: David C. Cook, 2015), 30.
7. Kendra Cherry, "20 Common Defense Mechanisms Used for Anxiety," VeryWell Mind, last modified July 18, 2019, verywellmind.com/defense-mechanisms-2795960.
8. "Addiction Statistics," Drug & Substance Abuse Statistics, last modified January 2, 2020, americanaddictioncenters.org/rehab-guide/addiction-statistics.
9. Nerissa L. Soh et al., "Nutrition, Mood and Behaviour: A Review," *Acta Neuropsychiatrica* 21, no. 5 (October 2009): 214–227, doi.org/10.1111/j.1601-5215.2009.00413.x; Michael Berk, "Should We Be Targeting Exercise as a Routine Mental Health Intervention?" *Acta Neuropsychiatrica* 19, no. 3 (June 2017): 217–218, doi.org/10.1111/j.1601-5215.2007.00201.x.
10. "Know the Warning Signs," NAMI: National Alliance on Mental Illness, nami.org/About-Mental-Illness/Warning-Signs-and-Symptoms; "Common Warning Signs of Mental Illness," NAMI: National Alliance on Mental Illness, accessed January 7, 2020, nami.org/NAMI/media/NAMI-Media/Infographics/NAMI-Warning-Signs-FINAL.pdf.
11. "The Ripple Effect of Mental Illness," NAMI: National Alliance on Mental Illness, accessed January 7, 2020, nami.org/NAMI/media/NAMI-Media/Infographics/NAMI-Impact-Ripple-Effect-FINAL.pdf.
12. "Find a Therapist, Psychologist, Counselor," Psychology Today, accessed August 2, 2020, psychologytoday.com/us/therapists.
13. "Daylio: Journal, Diary, and Mood Tracker," Daylio, accessed August 2, 2020, daylio.net.

14. "Self Tests," Psychology Today, accessed August 2, 2020, psychologytoday.com/us/tests; "Psychological Quizzes and Tests," Psych Central, last modified May 6, 2020, psychcentral.com/quizzes.
15. Jeremy Vohwinkle, "How to Make a Budget in 6 Easy Steps," The Balance, last modified March 6, 2020, thebalance.com/how-to-make-a-budget-1289587.
16. Candice Elliott, "What the Ideal Fiscally Responsible Person Looks Like," Listen Money Matters, last modified March 22, 2020, listenmoneymatters.com/fiscally-responsible.
17. "Definition of Addiction," American Society of Addiction Medicine, accessed October 15, 2020, asam.org/Quality-Science/definition-of-addiction.

CHAPTER 3: RESPONSIBILITY

1. Daniel L. Kirsch, "Burnout Is Now an Official Medical Condition," American Institute of Stress, date modified May 29, 2019, stress.org/burnout-is-now-an-official-medical-condition.
2. Michael Korda, *Making the List: A Cultural History of the American Bestseller 1900–1999* (New York: Barnes & Noble, 2001).
3. Donald G. Gardner and Jon L. Pierce, "The Core Self-Evaluation Scale" *Educational and Psychological Measurement* 70, no. 2 (August 2009): 291–304, doi.org/10.1177/0013164409344505.
4. Gardner and Pierce, "Core Self-Evaluation Scale," Ali Zadeh Mohammadi, Alireza Abedi, and Fereshteh Moradi Panah, "Group Narrative Therapy Effect on Self-Esteem and Self-Efficacy of Male Orphan Adolescents," *Practice in Clinical Psychology* 1, no. 1 (January 2013): 55–60, jpcp.uswr.ac.ir/article-1-28-fa.html.
5. Priyanka Bagade, *When Life Makes You Hit a Pause Button* (New Delhi: Educreation Publishing, 2018).
6. David Rakel, *Integrative Medicine*, 4th ed. (Philadelphia: Elsevier, 2018).
7. Manfred F. R. Kets de Vries, "Are You a Victim of the Victim Syndrome," *Organizational Dynamics* 43, no. 2 (June 2014): 130–137, doi.org/10.1057/9781137382337_4.
8. Carrie Fisher, *Wishful Drinking* (New York: Simon & Schuster, 2008).
9. Gary D. Chapman and Jocelyn Green, *The 5 Love Languages: The Secret to Love That Lasts* (Chicago: Northfield Publishing, 2015), 45.
10. Laura E. Wagner-Moore, "Gestalt Therapy: Past, Present, Theory, and Research," *Psychotherapy: Theory, Research, Practice, Training* 41, no. 2 (June 2004): 180–189, doi.org/10.1037/0033-3204.41.2.180.
11. Ryan S. Bisel and Amber S. Messersmith, "Organizational and Supervisory Apology Effectiveness: Apology Giving in Work Settings," *Business Communication Quarterly* 75, no. 4 (December 2012): 425–448, doi.org/10.1177/1080569912461171; Caroline Bologna, "The Biggest Mistakes People Make When Apologizing," HuffPost,

last modified July 30, 2018, huffpost.com/entry/biggest-apology-mistakes_n_5b575e3ce4b0de86f4910f69.
12. Hannes Leroy, Michael E. Palanski, and Tony L. Simons, "Authentic Leadership and Behavioral Integrity as Drivers of Follower Commitment and Performance," *Journal of Business Ethics* 107, no. 3 (May 2012): 255–264, doi.org/10.1007/s10551-011-1036-1.
13. Madeline Farber, "Financial Literacy: Two-Thirds of Americans Can't Pass Basic Test," *Fortune*, June 27, 2019, fortune.com/2016/07/12/financial-literacy.
14. Mark Manson, "The Responsibility/Fault Fallacy," Mark Manson, last modified January 19, 2019, markmanson.net/responsibility-fault-fallacy.

CHAPTER 4: PRESENCE

1. "KonMari," accessed January 23, 2020, konmari.com.
2. Hiltraut M. Paridon and Marlen Kaufmann, "Multitasking in Work-Related Situations and Its Relevance for Occupational Health and Safety: Effects on Performance, Subjective Strain and Physiological Parameters," *Europe's Journal of Psychology* 6, no. 4 (November 2010): 110–124, doi.org/10.5964/ejop.v6i4.226.
3. Paul Ratner, "An Average Human Lifetime Described in Stunning Statistics," Big Think, last modified October 5, 2018, bigthink.com/paul-ratner/how-many-days-of-your-life-do-you-have-sex-your-lifetime-by-the-numbers.
4. Cherilynn M. Veland, *Stop Giving It Away: How to Stop Self-Sacrificing and Start Claiming Your Space, Power, and Happiness* (Berkeley, CA: She Writes Press, 2015).
5. Samuel Johnson, "No. 48. The Miseries of an Infirm Constitution," *The Rambler*, johnsonessays.com/the-rambler/miseries-infirm-constitution.
6. Jon Kabat-Zinn, "Mindfulness-Based Interventions in Context: Past, Present, and Future," *Clinical Psychology: Science and Practice* 10, no. 2 (June 2003): 144–156, doi.org/10.1093/clipsy.bpg016; Kirk Warren Brown, Richard M. Ryan, and David Creswell, "Mindfulness: Theoretical Foundations and Evidence for Its Salutary Effects," *Psychological Inquiry: An International Journal for the Advancement of Psychological Theory* 18, no. 4 (October 2007): 212, doi.org/10.1080/10478400701598298.
7. Darren J. Good et al., "Contemplating Mindfulness at Work: An Integrative Review," *Journal of Management* 42, no. 1 (January 2016): 114–142, doi.org/10.1177/0149206315617003.
8. Good, "Contemplating Mindfulness at Work," 114–142.
9. "NCHS Data Brief," Centers for Disease Control and Prevention, accessed February 13, 2020, cdc.gov/nchs/data/databriefs/db325-h.pdf.
10. Marissa Levin, "Why Google, Nike, and Apple Love Mindfulness Training, and How You Can Easily Love It Too," Inc., last modified June 21, 2018, inc.com/marissa-levin/why-google-nike-and-apple-love-mindfulness-training-and-how-you-can-easily-love-.html.

11. Lillian T. Eby, "Mindfulness-Based Training Interventions for Employees: A Qualitative Review of the Literature," *Human Resource Management Review* 29, no. 2 (June 2019): 156–178, doi.org/10.1016/j.hrmr.2017.03.004.
12. Tammy D. Allen, Lillian T. Eby, Kate M. Conley, and Rachel L. Williamson, "What Do We *Really* Know About the Effects of Mindfulness-Based Training in the Workplace?" *Industrial and Organizational Psychology* 8, no. 4 (December 2015): 652–661, doi.org/10.1017/iop.2015.95.
13. Good, "Contemplating Mindfulness at Work," 114–142; Amishi P. Jha et al., "Examining the Protective Effects of Mindfulness Training on Working Memory Capacity and Affective Experience," *Emotion* 10, no. 1 (February 2010): 54–64, doi.org/10.1037/a0018438; Nate Klemp, "5 Reasons Your Company Should Be Investing in Mindfulness Training," Inc., last modified October 27, 2019, inc.com/nate-klemp/5-reasons-your-company-should-be-investing-in-mindfulness-training.html; Saleh Bajaba et al., "Does Mindfulness Enhance the Beneficial Outcomes that Accrue to Employees with Proactive Personalities?" *Current Psychology* 40 (February 2021): 475-484, doi.org/10.1007/s12144-018-9995-3.
14. Eby, "Mindfulness-Based Training Interventions for Employees," 156–178.
15. Klemp, "5 Reasons Your Company Should Be Investing in Mindfulness Training."
16. Susan Philips, *Mother Teresa* (Gahanna, OH: Prodigy Books, 2017).
17. Matthew A. Killingsworth and Daniel T. Gilbert, "A Wandering Mind Is an Unhappy Mind," *Science* 330, no. 6006 (November 2010): 932, doi.org/10.1126/science.1192439.
18. Fadel K. Matta et al., "Significant Work Events and Counterproductive Work Behavior: The Role of Fairness, Emotions, and Emotion Regulation," *Journal of Organizational Behavior* 35, no. 7 (October 2014): 920–944, doi.org/10.1002/job.1934.
19. Killingsworth and Gilbert, "A Wandering Mind Is an Unhappy Mind."
20. Thomas E. Smith, Kristin V. Richards, and Victoria M. Shelton, "Mindfulness in Financial Literacy," *Journal of Human Behavior in the Social Environment* 26, no. 2 (February 2016): 154–161, dx.doi.org/10.1080/10911359.2015.1052914.
21. Philip A. Hensler, Antoinette Somers, and Sheri Perelli, "Mindfulness and Money Management: The Post-Crisis Behavior of Financial Advisors," *Academy of Management Proceedings* (Briarcliff Manor, NY: Academy of Management, 2013), 65–81.
22. Hensler, Sommers, and Perelli, "Mindfulness and Money Management."
23. Jean Chatzky, "How to Use Mindfulness to Manage Your Money Better," NBC, last modified January 19, 2018, nbcnews.com/better/business/how-use-mindfulness-manage-your-money-better-ncna839111.

CHAPTER 5: ESSENCE

1. Lachlan Brown, "Eckhart Tolle's Pain-Body: How to Deal with Anxiety and Depression," Hack Spirit, last modified October 10, 2019, hackspirit.com/eckhart-tolle-reveals-best-strategy-deal-anxiety-depression.
2. Elisabeth Kübler-Ross and David Kesler, *Life Lessons: Two Experts on Death and Dying*

Teach Us About the Mysteries of Life and Living (New York: Scribner, 2014), 118.

3. Roger Gabriel, "Is the Ego Your Friend or Foe?" The Chopra Center, last modified January 23, 2017, chopra.com/articles/is-the-ego-your-friend-or-foe.

4. Athena Staik, "Ego versus Ego-Strength: The Characteristics of a Healthy Ego and Why It's Essential to Your Happiness," Psych Central, last modified August 5, 2017, blogs.psychcentral.com/relationships/2012/01/ego-versus-ego-strength-the-characteristics-of-healthy-ego.

5. Eckhart Tolle, *A New Earth: Awakening to Your Life's Purpose* (New York: Plume, 2008), 86.

6. Ronald Alexander, "What Are the Limitations of Your Ego Mind?," Psychology Today, accessed February 3, 2020, psychologytoday.com/us/blog/the-wise-open-mind/201007/what-are-the-limitations-your-ego-mind.

7. Nicole M. Cain, Aaron L. Pincus, and Emily B. Ansell, "Narcissism at the Crossroads: Phenotypic Description of Pathological Narcissism Across Clinical Theory, Social/Personality Psychology, and Psychiatric Diagnosis," *Clinical Psychology Review* 28, no. 4 (April 2008): 638–656, doi.org/10.1016/j.cpr.2007.09.006.

8. Richard J. Harnish and K. Robert Bridges, "Compulsive Buying: The Role of Irrational Beliefs, Materialism, and Narcissism," *Journal of Rational-Emotive & Cognitive-Behavior Therapy* 33, no. 1 (March 2015): 1–16, doi.org/10.1007/s10942-014-0197-0.

9. Matthew J. Pearsall and Aleksander P. J. Ellis, "The Effects of Critical Team Member Assertiveness on Team Performance and Satisfaction," *Journal of Management* 32, no. 4 (August 2006): 575–594, doi.org/10.1177/0149206306289099.

10. Joshua D. Foster, Jessica W. Shenesey, and Joshua S. Goff, "Why do Narcissists Take More Risks? Testing the Roles of Perceived Risks and Benefits of Risky Behaviors," *Personality and Individual Differences* 47, no. 8 (December 2009): 885–889, doi.org/10.1016/j.paid.2009.07.008; Charles A. O'Reilly III, Bernadette Doerr, and Jennifer A. Chatman, "'See You in Court': How CEO Narcissism Increases Firms' Vulnerability to Lawsuits," *Leadership Quarterly* 29, no. 3 (June 2018): 365–378, doi.org/10.1016/j.leaqua.2017.08.001; Emily Grijalva and Daniel A. Newman, "Narcissism and Counterproductive Work Behavior (CWB): Meta-Analysis and Consideration of Collectivist Culture, Big Five Personality, and Narcissism's Facet Structure," *Applied Psychology: An International Review* 64, no. 1 (January 2015): 93–126, doi.org/10.1111/apps.12025.

11. Brené Brown, *Daring Greatly: How the Courage to Be Vulnerable Transforms the Way We Live, Love, Parent, and Lead* (New York: Avery, 2015).

12. Maya Angelou, *Rainbow in the Cloud: The Wisdom and Spirit of Maya Angelou* (Highland City, FL: Rainbow House, 2014), 84.

13. Kristin D. Neff and Susan Harter, "The Role of Power and Authenticity in Relationship Styles Emphasizing Autonomy, Connectedness, or Mutuality Among

Adult Couples," *Journal of Social and Personal Relationships* 19, no. 16 (December 2002): 835–857, doi.org/10.1177/0265407502196006; Ralph van den Bosch and Toon W. Taris, "The Authentic Worker's Well-Being and Performance: The Relationship Between Authenticity at Work, Well-Being, and Work Outcomes," *Journal of Psychology* 148, no. 6 (November 2014): 659–681, doi.org/10.1080/00223980.2013.820684; Carol A. Wong and Heather K. S. Laschinger, "Authentic Leadership, Performance, and Job Satisfaction: The Mediating Role of Empowerment," *Journal of Advanced Nursing* 69, no. 4 (April 2013): 947–959, doi.org/10.1111/j.1365-2648.2012.06089.x.

14. Holly M. Hutchins, "Outing the Imposter: A Study Exploring Imposter Phenomenon Among Higher Education Faculty," *New Horizons in Adult Education and Human Resource Development* 27, no. 2 (April 2015): 3–12, doi.org/10.1002/nha3.20098.

15. Gill Corkindale, "Overcoming Imposter Syndrome," Harvard Business Review, last modified December 2, 2019, hbr.org/2008/05/overcoming-imposter-syndrome.

16. Kori A. LaDonna, Shiphra Ginsburg, and Christopher Watling, "'Rising to the Level of Your Incompetence': What Physicians' Self-Assessment of Their Performance Reveals About the Imposter Syndrome in Medicine," *Academic Medicine* 93, no. 5 (May 2018): 763–768, doi.org/10.1097/ACM.0000000000002046; Hutchins, "Outing the Imposter," 3–12.

17. LaDonna, Ginsburg, and Watling, "'Rising to the Level of Your Incompetence,'" 763–768.

18. Elke Rohmann et al., "Grandiose and Vulnerable Narcissism: Self-Construal, Attachment, and Love in Romantic Relationships," *European Psychologist* 17, no. 4 (2012): 279–290, doi.org/10.1027/1016-9040/a000100; Shohreh Ghorbanshirodi, "The Relationship Between Self-Esteem and Emotional Intelligence with Imposter Syndrome Among Medical Students of Guilan and Heratsi Universities," *Journal of Basic and Applied Scientific Research* 2, no. 2 (2012).

19. Hutchins, "Outing the Imposter," 3–12.

20. Corkindale, "Overcoming Imposter Syndrome."

21. Simon B. Sherry et al., "Perfectionism Dimensions and Research Productivity in Psychology Professors: Implications for Understanding the (Mal)Adaptiveness of Perfectionism," *Canadian Journal of Behavioural Science* 42, no. 4 (October 2010): 273–283, doi.org/10.1037/a0020466; Dianna T. Kenny, Pamela Davis, and Jenni Oates, "Music Performance Anxiety and Occupational Stress Amongst Opera Chorus Artists and Their Relationship with State and Trait Anxiety and Perfectionism," *Journal of Anxiety Disorders* 18, no. 6 (January 2004): 757–777, doi.org/10.1016/j.janxdis.2003.09.004.

22. Sandra Sassaroli et al., "Perfectionism in Depression, Obsessive-Compulsive Disorder and Eating Disorders," *Behaviour Research and Therapy* 46, no. 6 (June 2008): 757–765, doi.org/10.1016/j.brat.2008.02.007; Malissa A. Clark, Ariel M. Lelchook, and Marcie L. Taylor, "Beyond the Big Five: How Narcissism, Perfectionism, and

Dispositional Affect Relate to Workaholism," *Personality and Individual Differences* 48, no. 7 (May 2010): 786–791, doi.org/10.1016/j.paid.2010.01.013; Jesse M. Crosby, Scott C. Bates, and Michael P. Twohig, "Examination of the Relationship Between Perfectionism and Religiosity as Mediated by Psychological Inflexibility," *Current Psychology* 30, no. 2 (June 2011): 117–129, doi.org/10.1007/s12144-011-9104-3; Sarah J. Egan et al., "The Role of Dichotomous Thinking and Rigidity in Perfectionism," *Behaviour Research and Therapy* 45, no. 8 (August 2007): 1813–1822, doi.org/10.1016/j.brat.2007.02.002.
23. Martin M. Smith et al., "Perfectionism and Narcissism: A Meta-Analytic Review," *Journal of Research in Personality* 64 (October 2016): 90–101, doi.org/10.1016/j.jrp.2016.07.012.
24. Smith, "Perfectionism and Narcissism," 90–101.

CHAPTER 6: SELF-LOVE

1. Darlene Lancer, "How Do Self-Love, Self-Esteem, Self-Acceptance Differ," Darlene Lancer, last modified December 9, 2019, whatiscodependency.com/difference-between-selfesteem-selfacceptance-self-love-self-compassion.
2. Abraham Maslow, "A Theory of Human Motivation," *Psychological Review* 50, no. 4 (1943): 370–396.
3. Robert Holden, *Happiness NOW!* (Carlsbad, CA: Hay House, 2011), 72.
4. Natalie Sachs-Ericsson et al., "Parental Verbal Abuse and the Mediating Role of Self-Criticism in Adult Internalizing Disorders," *Journal of Affective Disorders* 93, no. 1–3 (July 2006): 71–78, doi.org/10.1016/j.jad.2006.02.014.
5. Mara Cadinu et al., "Why Do Women Underperform Under Stereotype Threat?" *Psychological Science* 16, no. 7 (July 2005): 572–578, doi.org/10.1111/j.0956-7976.2005.01577.x.
6. Annakeara Stinson, "How to Have More Self-Confidence, Even When You're Feeling Down, According to Experts," Bustle, last modified July 16, 2019, bustle.com/p/how-to-have-more-self-confidence-even-when-youre-feeling-down-according-to-experts-18200024; Annakeara Stinson, "How Do You Stop Negative Thoughts? I Gave My Inner Voice a Name & Learned a Lot About My Thinking Patterns," Bustle, last modified August 18, 2019, bustle.com/p/how-do-you-stop-negative-thoughts-i-gave-my-inner-voice-a-name-learned-a-lot-about-my-thinking-patterns-18557463.
7. Stinson, "How Do You Stop Negative Thoughts?"
8. Andy Martens et al., "Combating Stereotype Threat: The Effect of Self-Affirmation on Women's Intellectual Performance," *Journal of Experimental Social Psychology* 42, no. 2 (March 2006): 236–243, doi.org/10.1016/j.jesp.2005.04.010.
9. Travor C. Brown and Gary P. Latham, "The Effect of Training in Verbal Self-Guidance on Performance Effectiveness in a MBA Program," *Canadian Journal of Behavioural Science* 38, no. 1 (January 2006): 1–11, doi.org/10.1037/h0087266.

10. Abira Reizer, "Bringing Self-Kindness Into the Workplace: Exploring the Mediating Role of Self-Compassion in the Associations Between Attachment and Organizational Outcomes," *Frontiers in Psychology* 10 (2019): 1–13, doi.org/10.3389/fpsyg.2019.01148.
11. Reizer, "Bringing Self-Kindness Into the Workplace," 1–13.
12. Lisa M. Yarnell and Kristin D. Neff, "Self-Compassion, Interpersonal Conflict Resolutions, and Well-Being," *Self and Identity* 12, no. 2 (March 2013): 146–159, doi.org/10.1080/15298868.2011.649545; Kristin D. Neff and Natasha Beretvas, "The Role of Self-Compassion in Romantic Relationships," *Self and Identity* 12, no. 1 (January 2013): 78–98, doi.org/10.1080/15298868.2011.639548; Deborah Grice Conway, "The Role of Internal Resources in Academic Achievement: Exploring the Meaning of Self-Compassion in the Adaptive Functioning of Low-Income College Students" (PhD diss., University of Pittsburgh, 2007), 1–112; Lisa K. Jennings and P. Philip Tan, "Self-Compassion and Life Satisfaction in Gay Men," *Psychological Reports: Relationships & Communications* 115, no. 3 (December 2014): 888–895, doi.org/10.2466/21.07.PR0.115c33z3.
13. S. M. Farrington, "Psychological Well-Being and Perceived Financial Performance: An SME Perspective," *South African Journal of Business Management* 48, no. 4 (December 2017): 47–56.
14. Farrington, "Psychological Well-Being and Perceived Financial Performance," 47–56.
15. George A. Kaplan, Sarah J. Shema, and Maria Claudia A. Leite, "Socioeconomic Determinants of Psychological Well-Being: The Role of Income, Income Change, and Income Sources Over 29 Years," *Annals of Epidemiology* 18, no. 7 (July 2009): 531–537, doi.org/10.1016/j.annepidem.2008.03.006.
16. Zhou Jiang et al., "Open Workplace Climate and LGB Employees' Psychological Experiences: The Roles of Self-Concealment and Self-Acceptance," *Journal of Employment Counseling* 56, no. 1 (March 2019): 2–19, doi.org/10.1002/joec.12099.
17. Rebecca Thompson Lindsey, "The Relation of Nutrition, Exercise, and Self-Efficacy to Job Performance" (PhD diss., Grand Canyon University, 2018), 1–162.
18. Christopher M. Barnes, "Working in Our Sleep: Sleep and Self-Regulation in Organizations," *Organizational Psychology Review* 2, no. 3 (August 2012): 1–24, doi.org/10.1177/2041386612450181.
19. Barry M. Popkin, Kristen E. D'Anci, and Irwin H. Rosenberg, "Water, Hydration, and Health," *Nutrition Reviews* 68, no. 8 (August 2010): 439–458, doi.org/10.1111/j.1753-4887.2010.00304.x.
20. Klodiana Lanaj, Russell E. Johnson, and Christopher M. Barnes, "Beginning the Workday Yet Already Depleted? Consequences of Late-Night Smartphone Use and Sleep," *Organizational Behavior and Human Decision Processes* 124, no. 1 (May 2014): 11–23, doi.org/10.1016/j.obhdp.2014.01.001.
21. Ajary K. Jain and Ana Moreno, "Organizational Learning, Knowledge Management Practices and Firm's Performance: An Empirical Study of a Heavy Engineering Firm

in India," *The Learning Organization* 22, no. 1 (January 2015): 14–39, doi.org/10.1108/TLO-05-2013-0024.

22. Gisela Sjogaard et al., "Exercise Is More Than Medicine: The Working Age Population's Well-Being and Productivity," *Journal of Sport and Health Science* 5, no. 2 (June 2016): 159–165, doi.org/10.1016/j.jshs.2016.04.004.

23. Lanaj, Johnson, and Barnes, "Beginning the Workday," 11–23; Orman, *Women & Money*.

CHAPTER 7: VISION

1. Amish Tripathi, *The Oath of the Vayuputras: Shiva Trilogy*, bk. 3 (Chennai, India: Westland, 2013).
2. Simon Grégoire, Thérèse Bouffard, and Carole Vezeau, "Personal Goal Setting as a Mediator of the Relationship Between Mindfulness and Wellbeing," *International Journal of Wellbeing* 2, no. 3 (August 2012): 236–250, doi.org/10.5502/ijw.v2.i3.5.
3. Marelisa Fabrega, "How to Write a Personal Manifesto," Daring to Live Fully, accessed March 13, 2020, daringtolivefully.com/personal-manifesto.
4. Fabrega, "How to Write a Personal Manifesto."
5. Nora Spinks, "Work-Life Balance: Achievable Goal or Pipe Dream?" *Journal for Quality and Participation* 27, no. 3 (October 2004): 4–11.
6. Jenny Dixon and Debbie S. Daugherty, "A Language Convergence/Meaning Divergence Analysis Exploring How LGBTQ and Single Employees Manage Traditional Family Expectations in the Workplace," *Journal of Applied Communication Research* 42, no. 1 (February 2014): 1–19, doi.org/10.1080/00909882.2013.847275.
7. Amanda Tarlton, "Stay-at-Home Parents Should Earn Over $160,000 Salary, Survey Finds," Fatherly, last modified January 17, 2019, fatherly.com/news/stay-at-home-parents-salary.
8. Tarlton, "Stay-at-Home Parents Should Earn Over $160,000 Salary."
9. Fabienne T. Amstad et al., "A Meta-Analysis of Work-Family Conflict and Various Outcomes with a Special Emphasis on Cross-Domain Versus Matching-Domain Relations," *Journal of Occupational Health Psychology* 16, no. 2 (April 2011): 151–169, doi.org/10.1037/a0022170.
10. Amstad et al., "Meta-Analysis of Work-Family Conflict and Various Outcomes," 151–169.
11. Jenet Jacob Erickson, Giuseppe Martinengo, and E. Jeffrey Hill, "Putting Work and Family Experienced in Context: Differences by Family Life Stage," *Human Relations* 63, no. 7 (July 2010): 955–979, doi.org/10.1177/0018726709353138.
12. Epictetus, *Discourses*, bk. 3 (New York: Thomas Nelson and Sons, 1890).
13. Les MacLeod, "Making SMART Goals Smarter," *Physician Executives* 38, no. 2 (March 2012): 68–72.
14. Wayne Dyer, *The Power of Intention* (Carlsbad, CA: Hay House, 2004).
15. "The What & Why of Sadhana," Isha Sadhguru, last modified October 15, 2019, isha.sadhguru.org/us/en/wisdom/article/the-what-why-of-sadhana.

16. Thomas Newmark, "Cases in Visualization for Improved Athletic Performance," *Psychiatric Annals* 42, no. 10 (October 2012): 385–387, doi.org/10.3928/00485713-20121003-07; Amar Cheema and Rajesh Bagchi, "The Effect of Goal Visualization on Goal Pursuit: Implications for Consumers and Managers," *Journal of Marketing* 75, no. 2 (March 2011): 109–123, doi.org/10.1509/jm.75.2.109.
17. Cheema and Bagchi, "The Effect of Goal Visualization on Goal Pursuit," 109–123.

CHAPTER 8: SUPPORT

1. Fred Rogers, *The World According to Mister Rogers: Important Things to Remember* (New York: Hachette Books, 2019).
2. Liu-Qin Yang et al., "Be Mindful of What You Impose on Your Colleagues: Implications of Social Burden for Burdenees' Well-Being, Attitudes and Counterproductive Work Behaviour," *Stress and Health* 32, no. 1 (February 2016): 70–83, doi.org/10.1002/smi.2581.
3. Brené Brown, *The Gifts of Imperfection: Let Go of Who You Think You're Supposed to Be and Embrace Who You Are* (Center City, MN: Hazelden Publishing, 2010), 20.
4. Ghulam R. Nabi, "The Relationship Between HRM, Social Support and Subjective Career Success Among Men and Women," *International Journal of Manpower* 22, no. 5 (August 2001): 457–474, doi.org/10.1108/EUM0000000005850.
5. "Dr. Phil's Ten Life Laws," Dr. Phil, last modified February 1, 2018, drphil.com/advice/dr-phils-ten-life-laws.
6. Joyce Marter, "Free Yourself from Toxic Relationships," Psych Central, last modified October 29, 2013, blogs.psychcentral.com/success/2013/10/free-yourself-from-toxic-relationships.
7. Nabi, "The Relationship Between HRM, Social Support and Subjective Career Success Among Men and Women," 457–474.
8. Marian M. Morry, "The Attraction-Similarity Hypothesis Among Cross-Sex Friends: Relationship Saitsfaction, Perceived Similarities, and Self-Serving Perceptions," *Journal of Social and Personal Relationships* 24, no. 1 (February 2007): 117–138, doi.org/10.1177/0265407507072615.
9. Jeffrey Dew, Sonya Britt, and Sandra Huston, "Examining the Relationship Between Financial Issues and Divorce," *Family Relations* 61, no. 4 (October 2012): 615–628, doi.org/10.1111/j.1741-3729.2012.00715.x.

CHAPTER 9: COMPASSION

1. Roger Ebert, "Cannes # 7: A Campaign for Real Movies," Roger Ebert, accessed April 29, 2020, rogerebert.com/roger-ebert/cannes-7-a-campaign-for-real-movies.
2. Enid R. Spitz, "The Three Kinds of Empathy: Emotional, Cognitive, Compassionate," Heartmanity's Blog, accessed March 24, 2020, blog.heartmanity.com/the-three-kinds-of-empathy-emotional-cognitive-compassionate.

3. Li-Chuan Chu, "Impact of Providing Compassion on Job Performance and Mental Health: The Moderating Effect of Interpersonal Relationship Quality," *Journal of Nursing Scholarship* 49, no. 4 (July 2017): 456–465, doi.org/10.1111/jnu.12307.
4. Chu, "Impact of Providing Compassion on Job Performance and Mental Health," 456–465.
5. Maria Ross, "4 Reasons Why Empathy Is Good for Business," Entrepreneur, last modified November 11, 2018, entrepreneur.com/article/322302.
6. Seung-Yoon Rhee, Won-Moo Hur, and Minsung Kim, "The Relationship of Coworker Incivility to Job Performance and the Moderating Role of Self-Efficacy and Compassion at Work: The Job Demands-Resources (JD-R) Approach," *Journal of Business Psychology* 32, no. 6 (December 2017): 711–726, doi.org/10.1007/s10869-016-9469-2.
7. Belinda Parmar, "The Most Empathetic Companies, 2016," Harvard Business Review, last modified December 20, 2016, hbr.org/2016/12/the-most-and-least-empathetic-companies-2016.
8. Mark C. Johlke, "Sales Presentation Skills and Salesperson Job Performance," *Journal of Business & Industrial Marketing* 21, no. 5 (August 2006): 311–319, doi.org/10.1108/08858620610681614.
9. Alice Walker, interview by Esther Iverem, *On the Ground: Voices of Resistance from the Nation's Capital*, Pacifica Radio, March 12, 2003.
10. Karyn Hall, "The Importance of Kindness," Psychology Today, accessed March 24, 2020, psychologytoday.com/us/blog/pieces-mind/201712/the-importance-kindness.
11. Martin Luther King, Jr., *Strength to Love* (Minneapolis: Harper & Row, 2010).
12. Tirath Singh, "Role of Spiritual Intelligence, Altruism and Mental Health in Predicting Academic Achievement," *International Journal of Education* 3 (December 2014): 1–8, ijoe.vidyapublications.com/Issues/Vol3/PDF/1.pdf.
13. Tracy D. Hecht and Kathleen Boies, "Structure and Correlates of Spillover from Nonwork to Work: An Examination of Nonwork Activities, Well-Being, and Work Outcomes," *Journal of Occupational Health Psychology* 14, no. 4 (October 2009): 414–426, doi.org/10.1037/a0015981.
14. Will Kenton, "What Is Conscious Capitalism?" Investopedia, last modified April 21, 2018, investopedia.com/terms/c/conscious-capitalism.asp.
15. AJ Willingham, "Patagonia Got $10 Million in GOP Tax Cuts. The Company's Donating It for Climate Change Awareness," CNN, accessed April 29, 2020, cnn.com/2018/11/29/business/patagonia-10-million-tax-climate-change-trnd/index.html.
16. Abraham Carmeli, Alexander S. McKay, and James C. Kaufman, "Emotional Intelligence and Creativity: The Mediating Role of Generosity and Vigor," *Journal of Creative Behavior* (December 2014): 1–21, doi.org/10.1002/jocb.53.

CHAPTER 10: DETACHMENT

1. Deepak Chopra, *The Seven Spiritual Laws of Success: A Practical Guide to the Fulfillment of Your Dreams* (Sydney, Australia: Read How You Want, 2009), 51.
2. Galen Buckwalter, interview, "Are You Struggling with Financial PTSD?" Goop, last modified December 6, 2019, goop.com/wellness/career-money/are-you-struggling-with-financial-ptsd.
3. Buckwalter, "Are You Struggling with Financial PTSD?"
4. John E. Grable, "Financial Risk Tolerance: A Psychometric Review," *Research Foundation Briefs* 4, no. 1 (June 2017).
5. Wiebke Eberhardt, Wändi Bruine de Bruin, and JoNell Strough, "Age Differences in Financial Decision Making: The Benefits of More Experience and Less Negative Emotions," *Journal of Behavioral Decision Making* 32, no. 1 (January 2019): 79–93, doi.org/10.1002/bdm.2097.
6. Gaurav Bagga, "Positive Steps to End Negativity in the Workplace: The Hidden Costs of an Individual and Organizational Phenomenon," *Human Resource Management International Digest* 21, no. 6 (August 2013): 28–29, doi.org/10.1108/HRMID-08-2013-0065.
7. Caitlin A. Demsky, Allison M. Ellis, and Charlotte Fritz, "Shrugging It Off: Does Psychological Detachment from Work Mediate the Relationship Between Workplace Aggression and Work-Family Conflict?" *Journal of Occupational Health Psychology* 19, no. 2 (April 2014): 195–205.
8. Wayne W. Dyer, Facebook posts, last accessed April 28, 2020, facebook.com/drwaynedyer/posts/how-people-treat-you-is-their-karma-how-you-react-is-yours-dr-wayne-dyer/157785317602653.
9. Thich Nhat Hanh, *True Love: A Practice for Awakening the Heart* (Boston: Shambhala Publications, 2011), 4.
10. Katarina Katja Mihelič and Metka Tekavčič, "Work-Family Conflict: A Review of Antecedents and Outcomes," *International Journal of Management & Information Systems* 18, no. 1 (2014): 15–26, doi.org/10.19030/ijmis.v18i1.8335.

CHAPTER 11: POSITIVITY

1. Guido Alessandri, et al., "The Utility of Positive Orientation in Predicting Job Performance and Organisational Citizenship Behaviors," *Applied Psychology: An International Review* 61, no. 4 (October 2012): 669–698, doi.org/10.1111/j.1464-0597.2012.00511.x.
2. Fit4D, "The Neuroscience of Behavior Change," Health Transformer, last modified May 27, 2018, healthtransformer.co/the-neuroscience-of-behavior-change-bcb567fa83c1.

3. Zameena Mejia, "How Arianna Huffington, Tony Robbins, and Oprah Use Gratitude to Succeed," CNBC, last modified February 16, 2018, cnbc.com/2018/02/16/how-arianna-huffington-tony-robbins-and-oprah-use-gratitude-to-succeed.html.
4. Michela Cortini et al., "Gratitude at Work Works! A Mix-Method Study on Different Dimensions of Gratitude, Job Satisfaction, and Job Performance," *Sustainability* 11, no. 14 (January 2019): 1–12, doi.org/10.3390/su11143902; Lukasz D. Kaczmarek, "Who Self-Initiates Gratitude Interventions in Daily Life? An Examination of Intentions, Curiosity, Depressive Symptoms, and Life Satisfaction," *Personality and Individual Differences* 55, no. 7 (October 2013): 805–810, doi.org/10.1016/j.paid.2013.06.013.
5. Richard E. Watts, "Reflecting 'As If,'" Counseling Today, last modified September 9, 2013, ct.counseling.org/2013/04/reflecting-as-if.
6. Shannon Polly, "Acting 'As If,'" Positive Psychology News, last modified June 25, 2015, positivepsychologynews.com/news/shannon-polly/2015062531882.
7. David Gooblar, "Looking for the Exceptions," Chronicle Vitae, accessed March 26, 2020, chroniclevitae.com/news/1368-look-for-the-exceptions.
8. Brené Brown, *The Gifts of Imperfection: Let Go of Who You Think You're Supposed to Be and Embrace Who You Are*, (Center City, MN: Hazelden Publishing, 2010).
9. Ans De Vos, Inge De Clippeleer, and Thomas Dewilde, "Proactive Career Behaviours and Career Success During the Early Career," *Journal of Occupational and Organizational Psychology* 82, no. 4 (September 2009): 761–777, doi.org/10.1348/096317909X471013.
10. Sheryl Sandberg, "Why We Have Too Few Women Leaders" (talk, TedWomen 2010, International Trade Center, Washington, DC, December 7–8, 2010), ted.com/talks/sheryl_sandberg_why_we_have_too_few_women_leaders?source=facebook&fbclid=IwAR0lqYFrUAHVVNguV2u2t7nu5XHYNSiUm2t1VVrhGA3qf8YPMD17DRxv8wI#t-54058.
11. Emily T. Amanatullah and Michael W. Morris, "Negotiating Gender Roles: Gender Differences in Assertive Negotiating Are Mediated by Women's Fear of Backlash and Attenuated When Negotiating on Behalf of Others," *Journal of Personality and Social Psychology* 98, no. 2 (February 2010): 256–267, doi.org/10.1037/a0017094.
12. Amanatullah and Morris, "Negotiating Gender Roles," 256–267.
13. Marcel Schwantes, "The CEO of Salesforce Found Out His Female Employees Were Paid Less Than Men. His Response Is a Priceless Leadership Lesson," Inc., last modified February 6, 2020, inc.com/marcel-schwantes/the-ceo-of-salesforce-found-out-female-employees-are-paid-less-than-men-his-response-is-a-priceless-leadership-lesson.html.

CHAPTER 12: RESILIENCE

1. Rita Mae Brown, "Untitled Essay," *The Courage of Conviction* (New York: Dodd, Mead & Company, 1985), 23.
2. Diane Coutu, "How Resilience Works," Harvard Business Review, last modified July 11, 2016, hbr.org/2002/05/how-resilience-works.
3. Brian Cooper et al., "Well-Being-Oriented Human Resource Management Practices and Employee Performance in the Chinese Banking Sector: The Role of Social Climate and Resilience," *Human Resource Management* 58, no. 1 (January 2019): 85–97, doi.org/10.1002/hrm.21934.
4. Tianqiang Hu, Dajun Zhang, and Jinliang Wang, "A Meta-Analysis of the Trait Resilience and Mental Health," *Personality and Individual Differences* 76 (April 2015): 18–27, doi.org/10.1016/j.paid.2014.11.039.
5. "Ramp Up Your Resilience!" Harvard Health Publishing, last modified September 24, 2019, health.harvard.edu/mind-and-mood/ramp-up-your-resilience.
6. "Ramp Up Your Resilience!"
7. Lisa S. Meredith et al., "Promoting Psychological Resilience in the US Military," *Rand Health Quarterly* 1, no. 2 (2011): 2.
8. Zakieh Shooshtarian, Fatemeh Emali, and Mahmood Amine Lori, "The Effect of Labor's Emotional Intelligence on Their Job Satisfaction, Job Performance and Commitment," *Iranian Journal of Management Studies* 6, no. 1 (January 2013), 27–42.
9. Robert D. Enright and Richard P. Fitzgibbons, F*orgiveness Therapy: An Empirical Guide for Resolving Anger and Restoring Hope* (Washington, D.C.: American Psychological Association, 2014); Manfred F. R. Kets de Vries, "Are You a Victim of the Victim Syndrome?" *Organizational Dynamics* 43, no. 2 (June 2014): 130–137, doi.org/10.1057/9781137382337_4.
10. Badri Bajaj and Neerja Pande, "Mediating Role of Resilience in the Impact of Mindfulness on Life Satisfaction and Affect as Indices of Subjective Well-Being," *Personality and Individual Differences* 93 (April 2016): 63–67, doi.org/10.1016/j.paid.2015.09.005.
11. Olivia Goldhill, "Psychologists Have Found That a Spiritual Outlook Makes Humans More Resilient to Trauma," Quartz, last modified January 30, 2016, qz.com/606564/psychologists-have-found-that-a-spiritual-outlook-makes-humans-universally-more-resilient-to-trauma.
12. Kristin D. Neff and Pittman McGehee, "Self-Compassion and Psychological Resilience Among Adolescents and Young Adults," *Self and Identity* 9, no. 3 (July 2010): 225–240, doi.org/10.1080/15298860902979307.
13. Ansley Bender and Rick Ingram, "Connecting Attachment Style to Resilience: Contributions of Self-Care and Self-Efficacy," *Personality and Individual Differences* 130 (August 2018): 18–20, doi.org/10.1016/j.paid.2018.03.038.

14. Sam J. Maglio, Peter M. Gollwitzer, and Gabriele Oettingen, "Emotion and Control in the Planning of Goals," *Motivation and Emotions* 38 (2014): 620–634, doi.org/10.1007/s11031-014-9407-4.
15. Fatih Ozbay et al., "Social Support and Resilience to Stress: From Neurobiology to Clinical Practice," *Psychiatry* 4, no. 5 (May 2007): 35–40.
16. Dorian Peters and Rafael Calvo, "Compassion vs. Empathy: Designing for Resilience," *Interactions* 21, no. 5 (September 2014): 48–53, doi.org/10.1145/2647087.
17. David Fletcher and Mustafa Sarkar, "Psychological Resilience: A Review and Critique of Definitions, Concepts, and Theory," *European Psychologist* 18, no. 1 (2013): 12–23, doi.org/10.1027/1016-9040/a000124.
18. Tamera R. Schneider, Joseph B. Lyons, and Steven Khazon, "Emotional Intelligence and Resilience," *Personality and Individual Differences* 55, no. 8 (November 2013): 909–914, doi.org/10.1016/j.paid.2013.07.460.
19. Michael A. Cohn et al., "Happiness Unpacked: Positive Emotions Increase Life Satisfaction by Building Resilience," *Emotion* 9, no. 3 (June 2009): 361–368, doi.org/10.1037/a0015952.
20. Arun Kumar and Vidushi Dixit, "Forgiveness, Gratitude and Resilience Among Indian Youth," *Indian Journal of Health and Wellbeing* 5, no. 12 (December 2014): 1414–1419, i-scholar.in/index.php/ijhw/article/view/88644.
21. Eleanor Roosevelt, *You Learn by Living* (Louisville, KY: Westminster John Knox Press, 1983), 29.
22. Dushad Ram et al., "Correlation of Cognitive Resilience, Cognitive Flexibility and Impulsivity in Attempted Suicide," *Indian Journal of Psychological Medicine* 41, no. 4 (2019): 362–367, doi.org/10.4103/IJPSYM.IJPSYM_189_18.
23. Jeffery A. Lepine, Nathan P. Podsakoff, and Marcia A. Lepine, "A Meta-Analytic Test of the Challenge Stressor-Hindrance Stressor Framework: An Explanation for Inconsistent Relationships Among Stressors and Performance," *Academy of Management Journal* 48, no. 5 (October 2005): 764–775, doi.org/10.5465/amj.2005.18803921.
24. Dave Ramsey, *The Total Money Makeover: A Proven Plan for Financial Fitness* (Nashville, TN: Thomas Nelson, 2013).
25. GOBankingRates, "57% of Americans Have Less Than $1,000 in Savings," Cision PR Newswire, September 12, 2017, prnewswire.com/news-releases/57-of-americans-have-less-than-1000-in-savings-300516664.html.
26. Denise Hill, "5 Ways to Boost Your Financial Resilience," Wise Bread, accessed April 25, 2020, wisebread.com/5-ways-to-boost-your-financial-resilience; Sarah Foster, "The U.S. Economy is Officially in a Recession. Here are 7 Steps to Recession-Proof Your Finances," Bankrate, last modified April 16, 2020, bankrate.com/personal-finance/smart-money/ways-to-recession-proof-your-finances.

27. Barbara O'Neill, "Steps Toward Financial Resilience," Rutgers NJAES, accessed April 25, 2020, njaes.rutgers.edu/SSHW/message/message.php?p=Finance&m=194.
28. Maya Angelou, interview by George Plimpton, *Paris Review* 116 (Fall 1990).
29. Leah R. Halper and Jeffrey B. Vancouver, "Self-Efficacy's Influence on Persistence on a Physical Task: Moderating Effect of Performance Feedback Ambiguity," *Psychology of Sport Exercise* 22 (January 2016): 170–177, sciencedirect.com/science/article/pii/S1469029215300042.
30. Carol Dweck, "What Having a 'Growth Mindset' Actually Means," Harvard Business Review, last modified January 13, 2016, hbr.org/2016/01/what-having-a-growth-mindset-actually-means; "Decades of Scientific Research That Started a Growth Mindset Revolution," Mindset Works, accessed April 25, 2020, mindsetworks.com/science.
31. Simon J. Golden, Abdifatah Ali, and Russell E. Johnson, "Goal Orientation," *The SAGE Encyclopedia of Industrial and Organizational Psychology*, ed. Steven G. Rogelberg (Thousand Oaks, CA: Sage Press, 2017).
32. Golden, Ali, and Johnson, "Goal Orientation," *The SAGE Encyclopedia of Industrial and Organizational Psychology.*
33. Paulo Coelho, *The Alchemist* (New York: HarperTorch, 2006).
34. Jim Haudan, "Adversity Is the Fuel of Greatness," Inc., accessed April 29, 2020, inc.com/jim-haudan/adversity-is-the-fuel-of-greatness.html.
35. Laird J. Rawsthorne and Andrew J. Elliot, "Achievement Goals and Intrinsic Motivation: A Meta-Analytic Review," *Personality and Social Psychology Review* 3, no. 4 (November 1999): 326–344, doi.org/10.1207/s15327957pspr0304_3.
36. Denby Sheather, "The Definition of Divine Timing," Thrive Global, accessed April 29, 2020, thriveglobal.com/stories/the-definition-of-divine-timing.
37. Joyce Marter, "15 Affirmations: Find the Courage to Live the Life You Want," HuffPost, accessed April 29, 2020, huffpost.com/entry/find-the-courage-to-live-the-life-you-want_b_5826674.

BOOK CLUB READER'S GUIDE

- What did you like most about the book?
- How in touch were you with your own mental health before starting The Financial Mindset Fix program?
- What did you learn about yourself by reading the book?
- Do you believe your mental health impacts your financial health? Why or why not?
- Did your attitudes or behavior around money change as a result of participating in this program?
- When it comes to your essence (ego), do you feel more like a Diva or a Doormat? Why?
- If you were to share your life vision, what would it look like?
- What are some of your gifts and strengths that make you uniquely you, and how can this help you create your vision for your future?
- Have you seen a correlation between your mental health and the size of your bank account while practicing the twelve mindsets in this book?
- When it comes to rating yourself on resiliency on a scale of 1 to 10, where would you rate yourself? How has this helped your success?
- What kind of change did you discover between The Financial Health Wheel you completed in the introduction and The Financial Health Wheel in the conclusion?
- What was your biggest takeaway from The Financial Mindset Fix program?
- Which aspects of this program will you practice regularly to help keep you balanced?

ABOUT THE AUTHOR

For more than twenty years, Joyce Marter, LCPC, has been a licensed clinical professional counselor and an expert in self-esteem, mindfulness, career development, and the psychology of money. She is the founder of Urban Balance, an insurance-friendly counseling practice she started and grew to over one hundred clinicians during her thirteen years as owner and CEO. Besides her private practice, she teaches counseling and provides clinical supervision to masters-level therapists-in-training as an adjunct faculty professor at The Family Institute at Northwestern University. Joyce earned a bachelor of arts with honors and distinction in psychology and a minor in Spanish from The Ohio State University and a masters of counseling psychology from Northwestern University.

A member of the National Speakers Association, Joyce is a national keynote speaker and corporate trainer for Fortune 500 companies, universities, and professional associations. She has blogged for multiple sites including Psych Central, *Spirituality & Health*, and HuffPost and has been quoted extensively in national publications. Joyce is routinely consulted as a counseling expert in the media and has been featured in such outlets as *The Wall Street Journal*, U.S. News & World Report, CNN, *Real Simple*, and MTV.

Her accolades include "Distinguished Alumni of the Year" from The Family Institute at Northwestern University (2008), "40 Under 40" from Crain's Chicago Business (2010), the "President's Award for Excellence in Leadership" from the Illinois Mental Health Counselors Association (2017), and the Robert J. Needle Distinguished Leadership Award from the Illinois Counseling Association (2020).

With a passion for advocating for mental health awareness and access to care, Joyce has held multiple volunteer board leadership positions including chair of the Midwest Region of the American Counseling Association, president of the Illinois Counseling Association, and two terms as president of the Illinois Mental Health Counselors Association.

As a true advocate for both financial health and mental health, Joyce embraces work-life balance. Recognizing she needed a bit more, she embraced the healing powers of yoga. She received a certificate of training from a Yoga Alliance-accredited, 200-hour yoga teacher training in Ashtanga Vinyasa from Heaven Meets Earth Yoga Studio & Center for Conscious Living in 2019. Yes, the same yoga studio she first stepped into!

Joyce lives in Evanston, Illinois, and Cape Coral, Florida, with her beloved husband, Jason Marotzke, who is also a counselor and professor. Together they enjoy a full life with their children, Celeste and Claudia Marter and Katelyn and Nick Marotzke, and their dogs, Phoebe and Nala. One day she hopes to add a few fluffy alpacas to the family, as they make her heart happy. She views life as an adventure; loves traveling with her husband, friends, and family; and admits roller coasters, zip lining, parasailing, and horseback riding are some of her favorite adventures.

Connect with Joyce through the following sites:

joyce-marter.com
urbanbalance.com
refreshmentalhealth.com
LinkedIn: Joyce Marter
Pinterest: Joyce Marter
Twitter: @Joyce_Marter
Instagram: Joyce.Marter
Facebook: Joyce Marter, LCPC
YouTube: Joyce Marter Licensed Therapist & National Speaker

ABOUT SOUNDS TRUE BOOKS

Sounds True was founded in 1985 by Tami Simon with a clear mandate: to disseminate spiritual wisdom. Since starting out as a project with one woman and her tape recorder, Sounds True has grown into a mission-driven learning and media company, partnering with many of the leading wisdom teachers and visionaries of our time.

Every Sounds True Book is designed to not only provide information to a reader but to also to embody the quality of a wisdom transmission, unlocking our greatest capacities to love, serve, and uplift others.

Sounds True Books are part of St. Martin's Essentials, an imprint of Macmillan Publishers.